GREAT COOKS and Their RECIPES
From TAILLEVENT to ESCOFFIER

GREAT COOKS and Their RECIPES
From TAILLEVENT to ESCOFFIER

ANNE WILLAN
Photographs by MICHAEL BOYS

A BULFINCH PRESS BOOK
LITTLE, BROWN AND COMPANY
BOSTON · TORONTO · LONDON

Dedicated to the memory of
Jane Grigson
(1928-1990)
Great Scholar, Great Cook and Great Friend

FIRST UNITED STATES EDITION

FIRST PUBLISHED IN GREAT BRITAIN BY PAVILION BOOKS LIMITED

DESIGNED BY DAVID FORDHAM

ISBN 0-8212-1922-7

LIBRARY OF CONGRESS CATALOG CARD NUMBER 91-58256

LIBRARY OF CONGRESS CATALOGING-IN-PUBLICATION INFORMATION IS AVAILABLE.

BULFINCH PRESS IS AN IMPRINT AND TRADEMARK OF LITTLE, BROWN AND COMPANY (INC.)

PRINTED IN HONG KONG BY IMAGO

FRONTISPIECE PHOTOGRAPHS:
FRANCESCO LEONARDI'S CASSATA PALERMITANA
TITLE PAGE:
"COSTUMES PARALLÈLES DU CUISINIER ANCIENT ET MODERNS"
FROM *LE MAÎTRE D'HÔTEL FRANÇAIS* BY ANTONIN CARÊME

PRINTED IN HONG KONG BY IMAGO

CONTENTS

A MASTER COOK

A master-cook! why, he's the man of men,
For a professor! he designs, he draws,
He paints, he carves, he builds, he fortifies,
Makes citadels of curious fowl and fish,
Some he dry-dishes, some motes round with broths;
Mounts marrow bones, cuts fifty-angled custards,
Rears bulwark pies, and for his outer works,
He raiseth ramparts of immortal crust;
And teacheth all the tactics, at one dinner:
What ranks, what files, to put his dishes in;
The whole art military. Then he knows
The influence of the stars upon his meats,
And all their seasons, tempers, qualities,
And so to fit his relishes and sauces.
He has nature in a pot, 'bove all the chymists,
Or airy brethren of the Rosie-cross.
He is an architect, an engineer,
A soldier, a physician, a philosopher,
A general mathematician.

Lickfinger in Ben Jonson's
"The Staple of News" (1631)

INTRODUCTION

THE MORE I HAVE BECOME involved in cooking, whether through reading, writing, teaching, or simply entertaining at home, the more I realize how much we owe to the cooks of the past.

This is what I wrote for the first edition of this book in 1977. And this is what I would repeat for this new, expanded edition which has been redesigned with such skill by Pavilion Books and enriched by some extraordinary recipe photography by Michael Boys, assisted by La Varenne chefs Claude Vauguet and Laurent Terrasson.

Many of us instantly recognize such names as Mrs Beeton, Fannie Farmer and Escoffier, but the identity of most other cooks on the profession's roll of honor remain unfamiliar. Taillevent enjoys some renown because his name is attached to a famous gastronomic temple in Paris – and perhaps the same can be said for La Varenne! – but few of us have any picture of who these two great chefs were, or how they shaped our culinary history.

This book attempts to fill in this gap by looking at the life and times – and the recipes – of fourteen great cooks in four different countries (Britain, France, Italy and the USA) over a time span of some 600 years. Many of these master cooks led a life of adventure. All would have echoed the sentiment of Robert May, who in 1660 looked back on six decades in English kitchens and informed his readers that "God and my own Conscience would not permit me to bury these my Experiences with my Silver Hairs in the Grave."

Cooking is constantly buffeted by extremes of fashion, not least in this media-conscious age when chefs strive to steal the limelight with new techniques, new recipes and new styles of presentation. We are tempted to echo Voltaire when in 1765 he wrote to a friend "... my digestion cannot tolerate *nouvelle cuisine*. I cannot endure veal sweetbreads drowned in a salty sauce one inch thick. I won't touch ground-up turkey, hare and rabbit which affect to be one meat. I don't like spatchcocked pigeon or bread without crust ... As for cooks, I won't stand for their ham glaze nor for a superfluity of morels, mushrooms, pepper and nutmeg used to disguise ingredients which are perfectly good in themselves."

Yet it is this urge towards experiment, towards new sensations of texture and taste, which has led us from the gallimaufries and gaudy "subtleties" of medieval times, when a grandiose display was the main justification for a feast, to the deceptive simplicity of modern cuisine, with its delicate balance of a few carefully chosen ingredients. Fine cooking is no longer the monopoly of the grand tables. Today a chef can make his mark in the profession without long years of menial apprenticeship, while more and more amateurs are cooking the specialties of the great chefs in their own homes. Good restaurants have become smaller and more personal, with the chef's presence often seen as well as felt. Modern life has done away with great *brigades* of cooks and with them the turn-of-the-century tomes that ordered their lives in the kitchen.

Among the old recipes themselves there are many surprises. The seemingly staid dishes of the Victorian Mrs Beeton turn out to be delicious, while the measurements and instructions given by the Renaissance Italian Bartolomeo Scappi survive 400 years with scarcely a change. Ironically, the recipes of the last of the master cooks in this book, Escoffier, with their interminable cross-references, are the most difficult to follow. Going back 600 years to Taillevent, when lavish spicing was the rule and ingredients were habitually ground to a purée, one finds that those of his recipes which can be interpreted with any degree of precision are astonishingly good, not unlike today's Indian cooking.

As originally drafted, many of the recipes in this book are difficult to follow, so alongside each one I have provided a contemporary version conforming to the original in both choice of ingredients and cooking method. They bring a glimpse of the past to the kitchens of the present and prove once more that the reputation of the master cooks who created them was, and is, well deserved.

ANNE WILLAN
Ecole de Cuisine La Varenne,
34 rue St. Dominique, 75007 Paris.

TAILLEVENT

about 1312-1395

I<small>N</small> THE LONG HISTORY OF cooking, the first professional whose name is still remembered is Taillevent, master chef in medieval times to an imposing roll of French royal households. Many before him had extolled the pleasures of good eating, but Taillevent's book *Le Viandier* marks the beginning of cooking as we know it; from his time on a succession of cooks and cookbooks records the development of the art.

Taillevent – his real name was Guillaume Tirel, but many apprentices in those days picked up nicknames that they never outgrew – must have been quite a character, for a remarkable amount is known about him in an age when most craftsmen, like the builders of the Gothic cathedrals, passed forgotten into history. In 1326, when he was about 14, he was a *happelapin* (kitchen boy) to Queen Jeanne of France and was charged with the unenviable task of turning the great roasting spits before the open fire. By 1346 Taillevent had risen to *keu* (cook) to King Philip VI, and in 1349 he was granted a house "in consideration of the good and pleasant service the king has received." Soon after, he was raised to the rank of *écuyer*, or squire, and passed from household to house-hold within the Valois family until, in 1381, he was at the top of his profession as master cook to King Charles VI. He probably compiled *Le Viandier* a few years earlier with

the encouragement of King Charles V, known as Charles the Wise for his fine judgment and cultivated tastes.

Today, the style of cooking described by Taillevent in *Le Viandier* seems strange. Where we try to develop the flavor and texture of ingredients to the full, medieval cooks pounded and puréed them out of all recognition, then spiced them in such profusion that the original taste was lost. There were very good reasons for this. Food was often so stale as to be almost rotten; it needed to be pounded and then disguised by strong spices or cheered up with coloring. The golden yellow of saffron was the favorite, but medieval cooks also brightened their drab purées with sandalwood (for red), herbs (for green), and mulberries (for blue). Such colorings are noted by Taillevent in his recipe for *blanc menger* (page 20).

Also, then as now, there was food snobbery. A pound of saffron cost as much as a horse, but this did not deter Taillevent from using it in more than half his recipes. The culinary luxuries of the day were spices like nutmeg, worth seven fat oxen per pound.

Taillevent also used a basic spice, *poudre fin*, resembling curry powder. In fact, modern Indian cookery probably comes closest to medieval, not only in its generous use of spices, but also in its habit of heightening flavor with sweet and acid ingredients. Savory dishes

A peacock in all its plumage, carried in procession by a lady of outstanding beauty and rank, was the high point of many medieval feasts. Throughout northern Europe, menus probably followed the pattern of the feast given for the enthronement of the English archbishop Nevill in 1467: frumentie (wheat porridge) with venison; potage ryall (royal soup); hart poudred for standard (deer spiced as usual); roo poudred for mutton (roe deer spiced like mutton); frumentie ryall (royal porridge); signettes roasted (roast baby swans); swanne with galendine (swan cooked with galingale root); capons with whole geese rost; corbettes (gobbets) of venison rost; beefe; venison baked; and as a "subtletie," a "great custard" – and all this was only the first of three similar courses.

were often seasoned with sugar as well as *vin aigre* (vinegar, literally sour wine) or *verjus,* made from the juice of any tart fruit. Sugar was treated as a seasoning like salt – both were precious commodities – and often sprinkled on a dish at the end of cooking. There was no distinction between sweet and savory dishes, and regardless of taste they were all placed on the table at once. Highly flavored meat dishes were served with bland porridges, or with purées of grains and legumes, a custom also evocative of modern Indian cooking.

In Taillevent's time, cooks had to prepare food for a table where there were few implements. It is no wonder that a "gobbet" the size of a finger was the largest permissible morsel or that meats are "hew'd," "smitten," or "grounde to douste" in almost every recipe. Forks were unknown and spoons were scarce, so food had to be eaten with the fingers. Meat was tough and teeth were poor, yet the knife – the only common table implement – was regarded as hazardous and its use was discouraged. (Two hundred years after Taillevent, a writer was still warning

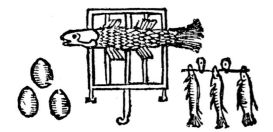

against the dangers of dipping into the communal pot without wearing a protective gauntlet.) A "trencher" (a thick slice or *tranche* of bread) was used instead of a plate, so gravies had to be thickened with breadcrumbs or egg yolks to stop them from running. Flour was not widely used as a binding agent until at least 200 years later.

Taillevent had a surprisingly wide range of ingredients at his disposal. He mentions over two dozen meats and birds, including stork, heron, and that medieval favorite, the peacock. The bird was skinned with the feathers intact, cooked, and then re-formed "in his hackell [coat]" with the tail erect (hence, the "hackles" of a dog). Contemporary menus make great play of roast meats, and though Taillevent devotes scant space to them, this is simply a reflection of the shorter directions needed, because of the common knowledge of techniques. Nonetheless, the popular picture of a medieval feast centered around a whole roast ox is inaccurate. Large animals must have been too tough to be roasted, and Taillevent mentions only young animals – calves, kids, and suckling pigs – in addition to birds. In winter even these were in short supply and almost the only meat available was salted.

Meat of any kind was reserved for the rich, and even they, for over half the days in the year, were restricted to a diet of fish by the fasting laws. Taillevent lists more than 50 different kinds of salt and freshwater fish. Fast days were strictly observed – the French called them *jours maigres* (i.e., meagre) – and to break them was a serious offence. Vegetables were regarded as the food of the poor (a fact confirmed by the vegetarian diet of the strictest religious sects) who were forced to subsist on milk, cheese, and what they could grow. This included cabbages, leeks, onions, and a multitude of half-forgotten herbs like borage, dittany, hyssop, and rue. This thin fare was supplemented by the occasional fowl, and it was another 200 years before Henry IV could claim that he had brought such prosperity to France that every house had a chicken in its pot (*poule au pot*) on Sundays.

Only a few medieval dishes have survived to the present day. *Hochepot* is very like a modern hot pot and *froumentée* is still known in some parts in England as frumenty, a wheaten porridge that is traditionally served on Christmas Eve. *Galentine* and *blanc menger* are familiar

In this manuscript illustration of 1390, two cooks present their master with pheasant baked in a crust, then carve it at the table on a trencher of bread to catch the juices.

words, but their modern equivalents are different. Taillevent's galantine was any dish flavored with the aromatic galingale root, while his blancmange (page 20) was a white purée, usually of poultry or fish, thickened with rice and ground almonds so it held a shape. Huge quantities of almonds were consumed in medieval times. They were ground for desserts, they were steeped in boiling water to make almond "milk," and they were pounded and used to bind sauces just as nuts and seeds are used for thickening in Mexican cooking.

Taillevent did a great deal more than simply supervise the cooking. As master chef he was also in

*In the foreground of this banquet a server is
tasting the wine – a precaution against poison.
The loaves at right will be trimmed as
trenchers – the slices of bread used as plates.*

charge of provisions, much like a modern quartermaster (*viandier* in fact means victualler). Toward the end of his life (he died in 1395, probably an octogenarian) he headed the half-dozen kitchens of the queen and the various royal dukes as well as those of the king. Whenever he left Paris in search of supplies he was given a travel allowance of "hay and oats for two horses," and with the poor communications and general lawlessness of the late Middle Ages, finding food day after day for the court must have been a Herculean task. According to *Le Ménagier de Paris* (a contemporary household treatise), the requirements each week for all the royal courts included 496 sheep, 70 cattle, 70 calves, 63 hogs, 17 salt hogs, 1,511 goats, 14,900 chickens, 12,390 pigeons, and 1,511 goslings. Such figures reflect the fact that hospitality was considered an important measure of power. Richard II of England is reputed to have enter- tained 10,000 of his subjects daily, and the French courts were probably organized on a similar scale, although large supplies could never have been kept up regularly and most eating must have followed a pattern of feast and famine. In normal times, the day began with dinner (corrupted from

déjeuner, to break the fast) taken four hours after sunrise and ended at sun- down with a supper consisting of something to sup (i.e., drink) like porridge or soup.

Of the feasts, or banquets, we have ample records. The lord and others of his rank occupied a high table raised on a dais at one end of the hall, set at right angles to the rest of the company, who were seated on long *banquets* or benches. Thus, everyone could observe the rituals of serving a meal – the washing of the hands, the presentation of the finest dishes, and the elaborate precautions taken against poison. All food and drink for the high table was tasted, often by the cook as well as the official taster, and dishes were covered on their journey from taster to table so no poison could be slipped in. The servings depended on rank; the high table was offered platter upon platter in three courses, with as many as 20 dishes in each course. Barons were entitled to only half the quantity given to the high table, knights to a quarter and everyone else to an eighth. The lord was served the meat of the animal, while its entrails were made into *oumble* pie for the lower ranks (hence the expression "to eat humble pie"). The climax of each course came with a

*The dinner for a German nobleman illustrates
the medieval convention of placing banquet
tables at right angles to the high table. The salt
cellar at the lord's left was designed not only to
display a valuable commodity, but also to
distinguish the host; anyone not seated at the
high table was thus "below the salt."*

"subtletie," a fanciful and often inedible creation several feet high echoing the colorful clothing of the spectators with their tall caps, parti- colored hose, and sweeping coats. The medieval mind was nothing if not literal – an exotic animal or a battle scene was often depicted, and at one wedding feast the cooks made a time- worn joke by sculpting the bride in childbed. More tactfully conceived *pièces montées*, or set pieces, were still in vogue a hundred years ago and are echoed today in the grandiose ice sculptures that adorn some stately dinners.

Entertainment on this scale called for literally an army of cooks (Richard II employed 2,000 cooks and 300 servitors) deployed with military precision. Taillevent commanded a dozen or more departments, some of whose names still echo a more ordered past. They demonstrate exactly how the catering of a household was organized – there was the pantry (where the *pain* or bread was stored), the cellar, the *bouteillerie* or buttery (where ale and wine were prepared for serving), the spicery, the acatery (the storeroom of the *acheteur* or caterer), the saucery, the larder (for meat, from *lard*, bacon), the pultery (for birds), the confectionery, the pastry (for pastry and pies), the scullery (for platters and dishes), and the wafery (where wafers that ended a meal were prepared). The importance of the master cook who ruled this little empire is shown by his rank, which was often that of squire with the right to a coat of arms.

Most writers link medieval cooking with the traditions of ancient Rome, and certainly there are parallels between the recipes of *Le Viandier* and those of the only surviving Roman cookbook, attributed to the epicure Apicius. Both medieval and Roman cooks shied away from the tough meat of larger animals; they had a penchant for purées, and they shared the odd (but hygienic) habit of parboiling food before roasting and part-roasting before boiling. Both set high store by songbirds and fowl of fine plumage, though these were supposed to be inferior in flavor to less showy birds like hen. For Taillevent and Apicius it was unthinkable to cook meat without using honey and spices on a lavish scale, and they both loved to transform the appearance and taste of ingredients "to make of a thousand flavors,

one flavor unique," as the Roman Seneca remarked. However, the seasonings listed by Apicius were quite different from those used by Taillevent and it is highly unlikely that Taillevent ever saw an Apician manuscript since in his day it was an extremely rare work studied by scholars rather than cooks. Similarities in the two cuisines therefore have less to do with the direct influence of Apicius than with oral traditions going back as far as the Roman occupation of France, combined with the rudimentary food technology of both eras.

Taillevent's world lacked the national traditions and frontiers we know today; the cooking described in *Le Viandier* was common to the court of England as well as France, and Taillevent's recipes differ little from those found in other works of the period. Indeed, there is a suspicion that a recently discovered manuscript, virtually identical to *Le Viandier*, was written 30 years before Taillevent's birth. Nonetheless, *Le Viandier* stands apart from other medieval writings on cookery in having been continuously recopied and reprinted from Taillevent's death in 1395 until the final edition of 1604. The rich harvest of French cookbooks did not begin until the 1650s and until then *Le Viandier* was the most successful French expression of the art.

TAILLEVENT RECIPES

C Le liure de taillevent grant cuy sinier du Roy de France.

C On les vend a Lyon/en la maison de feu Barnabe Chauffard/pres nostre dame de Confozt.

LEFT: *Blanc Menger Party.*
ABOVE: *Taillevent's* Le Viandier *was first printed in 1490, almost 100 years after his death. This title page comes from an early sixteenth-century edition from Lyon.*

Some of Taillevent's recipes are little more than lists of ingredients strung together with a few instructions, but many are more detailed, giving a clear outline of medieval cooking methods and finished dishes. Salt is often lacking from his recipes, partly because it was a valuable commodity usually sprinkled at the table according to individual taste and rank, and partly because so many meats were already salted through preservation in brine. Some of the following recipes may therefore require salt, although to some extent the other medieval flavorings will compensate for its omission.

GORNAULT, ROUGET, GRIMODIN

These are three similar types of mullet. Taillevent suggests poaching and serving them with a favorite medieval spiced sauce called *cameline*, which resembles a relish. Alternatively, he describes how to broil/grill them while basting with verjuice and spices, exactly as fish is barbecued today. Long pepper is a variety of peppercorn, not related to chili peppers which came from the New World about 150 years later.

Clean the stomach of the fish, and wash them well, then put them in the pan, with salt on top, then water, and cook them; and eat them with cameline sauce; or, if you wish, the shoulders should be split along the back, and then wash them, and put them to roast, plunge them often in verjuice and spice powder.

For cameline, pound ginger, plenty of cinnamon, clove, cardamom, mace, long pepper if you like, then sieve bread soaked in vinegar and moisten all and salt it to taste.

POACHED MULLET WITH CAMELINE SAUCE

Serves 4
4 mullet or other small fish such as red snapper or trout, 12 oz-1 lb/375-500 g
FOR THE SAUCE:
4 fl oz/½ cup/125 ml wine vinegar or cider vinegar
5 slices bread, crusts discarded
1½ tsp ground cinnamon
1 tsp ground ginger
seeds of 2 cardamom pods, crushed
½ tsp ground cloves
½ tsp ground mace
½ tsp pepper and salt

1. For the sauce: pour the vinegar over the bread and let stand 5 minutes or until soft. Add the cinnamon, ginger, cardamom, cloves, mace and pepper and purée the mixture in a food processor; it should be just thick enough to fall from a spoon. Add salt to taste.
2. Heat the oven to No 4/350°F/175°C. Clean and scale the fish. Wash them thoroughly and dry them on paper towels. Put them in a baking dish, and add salted water to almost cover. Cover with foil or a lid and poach in the oven

until the fish flakes easily when tested with a fork, 20-25 minutes. Drain them on paper towels and serve with the sauce separately.

BARBECUED MULLET

Serves 4
2 medium mullet, striped bass, or bream, 1½-2 lb/750 g-1 kg each, or 4 small mullet or other fish such as mackerel or trout, 12 oz-1 lb/375-500 g each
8 fl oz/1 cup/250 ml verjuice (see page 17)
1 tsp ground ginger
1 tsp ground cinnamon
½ tsp pepper
½ tsp ground nutmeg
¼ tsp ground cloves
seeds from 1 cardamom pod, crushed
salt, to taste

1. Scale the fish. Wash them and pat them dry with paper towels. Slit along the backbone, then continue cutting horizontally to detach flesh from the bone. Repeat on the other side, then snip the backbone at each end and discard it. Clean the stomach cavity of the fish and reshape it. Deeply slash each side so they cook evenly.
2. Mix 2 tablespoons of the verjuice with the ginger, cinnamon, pepper, nutmeg, cloves, cardamom and salt. When it is a smooth paste, stir in the

remaining verjuice. Brush the fish with the mixture, set them on a barbecue rack and broil/grill, basting with the verjuice mixture, for 5-10 minutes, depending on the thickness of the fish. Turn over, baste again, and continue cooking until the fish flakes easily when tested with a fork.

CIVÉ DE VEEL

Civet, meaning stew, is still a common French dish, though we would call Taillevent's recipe a curry. The sauce is thickened with breadcrumbs or with a purée of peas, in much the same way that legumes are added to give body to curries in southern India. Grain of paradise is a pepper-flavored variety of cardamom, and verjuice is tart fruit juice.

Roast on the spit or on the grill without cooking the meat too much, cut it in pieces and let it fry in fat in a casserole, and cut onion very finely and fry with it, then take toasted bread softened in wine and beef bouillon or purée of peas and bring to a boil with your meat; then prepare ginger, cinnamon, clove, grain of paradise and saffron to give it color, and dilute with verjuice and vinegar; and let it be well thickened, and plenty of onions, and the bread be browned, and all piquant with vinegar and highly spiced; and it should be yellow.

Cooked food is cut up for serving on three-legged tables designed to balance firmly on uneven floors. On the right dishes are carried in procession to the tables.

VEAL STEW

Serves 4
FOR THE THICKENING I:
3 slices bread
6 fl oz/¾ cup/175 ml red or white wine
8 fl oz/1 cup/250 ml beef stock
FOR THE THICKENING II:
2 oz/¼ cup/60 g dried split green peas,
*   soaked overnight in water and drained*
12 fl oz/1½ cups/375 ml water
salt and pepper
FOR THE STEW:
2 lb/1 kg piece boneless shoulder or leg of
*   veal*
2 tbsp lard or oil
4 medium onions, chopped
2 tsp ground ginger
2 tsp ground cinnamon
½ tsp ground cloves
seeds of 1 cardamom pod
pinch of saffron
salt and pepper
2-3 tbsp verjuice (see below)
2-3 tbsp vinegar

1. For the thickening: if using bread with wine and stock, heat the oven to No 2/300°F/150°C. Bake the bread in the heated oven until well browned, about 30 minutes. Let cool and grind it to fine crumbs in a food processor or blender. Stir in the wine, let stand 5 minutes until the crumbs are soft, then add the beef stock. If using dried peas, simmer them, covered, in water until very soft, 1½-2 hours. Purée the mixture in a food processor or blender; it should be thick but still pour easily. Season to taste with salt and pepper.

2. For the stew: sear the veal over an open flame, preferably charcoal, so the outside is slightly charred; cut it in 1 inch/2.5 cm cubes. In a casserole, heat the lard or oil and fry half the veal until browned on all sides. Take out, fry the remaining veal and remove it. Add the onions and cook until soft but not brown. Put back the meat, pour over the bread and wine mixture or the pea purée, cover and bring to a boil. Stir a few spoonfuls of the sauce into a mixture of the ginger, cinnamon, cloves, cardamom and saffron, and stir this mixture back into the meat. Add salt and pepper, cover, and simmer on top of the stove or cook in an oven heated to No 3/325°F/160°C until the meat is very tender, 1-1½ hours. Stir in the verjuice and vinegar, adding more to taste (the amount needed depends on their tartness).

FOR THE VERJUICE:
Work tart grapes, tart apples, crab apples, or any other tart or unripe fruit in a food processor then strain to obtain the sour juice. Alternatively, chop the fruit and work it through a vegetable mill, then strain to obtain the juice.

HOCHEPOT DE POULLAILLE

In medieval times the name *hochepot* meant a pot on a hook, suggesting that the food in it was simmered a long time. An *hochepot* resembles a hot pot; it is also the origin of the expressions "hodgepodge" and "hotchpotch."

Take your chicken and cut it in pieces and put it to fry in lard in a casserole; then take a little browned bread and the livers of the chicken and soften them with wine and beef stock, and put them to boil with your chicken; then peel ginger, cinnamon and grain of paradise [cardamom] and dissolve them in verjuice; and it should be clear and dark, but not too much.

In medieval times, birds and small animals like suckling pig were tender enough to be roasted. Other tougher meats needed to be simmered in a cauldron or chopped — cleavers were still the quickest method of chopping by hand.

CHICKEN CASSEROLE

Serves 4

2 slices bread
3½-4 lb/1.6-1.8 kg roasting chicken, cut in pieces, with the liver
6 fl oz/¾ cup/175 ml red wine
6 fl oz/¾ cup/175 ml beef stock
2 tbsp lard
salt and pepper
2 tbsp verjuice (see page 17)
1 tsp ground ginger
1 tsp ground cinnamon
seeds of 1 cardamom pod, crushed

1. Heat the oven to No 2/300°F/150°C. Bake the bread in the heated oven until thoroughly browned. Let cool, then grind it to fine crumbs in a food processor or blender. Remove any membrane from the chicken liver and purée in a food processor or blender. Alternatively, chop the chicken liver finely and work it through a strainer to remove the membrane. Add the liver to the breadcrumbs, stir in the wine, and let stand until the breadcrumbs are soft, about 5 minutes. Stir in the beef stock.

2. In a casserole heat the lard and brown the pieces of chicken on all sides. Add the breadcrumb mixture with salt and pepper, cover, and simmer on top of the stove or cook in an oven heated to No 4/350°F/175°C until the chicken is almost tender, about 30 minutes. Stir the verjuice into the ginger, cinnamon and cardamom and stir this mixture into the chicken sauce. Continue cooking until the chicken is very tender, about 10 minutes longer. Take out the chicken and keep warm on a serving dish. Boil the sauce until it is dark, glossy, and very thick; spoon it over the chicken on the dish.

SUTIL BROUET d'ENGLETERRE

A *brouet*, or purée, could contain almost anything – meat, fish, or fowl. This *brouet* made of chestnuts *(purée de marrons)* is still a popular accompaniment to game in Europe.

Take cooked peeled chestnuts, and cooked egg yolks, and a little pig's liver and pound all together, soften the mixture with a little warm water and sieve it, season with long pepper and saffron and boil all together.

The lady of the house is being served a platter of small birds to a chorus of trumpets. Medieval nobles loved to dine to the sound of music.

CHESTNUT PURÉE FROM ENGLAND

Serves 6
2 lb/1 kg chestnuts
1¼ pints/3 cups/750 ml water
4 hard-boiled/cooked egg yolks
8 oz/250 g pig's liver, cut in pieces and any membrane discarded
2 tsp pepper, or to taste
pinch of saffron, infused in 2 tbsp boiling water
salt, to taste

1. Pierce each chestnut with the point of a knife, put them in a saucepan with water to cover and bring to the boil. Drain them a few at a time and peel them, removing both shell and inner skin. If the chestnuts become hard to peel, bring them just back to the boil, but do not let them cook.

2. Put the peeled chestnuts in a pan with the water, cover and simmer until the chestnuts are very tender, about 30 minutes. Drain them, reserving the liquid. Purée them in a food processor or a blender a little at a time with the hard-cooked/boiled egg yolks and pig's liver, adding just enough of the re-served cooking liquid to make a purée that will drop from the spoon. Return the purée to the pan, add the pepper and saffron with its liquid, and heat, stirring constantly. Cook the purée 4-5 minutes – it should just hold a shape, but as it dries add more cooking liquid if necessary. Taste it for seasoning; it should be quite peppery.

BLANC MENGER PARTY

This recipe for *blanc menger* is unusual in that it contains no chicken or fish, but only almonds and rice, exactly like the old-fashioned children's blancmange. *Party* here means "in parts" and the mold is set in gaily striped layers, showing the medieval love of colored foods. Preparing the red, green, blue, and yellow dyes must have been a major task; Taillevent uses bugloss or sunflower for red, azur fin (probably made from mulberries) for blue, parsley or herb bennet for green, and saffron for orange.

Take scalded peeled almonds and pound them very well, and soften them with boiled water; then, to make the liaison to bind them, pounded rice or starch are needed. And when the milk has stopped boiling, it must be divided in several parts, in two pots, if only two colors are needed, or whoever wishes can make three or four parts; and it is right that it be very thick, as thick as frumenty, so that it cannot fall when it is set on a plate or in a bowl; then take bugloss or sunflower or mulberries, or parsley, or herb bennet, or a little saffron sieved with some greenery, so that it keeps its color better when it is boiled; and it is best to have lard and let the bugloss and sunflower soak in it, and the mulberries also. Then throw sugar into the milk when it boils, draw it aside and salt it, and stir vigorously until it is thick and has taken on the color you want.

STRIPED BLANCMANGE

Serves 6-8

3 oz/90 g spinach and/or parsley
2½ oz/½ cup/75 g mulberries, black
*   currants or blackberries*
1⅔ pints/1 quart/1 liter milk
pinch of saffron
6 oz/1 cup/175 g whole blanched almonds,
*   finely ground*
6 oz/1 cup/175 g cream of rice
3¼ oz/½ cup/100 g sugar
1 tsp salt
2 tbsp lard or shortening
1 tsp ground cinnamon (optional)
½ tsp ground cloves (optional)
½ tsp ground ginger (optional)
2 pint/5 cup/1.25 liter peaked mold

1. Lightly oil the mold. Discard stems from spinach and/or parsley, thoroughly wash them, squeeze dry and coarsely chop them in a food processor. Pick over the berries and crush them in a small bowl. Pour equal amounts of the milk into 4 saucepans. Add the spinach and/or parsley to one pan, the crushed berries to the second pan and the saffron to the third. (The fourth mixture will remain white.) Bring these three pans of milk to a boil, cover and remove from the heat and leave in a warm place to draw the colors into the milk, about 10 minutes. Strain each batch of colored milk into a clean saucepan.

2. Bring each of the four pans of milk to a boil. Remove them from the heat and stir into each pan an equal portion of the ground almonds, cream of rice, sugar, salt, lard and any of the optional spices you are using. Return the pans to the heat and simmer, stirring often, until the mixture pulls away from the sides of the pan, about 10 minutes. The mixture should just fall easily from the spoon. Pour one colored portion into the mold and smooth the surface with the back of a spoon dipped in water, pressing the mixture well into the crevices of the mold. Repeat with each of the other colored portions, cover the mold with wax/greaseproof paper, and chill overnight or until firmly set. A short time before serving, run a knife around the edge of the mold and turn it out on to a platter.

TARTRES DE POMMES

Medieval cooks were adept at finding substitutes for sugar, which was an expensive import. Here wine and dried fruits are used to sweeten apples. Purslane, a common herb in medieval times, has large leaves and a sharp taste like sorrel. If you want to use it in this apple pie recipe, add 3 tablespoons chopped sorrel or spinach to the chopped apple mixture, with the spices.

Cut up each apple and add figs and put in well-cleaned raisins and mix them together, and put in onion fried in butter or oil, and wine and some pounded apples, soaked in wine, and with the remaining apples, crushed, put saffron and a little of various spices – cinnamon, white ginger, anise and purslane if you have it; and make two large bases of pastry and put all the mixtures in together, and press a thick layer of apple down well with the hand, and the other mixture, and after put on the lid and seal it and gild it with saffron and put it in the oven and cook it.

The medieval bakery changed little for the next 500 years. At right, a wood-fired oven with long-handled "peel" for handling loaves.

APPLE PIE

Serves 6

FOR THE PASTRY:

8 oz/2 cups/250 g flour
½ tsp salt
2½ oz/⅓ cup/75 g butter
2 tbsp shortening or lard
4-5 tbsp cold water

FOR THE FILLING:

1 onion, chopped
2 tbsp butter or oil
5 dessert apples
3 dried figs, chopped
2½ oz/½ cup/75 g raisins
6 fl oz/¾ cup/175 ml port or sweet white wine
1 tsp ground cinnamon
½ tsp ground ginger
½ tsp crushed aniseed
pinch of saffron, infused in 1 tbsp boiling water
Deep 9 inch/22 cm pie pan/tin

1. For the pastry: sift the flour into a bowl with the salt, add the butter and shortening or lard and cut them into small pieces. Rub with the fingertips until the mixture resembles crumbs, stir in enough water to make a pastry that is soft but not sticky, and knead lightly until smooth. Wrap and chill 30 minutes. Heat the oven to No 5/375°F/190°C.

2. For the filling: fry the onion in the butter or oil until soft but not brown, 2-3 minutes. Peel the apples, core and chop two of them, and mix them with the onion, figs, raisins and two-thirds of the port or wine. Grate the remaining apples and mix them at once with the remaining port or wine so they do not discolor. Add about a third of this mixture to the raisin mixture. Stir the cinnamon, ginger, aniseed, and half the saffron and liquid into the remaining grated apples.

3. Roll out just over half the pastry dough and line the pie pan/tin. Spread the raisin mixture in the bottom, put the spiced apple mixture on top, and press it down well. Roll out the remaining pastry to form a lid, place it on top, and seal the edges. Brush the top of the pie with the remaining saffron liquid and make a hole in the center for steam to escape. Bake in the heated oven until the pastry is browned, 50-60 minutes. Serve hot or cold.

Maiorana.

MARTINO

flourished 1450–1475

COOKING HAS COME TO BE regarded so much as a French art that its Italian origins are often overlooked. But they are there, firmly rooted in the rich traditions of Italy that Renaissance cooks developed to such splendid effect. It was the Italians who found in antiquity new inspirations for their feasts; it was they who happily blended the sturdy cooking of the different regions with ideas brought by the Arabs and crusaders, and founded the sophisticated cuisine that was an inspiration to the rest of Europe, much like the other Renaissance arts. An Italian cook was also the first to get his recipes in print in a book called *De honesta voluptate et valetudine* ("Of Honest Indulgence and Good Health"). The name of the cook was Martino.

De honesta voluptate was printed in Rome in 1474, the work of a humanist philosopher and man of letters called Platina, who spent his last years as Vatican librarian. In the first five chapters he discourses on good food and sober living with the rational elegance, based on ancient models, that was the hallmark of humanist writing. Then, abruptly, the book plunges into five chapters of practical recipes covering the best of Italian contemporary cooking, from the cheese tarts so dear to the ancient Romans to Saracen-inspired stews and native pasta. This curious change of tone in Platina's book attracted no comment until the 1930s when a fifteenth-century recipe manuscript was found,

OPPOSITE: *Sweet marjoram "helps the stomach, the brain and all the intestines," from* Tacuinum Sanitatis, *an illuminated health handbook probably known to Martino.*

"composed by the respected Maestro Martino, former cook to the Most Reverend Monsignor the Chamberlain and Patriarch of Aquileia." The manuscript (now in the Library of Congress) is written in the Italian of Tuscany, not in the Latin used by Platina, but the 250 recipes are identical to those in *De honesta voluptate*.

With this discovery, an acknowledgment tucked away in Platina's book suddenly assumed new significance – "O ye immortal Gods," he exclaims in a recipe for *bianco mangare*, "which cook could compete with my friend Martino of Como, with whom originates to a large extent that which I am writing here." Whether the particular manuscript in the Library of Congress was actually written before *De honesta voluptate* is uncertain, but Platina's dependence on Martino for his recipes seems beyond dispute. Platina was no cook and he clearly felt some embarrassment about applying his scholarship to so lowly a subject as food, for in the dedication to his book he hastens to explain that he is writing to "assist the well-bred man who desires to be healthy and to eat in a decorous way, rather than he who searches after luxury and extravagance."

The recipes in *De honesta voluptate* are clearly those of an expert cook – detailed and precise. Martino goes to great pains to explain the reasoning behind his instructions. For example, he advises using a large kettle for boiling meat so it is not packed too

23

tightly, and describes how to cover soup with a damp cloth to prevent it acquiring a smoky taste (one of the persistent problems when cooking over an open fire). His understanding of ingredients is intimate to the point of affection: "Salmon," he remarks, "is a most agreeable fish, most natural boiled, and yet again it is good any way you like to cook it. . . . For whole fish, you need big dishes like my master has, because all fish are much better cooked whole rather than in pieces."

Martino mentions the sausages of Bologna, the rice dishes of Lombardy, the crayfish of Venice and Rome, and the vegetables and fried dishes for which Florence was so famous. His easy familiarity with them all shows that by the fifteenth century a recognizably Italian style of cooking had already developed. Indeed, there are already signs of common methods and recipes in the few cookery manuscripts that antedate Martino, but none of them is nearly so well organized or complete as his work. Most include, for example, versions of *brodo saracenico* (ground chicken liver blended with bread and spice and often flavored with white wine and dried fruit) and *peverata*, an all-purpose sauce of toasted bread, spices, and liver pounded with wine and vinegar, which Martino uses as a base for his *peperata de salvaticina*, a game stew.

Most of these early Italian cookbooks feature pasta. Its introduction is often credited to Marco Polo, but a chest of macaroni was listed as part of a Genoese inheritance in 1279, a decade or more before he returned to Venice from his travels. Lasagne was the oldest and most common variety, invariably cooked in broth, then baked with layers of cheese; the word comes from the Latin *lasanum* (cooking pot). By the 1350s *lasagnari*, or pasta sellers, were well established. Boccaccio, who wrote the *Decameron* around this time, describes with delight a Utopian region called Bengodi where the vines were bound with sausages and a mountain was made of grated Parmesan cheese. People stood on top with nothing to do but make macaroni and ravioli and cook them in capon broth, then roll them down the hill; and as fast as they were eaten, the more there were.

By the time Martino was active, a century after Boccaccio, pasta had become a good deal more sophisticated, although it was still a luxury and in lean years its fabrication was forbidden. Martino describes what he

In the benign Italian climate dinner was often taken outdoors. The kitchen is primitive, with the spits turned by hand. Not until the 1500s would more sophisticated mechanisms become common.

calls *vermicelli*, squares "the size of dice" that were dried in the sun and would keep two years. His *macaroni siciliani*, made by wrapping dough around a stick, were very like modern Neapolitan pasta with the addition of eggs. Nor does he forget the crisp, deep-fried Florentine *crespelli*, usually sprinkled with sugar and spices, that are now called *cenci*. They can be all shapes, he says – rings, buckles, letters; horses or other animals.

The monsignor Martino worked for was almost certainly Ludovico Trevisan, a wealthy, worldly cardinal

Native workers gathering pepper in the kingdom of Quilon (Malabar coast). At right, a European merchant sniffs the pepper to test its quality. Venice was the great center of the spice trade with the East.

who became patriarch of Aquileia in 1439 and papal chamberlain a year later. He held both posts through five papacies and by the time he died, in 1465, he wielded so much power that the incumbent pope (Paul II) let both these offices lapse for several years. Ludovico must have been a master to warm any cook's heart. Called the Lucullan cardinal, he spent an extravagant 20 ducats a day on his food. It was said of him that "forgetting his origins he took on such airs that he was the first of the cardinals to dare to breed dogs and horses, to introduce licentious parties and banquets more splendid than were suited to his rank, and to restore a more civilized way of life to the Romans, who had declined to such a low state." In fact, he was just the sort of cardinal that later popes tried (with little success) to reform, but fortunately for Ludovico the

masters whom he served were anxious to restore Rome to her former glory and oust the Florentines and Venetians from their pre-eminence.

As the pope's chamberlain, Ludovico headed a household of about 600 and his personal staff probably amounted to half that number. He was responsible for organizing Rome's official banquets and entertainments, which were often held in the open air – today's *corso*, for example, is where races were run. One famous feast of which records survive is that given in 1473 (shortly after Ludovico's time) by Cardinal Pietro Riario for Eleanora of Aragon. It began with little hors d'oeuvres of ten sweet dishes (with gilded oranges and Malvasey wine) and then, after the ceremonial washing of hands, the assembled company tucked into roast chicken and goat's

liver, sweetbreads flavored with white wine, capons in white sauce with gilded pomegranate seeds, poultry in purple sauce, and a dozen other delicacies. A pastry figure entitled "Andromeda and the dragon" rounded off this course, which was followed by two more of equal luxuriance. At least half the entertainment must have been the sight of the lords at table – it was all very good publicity. As one sarcastic observer of the time remarked, the enormous treasure of the church had to be used up in some way or other.

"The Wedding Feast" by Sandro Botticelli; the Renaissance table settings are sparse and valuable dishes displayed on the "credenza" sideboard.

Finding no peacocks available, he told the cooks to use ducks instead and dress them in the feathers of an old peacock. A grand molded gelatin, portraying the papal arms in full color, taxed his ingenuity to the full, but he did his best with verdigris, white lead, vermilion, and other paints, never thinking of edible colors like saffron and herbs. The guests came, admired, ate, and were extremely ill the next morning.

The riches of the church during the Renaissance were second to none; to cook for a cardinal was the equivalent of cooking for a prince, and Martino must have supervised many an opulent feast. Yet his food is unpretentious, at least by the standards of ancient and medieval tables, and more like the fare of a merchant household. Simplicity was the style in Florence, leader of all the arts until the end of the fifteenth century, and like everyone else Martino was strongly influenced by it.

Not all the would-be imitators of Florentine cooking were as skilled as he; a certain Siennese nobleman, stunned by the magnificence of a feast given for Pius II in Florence in 1459, determined to reproduce it at home.

These Renaissance banquets were part of a deliberate evocation of the splendors of ancient Rome. Nostalgia also found a more intellectual outlet, for it was in 1457 that the most famous Roman cookery manuscript, attributed to the epicure Apicius (who lived at the time of Christ), was acquired by the Vatican. Platina undoubtedly was familiar with Apicius since he planned *De honesta voluptate* on the same classical ten-book pattern, and through oral traditions Martino must have had a good idea of what the Roman table was like. Both ancient and Renaissance Italians used a wide variety of vegetables and fruit with great imagination (a taste that was slow to reach the rest of Europe) and both shared a love of the macabre – the flamboyant Ascanio Sforza, for example, invited his fellow cardinals to a banquet where there

In one of the earliest pictures of pasta, a Boccaccian gastronome is treated to plump gnocchi with lasagne; gnocchi are thought to be the earliest pasta, although the Arab geographer Al Idrisi describes a variety called tria *in the twelfth century.*

were bones fashioned in sugar and drinking cups shaped as skulls. The fascination for Roman "flying pies" concealing live birds enjoyed a long life, still lingering in England 200 years after Martino.

However, the actual cooking of Renaissance Italy, as illustrated by Martino's recipes, was far removed from the crudities of ancient Rome and even of the Middle Ages. Martino has little time for outmoded purées and porridges, preferring more substantial dishes containing pieces of meat or whole birds in a sauce – the ancestors of French ragoûts. His vegetables are usually cooked whole, then sliced and served with a sprinkling of cheese or fried as fritters. The old tendency to disguise foods, whether by spicing them heavily or mixing them indiscriminately, began to disappear – no longer would a cook like Martino exclaim triumphantly, as had Apicius, that "no one will recognize this!" Martino thought little of this principle. He prides himself instead on bringing out the flavor of a single ingredient by careful seasoning and moderate cooking. He pays attention to texture, as in his recipe for veal rolls – thin escalopes of veal which are sprinkled with herbs, rolled, then broiled on a spit (page 33). Martino also has several soups based on meat broth, thickened with eggs and breadcrumbs or almonds. Soups were of ever-increasing importance during the Renaissance; often they were substantial dishes, more like our stews, and they were destined to have considerable influence in France, where *potages* occupied a prominent place in menus until the French Revolution.

Far more important to Martino than the cooking of ancient Rome was that of the Arabs, which had flourished hrough the Dark Ages (a tenth-century history lists a dozen writers on cookery in Baghdad). Italy, particularly Venice, had long been the gateway through which crusaders and spice merchants passed on their way to the East, and Italian scholars had translated several Arab treatises on food and medicine. Martino's habit of sprinkling dishes with sugar and spices is very Arabic as are his sauces flavored with raisins, prunes, and grapes. The appearance of aniseed, rice, dates, pomegranates, and bitter oranges can be traced to the long Arab occupation of Sicily and Spain. The sugar cane the Arabs introduced in Cyprus (and later Sicily) allowed them to indulge their sweet tooth – a passion they passed on to the Italians. Martino is one of the first cooks to use sugar in large quantities to make dishes that are specifically sweet, such as fritters, almond paste cookies, and sugared apples, rather than treating it as a seasoning like salt, in the medieval manner.

It took the Renaissance genius to fuse all these diverse elements into a coherent cuisine, blending the traditional and the exotic with the dishes indigenous to each region. *De honesta voluptate* was the first major step in this direction and its success was well deserved – it ran to over 30 editions in under a hundred years, including many translations into German, French, and Italian. Martino's recipes also led a double life in *Epulario* ("Of Feasting"), an Italian cookbook almost identical to the Library of Congress manuscript. Much translated, *Epulario* appeared in English as well and was still being printed in the mid 1600s, so that Martino's influence stretched throughout Europe for two centuries or more. Yet, by an irony of history, throughout its long life *Epulario* was attributed to one Giovanne de Rosselli and it is almost by accident that Martino's identity and achievement have been rediscovered today.

MARTINO RECIPES

LEFT: *Gambari Pieni.*
ABOVE: *Frontispiece to* Epulario, *a cookbook based on Martino's original work which was popular for over 200 years.*

Martino is the first cook to give detailed cooking instructions and tips that show he is thoroughly at home with his recipes. Like Taillevent, he rarely calls specifically for salt; often lemon juice, verjuice (sour grape juice), or cheese take its place, but in the following recipes salt and pepper can be added to taste.

GAMBARI PIENI

Already during the Renaissance Romans were eating a good deal of shellfish, including oysters and the crayfish that came from the water-threaded region along the Po and Piave rivers.

Boil them [the crayfish] in a little water and vinegar, with as much water as vinegar and plenty of salt, and since the crayfish add liquid do not put too much of this mixture, and boil them hard until the scum rises. And to know when they are cooked note when this scum has boiled two or three times over the caldron; then they should be done, but to be sure you can taste them and you will be content. With the point of a knife open the stomach between the legs, and pound the flesh from the tail and the legs with almonds and a little verjuice; and at times when eggs are permitted you can add the yolk of an egg to this mixture, or more depending on the quantity you want, also a little cheese, a little finely chopped parsley and marjoram. And fill the crayfish with this mixture and fry them in good oil as slowly and gently as possible; and in Lent you will not add egg or cheese.

Three ways of catching fish: with a net, with a spear, and on a line.

STUFFED CRAYFISH

Serves 6
2 lb/1 kg crayfish
12 fl oz/1½ cups/375 ml water
12 fl oz/1½ cups/375 ml vinegar
4 oz/⅔ cup/125 g whole blanched
  almonds, ground
2 tbsp verjuice (see page 17) or lemon juice
4 egg yolks
3¼ oz/½ cup/100 g grated Parmesan or
  Romano cheese
4 tbsp chopped parsley
1 tbsp chopped marjoram
salt and pepper
2 fl oz/¼ cup/60 ml olive oil (for sautéing)

1. Bring the water and vinegar to a boil, add the crayfish and boil 5-7 minutes, depending on their size. Drain them, rinse with cold water, and drain well. Cut along the tail on each side near the hard shell and discard the soft underside. Lift out the tail meat and discard the intestinal vein. Cut open the body and scoop out and reserve any soft meat. Set aside the shells and heads of the crayfish.

2. Purée the tail meat and any soft meat in a food processor or chop it very finely. Stir in the ground almonds, verjuice or lemon juice, egg yolks, cheese, parsley, marjoram and pepper and taste for seasoning. Salt may not be needed as the cheese is already salty. Fill the empty shells with the mixture, pressing it well. A short time before serving, heat the oil and sauté the stuffed shells over medium heat until lightly browned, 4-5 minutes, turning them half way through. Arrange the shells on a platter, topping them with the reserved heads. Serve them hot, or at room temperature.

ZUCCHE FRITTE

These fritters are typically Florentine as the best oil came from that region. The *zucche* used by Martino were most likely the large marrows that are common in Europe (though in his day they were certainly smaller in size). Zucchini (Courgettes) were probably brought later from the New World but they must closely resemble Martino's marrows.

Take marrows and clean them well. And then cut them crosswise in slices as thin as the blade of a knife. And then put them in water and bring to the boil, and then take them out and leave them to dry. Put a very little salt on the slices and cover them with good flour and fry them in oil. Then remove them, and take a little fennel flower, a little garlic and soft bread, and pound well and mix with agresto (tart grape juice) to make a good liquid, and put through a sieve and pour this relish on the slices of marrow. They are also good served only with vinegar and fennel flower. And if you desire this relish to be yellow add a little saffron.

Originating in India and brought to Europe by the Arabs, the eggplant/aubergine was popular in southern Italy early on.

ZUCCHINI/COURGETTE SALAD

Serves 6
*2 lb/1 kg zucchini/courgettes, cut in
 ¼ inch/6 mm rounds*
2 oz/½ cup/60 g flour
salt
4-6 tbsp olive oil (for frying)
FOR THE DRESSING:
*2 tbsp chopped leaf fennel, or 1 tsp fennel
 seed*
1 clove garlic, crushed
2 slices white bread, crusts discarded
*4 fl oz/½ cup/125 ml white wine vinegar
 or cider vinegar*
*pinch of saffron infused in 2 tbsp boiling
 water (optional)*
salt

1. Blanch the zucchini/courgette rounds in boiling water for 30 seconds and spread out on paper towels to dry thoroughly. Toss them with the flour and a pinch of salt in a bowl, turning until coated. In a frying pan, heat 2-3 tablespoons oil and lay in some of the zucchini/courgettes, separating any slices that stick together. Cook over high heat until just beginning to brown, ½-1 minute, turn over and brown the other side. Take out and spread them in a shallow serving dish; fry the remaining zucchini/courgettes in the same way.

2. For the dressing: purée the fennel, garlic, bread, vinegar, saffron with its liquid (if using), and salt to taste in a food processor or blender. Spoon the dressing over the zucchini/courgettes and leave 1-2 hours for the flavors to blend before serving.

If you prefer, a dressing can be made simply of vinegar and fennel with the bread and garlic omitted.

RAPE ARMATE

Martino's custom of making a special dish of an ordinary vegetable like turnips was typically Italian; elsewhere in Europe cooks regarded most root vegetables as food for the poor. This particular dish, to be served at the end of a meal, obviously forms what we call a dessert. The combination of sugar with turnips is not as strange as it seems, for the vegetable is already slightly sweet.

Cook the turnips in the hot cinders or boil them whole and uncut, and slice them as thickly as the blade of a knife, and have good moist *cacio* [cheese] cut in slices as big as the turnip slices, but thinner, and take sugar, pepper and sweet spices and mix these together, and arrange in a pan in this order starting at the bottom, slices of cheese to make a crust, and on top a layer of turnips with the said spices and much good fresh butter; and so on in this way arrange the turnip, and the cheese until the pan is full, and cook this for a quarter of an hour or more, like a tart. And this dish should be served after the others.

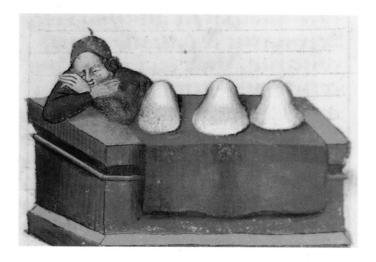

*A trader sleeps vigilantly beside his sugar
cones, an expensive import.*

TURNIP CAKE

Serves 8 as an accompaniment
2 lb/1 kg large white turnips
2 oz/⅓ cup/60 g sugar
2 tsp ground cinnamon
1 tsp pepper
½ tsp ground mace
½ tsp ground cloves
1¼ lb/625 g Bel Paese cheese, thinly sliced
Shallow 9 inch/22 cm cake pan/tin

1. Boil the unpeeled turnips in water to cover until just tender, 15-30 minutes (depending on their size). Drain them, let cool and peel off the skins; cut them in ¼ inch/6 mm slices. Mix the sugar with the pepper, cinnamon, mace and cloves. Heat the oven to No 5/375°F/190°C.
2. Thickly butter the cake pan/tin and arrange a layer of turnip slices in the bottom. Add a layer of cheese overlap-ping on top and sprinkle it with the sugar mixture. Continue adding layers of turnip, cheese and sugar until all the ingredients are used, ending with a layer of cheese.
3. Bake the dish in the heated oven until the top is browned, 30-35 minutes. Turn out the mold on to a platter, like a cake, and cut it in wedges or squares for serving. As a dessert it can be served hot or cold. As an accompaniment to meats, it is best hot.

PER FARE POLPETTE DI CARNE DE VITELLO O DE ALTRA BONA CARNE

This recipe for making meat rolls turns up in many old cookbooks. In England they are called veal olives (presumably because of their shape) and in France *oiseaux sans têtes* (birds without heads) because they also resemble little stuffed birds. By Martino's time a trencher (used below for pounding) had developed from the medieval slice of stale bread into a flat plate of wood or metal.

First cut some lean meat from the leg of the animal and slice it in long thin slices and beat it well on a trencher or table with the flat of a knife, and take salt and pounded fennel and put these on the slices of meat. Then take parsley, marjoram and good lard and beat them together with a little good spice, and spread this well over the slices. Then roll up each slice and put it on the spit to cook; but do not let the heat dry the meat too much.

VEAL ROLLS

Serves 4
1½ lb/750 g thinly sliced veal escalopes
1 tsp salt
1 tsp fennel seeds, crushed
3 oz/6 tbsp/90 g lard
4 tbsp chopped parsley
2 tsp chopped marjoram
½ tsp ground allspice
¼ tsp ground cloves or nutmeg
Thread for tying

1. Put the veal escalopes between two sheets of wax/greaseproof paper and pound them with a rolling pin or mallet until very thin; sprinkle them with the salt and crushed fennel. Cream the lard and add the parsley, marjoram, allspice and cloves or nutmeg. Spread the mixture over the veal escalopes right to the edges. Bring the edges to the center, then roll into neat bundles and tie them with thread.

2. If cooking in a rotisserie, spear the rolls on the spit and cook in front of a high heat until lightly browned, 10-15 minutes depending on the heat. Alternatively, roast the rolls in an oven heated to No 10/500°F/260°C. Baste the rolls with their juices half way through cooking. Untie the thread before serving.

RISO CON BRODO DI CARNE

This is an ancestor of the famous risotto Milanese, rice cooked in broth colored with saffron and flavored with cheese. In this recipe, cheese is omitted and eggs are added instead; the eggs have a similar thickening effect without adding flavor. The recipe is probably of Arabic origin, since the Arabs brought rice to Europe; Taillevent mentions rice and by 1475 it was being grown in the Po valley, where it is still an important crop.

For ten servings: First clean and wash the rice very well, and cook it in a good broth made from capon or a large chicken, and it needs to boil quite long. And when it is cooked add good spices, and take three egg yolks and a little of the cooked rice and mix well together. And then add to the rest of the rice and mix together. And it should be colored yellow with saffron. But many people do not like eggs with rice. In this case, follow your master's taste.

In Martino's Italy, the common accompaniment to pasta was cinnamon (here), sugar, and parmesan cheese. Generally, spices were used in much smaller quantities than in medieval times.

RISOTTO

Serves 4
1 pint/2½ cups/600 ml chicken stock
8 oz/1 cup/250 g round-grain rice
½ tsp ground cinnamon
½ tsp ground ginger
pinch of saffron, infused in 2 tbsp boiling water
salt
3 egg yolks

Bring the stock to a boil, add the rice, cover and simmer 20 minutes or until all the liquid has been absorbed. Let the rice stand 10 minutes for the grains to contract slightly, then stir in the cinnamon, ginger, saffron with its liquid and salt to taste. Stir 2 tablespoons of the rice into the egg yolks and stir this mixture back into the rice; it will thicken slightly. Taste for seasoning.

RAVIOLI IN TEMPO DI CARNE

The name ravioli probably comes from *rabiole* meaning "leftovers" in Ligurian dialect. The filling can be made of almost any meat or vegetable and was originally fried like a fritter; Martino seems to be the first cook to enclose it in pasta to make the ravioli we know, and he does not bother to give a recipe for the dough, which would have been a simple flour and water paste. He also uses a cheese called *cacio* still made in parts of Italy today.

To make ten servings: take ½ pound old *cacio*, and a little fresh *cacio* and 1 pound of fat belly of pork, or a calf's head that has been boiled until it falls apart. Then pound these well and add good well chopped herbs, and pepper, cloves and ginger; and add a pounded chicken breast and it will be even better. And mix all these things well together. Then make a good thin paste and fill it in the normal way with this filling. And these ravioli should not be bigger than a half chestnut, and should be put to cook in broth made from capon or from good meat, and it should be colored with saffron when it boils. And let the ravioli boil for the length of two paternosters. Then serve them and put on them grated *cacio* and sweet spices mixed. And these ravioli can be made the same with breast of pheasant, partridge or other birds.

RAVIOLI FOR MEAT DAYS

Serves 6-8
FOR THE PASTA DOUGH:
1 lb/4 cups/500 g semolina or all-purpose flour
1 tsp salt
1 tbsp olive oil
4 eggs, beaten to mix
2½-4 fl oz/⅓-½ cup/75-125 ml water

1 lb/500 g boneless fresh belly of pork, cut in 1 inch/2.5 cm cubes
4 pints/2½ quarts/2.5 liters chicken stock
1 whole boneless chicken breast, cut in 1 inch/2.5 cm cubes
8 oz/2 cups/250 g grated Parmesan or Romano cheese
4 oz/125 g Bel Paese or mozzarella cheese, chopped
1 tbsp chopped parsley
1 tbsp mixed chopped herbs (thyme, basil, oregano)
½ tsp pepper
¼ tsp ground cloves
¼ tsp ground ginger
salt
pinch of saffron, infused in 2 tbsp boiling water

1. For the dough: sift the flour with the salt on to a board or marble slab, make a well in the center and add the oil, eggs, and half the water. Start mixing the oil, eggs, and water together with the fingertips, gradually drawing in the flour and adding more liquid as it is needed. Knead the dough until it is smooth and very elastic, about 5 minutes. It should be very firm, almost dry. Cover it with an upturned bowl and leave 30 minutes for it to lose its elasticity before rolling.
2. Put the pork in a pan with enough of the stock to cover, add the lid and simmer until just tender, about 1 hour. Add the chicken breast and continue simmering until both the chicken and pork are very tender, about 30 minutes longer. Drain them, reserving the stock, and work them in a food processor to chop them finely. Add the Parmesan or Romano cheese, Bel Paese or mozzarella cheese, parsley, herbs, pepper, cloves and ginger and continue working until smooth in the food processor, with a little cooking liquid to moisten. Taste the filling for seasoning.

3. Divide the pasta dough in half and roll out as thinly as possible to a large rectangle. Brush the dough with water and put little mounds of the filling (about a teaspoonful) on the dough at regular intervals about 1½ inch/4 cm apart. Roll out the remaining dough to a rectangle of the same size, put it on top and with a small ball of dough dipped in flour, press the top piece down to seal around each little mound of filling. With a fluted ravioli cutter or a knife, cut the ravioli into squares and let dry 2-3 hours.
4. Bring the remaining chicken stock and the stock from cooking the pork to a boil with the saffron and its liquid. Simmer the ravioli in the mixture for 15-20 minutes or until they are tender but still *al dente*. Either taste the broth for seasoning and serve the ravioli and broth in soup bowls, or drain the pasta before serving. A bowl of grated Parmesan or Romano cheese and a bowl of cinnamon sugar for sprinkling are the authentic accompaniments.

BARTOLOMEO SCAPPI

flourished 1540–1570

BARTOLOMEO SCAPPI IS TO cooking as Michelangelo is to the fine arts. His cookbook *Opera*, in its beauty as a printed work, in its ordered presentation and comprehensiveness, exemplifies the practical elegance of the High Renaissance. No comparably authoritative work appeared again until the mid-eighteenth century in France, and none has ever matched *Opera* for its series of bold but scrupulously accurate drawings depicting the ideal kitchen furnished with all the equipment of the expert cook. Here is the fish tank full of fish, there the ravioli wheel, the nutmeg grater, and the slotted spoon for draining pasta, and there the kitchen boy manipulating a whisk by rolling the handle between his hands exactly as is done today. The text of *Opera* is as accomplished as the illustrations, and the recipes are so thorough in their detail and so clearly indexed that they put many a modern cookbook to shame. Scappi leaves nothing to chance; he even illustrates the perfect traveling saddle with leather bottles and containers, like a modern picnic basket – and stipulates that it needs a strong horse.

Opera was printed in 1570, at a time when the arts of good living were studied and enjoyed in Italy with unparalleled ardor; Italian manners were considered models by the ruder gentry of the north, as was the Italian taste in clothes, furnishing, and fine cooking. Gourmet clubs flourished. The members of the *Compagnia del*

Paiolo (Caldron Club), to which the painter Andrea del Sarto belonged, competed in preparing the most amusing as well as the most edible feasts. When it was del Sarto's turn to entertain his eleven fellows, he constructed a temple of sausage columns and Parmesan pillars, which housed a songbook of lasagne (the pages inscribed with notes of peppercorns) set on a lectern of sliced veal. Another group, the *Compagnia della Cazzuola* (Casserole Club) dressed up as construction workers and built an edifice of bread bricks and sweetmeat stones cemented with lasagne. Leonardo da Vinci put a rather more practical finger in the pie and invented a spit with a propeller that turned in the heat of the fire; his cook Matrina is the only woman ever mentioned in his writings, and he used to sketch the food he wanted so she could do the shopping properly.

Scappi rises easily to the demands of his knowledgeable audience. He was obviously an educated man. From a few scattered allusions in *Opera*, it seems probable that Scappi's first major position was as cook to Cardinal Campeggio, since Scappi describes in detail the banquet which the cardinal organized in 1536 in honor of the Holy Roman Emperor Charles V. (Campeggio was a shrewd lawyer and frequent choice as papal legate for difficult negotiations, as over the divorce of Henry VIII and Catherine of Aragon.) The fact that it was a fast day made little difference to the spread. No fewer than 13 courses

---

OPPOSITE: In Veronese's biblical painting of "The Marriage in Cana" (1593), the jewels of the women, the laden table, and the little black boy all reflect the wealth and cosmopolitan outlook of sixteenth-century Italy.

In this illustration from Opera *we see how Scappi applies the Renaissance love of invention to the kitchen with conspicuous success. A chimney hood catches the smoke of the fire, the cauldron hangs from a hinged crane and the turnspit is sheltered by a firescreen. On the right stretches a row of stoves with simmering pots, and above them is a hatch for calling orders to the market boys. In the corner knives and spoons are speared in a bale of straw, and bread rests on a high shelf, safe from animals. On the left stands a sink with running water and the all-important mortar and pestle.*

followed each other in dizzy succession, with soups, fish, pastries, vegetables, and sweet dishes mingled in apparently random combination, though there is a perceptible lightening towards the end of the meal. One representative course offered fried baby squid with lemon, prune pastries, fried lobster tails, fried spinach with vinegar and must (unfermented grape juice), caviar pie, and broccoli cooked in hot oil *alla napolitana* and sprinkled with orange juice.

When Cardinal Campeggio died in 1539, Scappi probably moved on to the household of Cardinal Carpi, member of an immensely wealthy family who possessed one of the greatest Roman palaces. Certainly he was working for another cardinal, since in *Opera* he describes the catering arrangements for the conclave in the winter of 1549-50 when Julius III was elected. The conclave was unusually long, lasting over two months. Cooking for it must have been quite a strain, as arrangements were complex. Each cardinal employed his own servants who cooked his food and in solemn procession brought it to a panel of bishops, who inspected it to make sure that no secret messages were being smuggled in. Once approved, the food was put in a revolving hatch so the cardinals were safely isolated from all contact with the outside world, as canonical law required. In such a long drawn-out struggle for election, the wealth and good taste of each cardinal's table must have been an important part of the psychological warfare.

To judge from *Opera*, the conclave was one of the highlights of Scappi's career. He apparently continued to work for the church, as he makes a casual reference in his book to the "happy year of 1564" when he served the pope. This was Pius IV, a Lombard renowned for his love of puddings and pies as well as, says Scappi, frogs' legs fried in garlic and parsley (page 48). Scappi seems to have spent his last years in the service of Pius V since he reports on the coronation banquet of 1566 and four years later describes himself in *Opera* as *cuoco secreto* or private cook to the pope.

The cooking of *Opera* has progressed far beyond the tentative steps of Martino, writing a hundred years earlier. Opening with a dialogue between himself and his apprentice (a favourite device for explaining the principles of good cooking), Scappi goes on to cover, in six lengthy

As cook to several cardinals and popes, Scappi was familiar with the elaborate ceremonial of serving food during a papal conclave. The procession of servants to the table carries scarlet and gold hampers of hot food (cucina), cold food (credenza), and drinks (bottigliaria), each emblazoned with a cardinal's coat of arms. To ensure no messages can reach the conclave, a panel of bishops (right) inspects the food (Scappi says he cannot make pies because the bishops must open them) as well as the steward's box and tableware, before passing everything through the revolving hatches behind. The fare of every cardinal in conclave was subject to the same scrutiny.

chapters, meat and poultry, fish, food for meat and fast days, pasta, and diets for the sick. Like all Renaissance cooks, he was interested in the scientific aspects of food. His experience with elderly popes – Pius IV had trouble with his digestion – must have made him particularly health-conscious. Many of the methods of classical cooking are already developed in Scappi – he is particularly fond of marinating and is also adept at braising and poaching. For example, he soaks chicken in white wine, vinegar, and spices, then bakes it in a sealed *stufatoro* (stewpot), serving the marinade as a sauce. The new interest in *stufatori*, which retained the meat juices and blended the flavors by gentle cooking, was typical of a more sophisticated approach to cooking.

Scappi also considers each subject in greater detail than ever before, and he is the first European cook to explore the Arab art of pastry-making. Martino mentions only a simple flour and water paste, but Scappi details several sophisticated methods for making pastry which he uses in over 200 recipes. One pastry layered with melted lard, then folded and rolled, marks the primitive beginnings of puff pastry. However, it must have been

far from today's flaky French delicacy – and equally far from the wafer-thin Arab pastry that probably served as the model (and is made by a totally different method). A similarly flaky dough was also used for an early type of *vol au vent* (called *crostate*) which was basted with a feather dipped in butter to help it rise during cooking, then filled. Medieval pies with a top crust remained as popular as ever, and often in the filling one meat was wrapped around another (ham around sweetbreads, for instance), making an attractive pattern when the pie was cut – a practice still seen today in French terrines.

Very Italian are Scappi's open pies filled with peas, artichoke hearts, and other vegetables; one crumbly pastry made of equal quantities of flour and butter and flavored with rosewater seems to be the ancestor of *pasta frolla*, now used for so many meltingly rich Italian pastries. Also included among Scappi's pastries are waffles (he illustrates the iron), several kinds of fritter, and cakes called *pizze*, bearing but a faint resemblance to the Neapolitan versions of today. Other recognizably Italian traits in Scappi's cooking are his love of cheese – he uses ricotta for stuffings and desserts, soft cheese for melting in layered dishes, and Parmesan for sprinkling as a seasoning – and a taste for veal and sausages, including mortadella and salami.

Scappi was well aware of the strong regional influence in Italian cooking. He mentions the fine oysters and prawns he saw in Venice; he calls several vegetable and fruit dishes *alla lombarda*; and he has a recipe for *zambaglione*, the fluffy mousse of egg yolks, sugar, and sweet Sicilian wine to which he adds chicken broth. Many dishes are named for gastronomic centers like Rome, Bologna, and Milan because of their traditional patronage of good food. The foreign influence in Scappi is equally strong, reflecting the cosmopolitan position of Rome, which by now had replaced Florence and Venice as the leader in taste. Scappi has a recipe for *succussu all moresca* (Moorish couscous) made in special steamers exactly as today; his trout is *alla tedesca* (German style) and so is his beef marinated with ham and spices. He

OPPOSITE: The fruits and vegetables of sixteenth-century Italy are brought vividly to life in this surrealist evocation of autumn by the Milanese artist Arcimboldo.

talks of the plentiful supplies of cod in English waters, reported to him by the cook of an English cardinal, and elsewhere explains that "*crema* is a French word, and it is made from flour, milk and eggs" – today's pastry cream or confectioners' custard.

A cook was under the nominal direction of the *scalco* or steward who ran the household, though Scappi says the steward must also know how to cook, implying that the two offices were not totally separate. This is confirmed by the influential cookbook *Banchetti*, written in 1548 by Cristoforo da Messisbugo, a steward who achieved such success that he was ennobled. True to his profession, Messisbugo goes into great detail on the serving as well as the cooking of food, and he is an authority on an Italian innovation, the *credenza*. The *credenza* (the word is now used to describe the side table or sideboard) was a course of cold dishes featuring pies, sausages, boiled shellfish, vegetables, salads, and other typical *antipasti*, as well as fruits, sweet cakes, and candies. Display was half the attraction, with fine Venetian glass and precious plate, wrought by masters like Benvenuto Cellini, standing cheek by jowl with sugar statues and gelatin molds. The *credenza* was the forerunner of the French cold buffet – apparently introduced to France by Pierre Buffet, a royal cook who was working in Verona in the early sixteenth century – but in the cooler northern climate cold food never had quite the same appeal as in Italy, where a *credenza* course alternated with a hot course, from the kitchen.

Italian table settings, a worthy complement to the opulence of the *credenza*, struck Montaigne's fancy during a visit to Rome in 1580: "In front of those to whom they want to do particular honor, who are seated beside or opposite the master, they place big silver squares on which their salt cellar stands, of the same sort as they put before the great in France. On top of this there is a napkin folded in four and on this napkin is the bread, knife, fork, and spoon." Forks were mentioned in an inventory as early as 1360 but Scappi shows one of the first pictures – a stubby, two-pronged implement that no doubt helped circumvent the voluminous ruffs that were in vogue, and

ABOVE LEFT: Scappi advises a cool place with high windows as a dairy. A kitchen boy twirls a whisk between both hands while another at right stirs honey butter.
ABOVE RIGHT: Here cooks knead dough for pasta, then roll it flat. At hand are a flour sifter, a ravioli wheel, a shallow padella *pan for baking, and a lemon squeezer.*

also made the job of eating slippery pasta easier. Protective table napkins, tied around the neck over the ruff and stretching down to cover the lap, were equally indispensable. They were folded into fantastic shapes – waterlilies, melons, bishop's mitres – but as the use of forks spread and eating became more discreet, the importance of napkins declined. Even so, pictures of Louis XIV at table a hundred years later show him wearing one of towel size, draped fashionably from the shoulder.

Such complex table-setting and serving arrangements needed the careful supervision of the *trinciante* or carver. He was the third man in the catering triangle, on an equal footing with the cook. His duties have been minutely described by Vincente Cervio in *Il Trinciante*, printed in 1581. As well as dismembering birds and large cuts of meat, the carver would personally serve his master, thus protecting him against poisoning – more a formality than a necessity by the sixteenth century.

Popes and cardinals always took their private cooks on their journeys, and Cervio describes how to set up a special kitchen when a dignitary comes to stay. No doubt the *trinciante* and *scalco* were often at odds with each other, since according to Messisbugo it was the steward's responsibility to welcome guests with due ceremony. He also saw that the servants discharged their duties correctly and supervised journeys to and from the summer villa, not forgetting the fishing rods, playing cards, and dice. Another steward, Domenico Romoli, writing in 1560, warns against admitting the public to a banquet, as had been the custom. They get drunk, interfere with the service of food, and gobble up the leftovers; much better, he says, to admit onlookers only when the dancing begins and the tables have been cleared.

Scappi's kitchen equipment includes a dozen knives (the handles riveted for extra strength), two-pronged fork, macaroni rolling pin, skewers, bellows, and waffle irons. Renaissance cooks developed flat gâteaux, little cakes, and waffles to an art.

In tune with Romoli's advice, Pope Pius V (a prudish pope who even had Michelangelo's nudes veiled) exercised restraint at his coronation in 1566, refraining from throwing money to the Roman crowd, as was the custom, and canceling altogether the usual anniversary banquet the following year. This reaction against the medieval tradition of free-for-all feasting ultimately spread throughout Europe. No longer was it considered the ruler's obligation to dine under the inquisitive gaze of his subjects. In England, this segregation of the classes had relatively little effect on the daily fare of the nobility, but in France two separate cooking styles evolved – the *haute cuisine* of the court and nobility, and the *cuisine bourgeoise* that varied from region to region and was based on local ingredients.

Scanning *Opera*, with its more than 1,000 recipes and dazzling display of a master cook's equipment (so much of it still in use today), it might seem that in 1570 Renaissance Italians were irrevocably established as the leaders of European cooking. Yet within 50 years the initiative had passed to Paris which, as the focal point of French culture, offered a more propitious setting for the development of cooking than the factious cities of Italy. With the end of the unifying spirit of the Renaissance, the destiny of Italian cooking lay in the regions rather than in a single town; Scappi's broad perspective on cooking fell from favor and by the 1650s *Opera* was out of print. Nonetheless, in its encyclopedic learning *Opera* marks the high point among Italian cookbooks. Even more importantly, its design, accuracy, and detail reflect the scientific method which was to so greatly influence Europe throughout the seventeenth century.

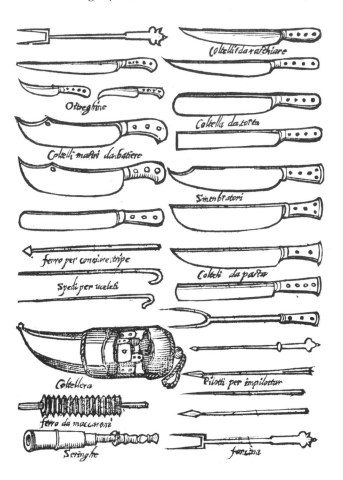

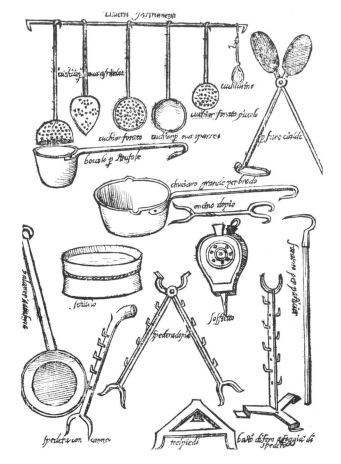

43

SCAPPI RECIPES

OPERA DI
BARTOLOMEO
SCAPPI
MASTRO DELL'ARTE DEL CVCINARE,
con laquale si può ammaestrare qual si voglia Cuoco,
Scalco, Trinciante, o Mastro di Casa.
DIVISA IN SEI LIBRI.

NEL
Primo si intende il ragionamento che fa l'Autore con Giouanni suo discepolo.
Secondo si tratta di diuerse viuande di carne, sì di quadrupedi come di volatili.
Terzo si parla della statura, e stagione di ogni sorte di pesci.
Quarto si mostra le liste del presentar le viuande in tauola di grasso, & magro.
Quinto si contiene l'ordine di far diuerse sorti di paste, & altri lauori.
Sesto si ragiona de'conualescenti, e molte altre sorte di viuande per gli infermi.

Con le Figure che fanno dibisogno nella Cucina.
Aggiontoui nuouamente il Trinciante, & il Mastro di Casa.
DEDICATE AL MAG. M. MATTEO BARBINI
Cuoco, e Scalco celeberrimo della Città di Venetia.

IN VENETIA, Per Alessandro de'Vecchi. MDCXXII.

OPPOSITE: *Per Friggere, Accomodare in Agresta Le Rane.*
ABOVE: *The frontispiece of the 1622 edition of* Opera *gives a glimpse of its magnificent contents. On the spit the small birds closest to the fire require quick cooking, while slower-cooking roasts are set further away.*

Scappi's pound measure derives from the Roman *libra* and weighed about 12 ounces. This value (called troy weight) is still used for gold and precious stones, but more bulky items come in avoirdupois weight – a term meaning "to have weight" and referring to a 16-ounce pound.

PER FAR MINESTRA DI TAGLIATELLI

Scappi's pasta dough is exactly the same as that made today, both in ingredients and method. After rolling the dough, he wraps it around the rolling pin so it can be cut across easily at narrow intervals (for noodles) or more widely spaced (for broad pasta such as lasagne). Like Martino, Scappi serves his pasta with sugar, cinnamon, and cheese for sprinkling and he gives no indication whether the pasta should be drained or served in its cooking broth. Nor does he mention draining meat or vegetables, where appropriate, so perhaps he simply assumed the cook knew all about it.

Knead together 2 pounds of fine white flour, 3 eggs and some lukewarm water, mixing them well on a table for the space of a quarter of an hour, and then roll out thinly

and leave the pasta to dry for a while, trimming untidy bits at the edge, and when dry, but not too dry as then it would crumble, sprinkle with flour from the sieve to prevent the pasta sticking, and then take the pasta roller [rolling pin] and take one end of the pasta and roll it lightly around the pasta roller, and then slice the rolled up pasta with a broad sharp knife, and when the *tagliatelli* are cut stretch them out and leave them to dry a while, and when dry cook them in fat broth or with milk and butter, and when cooked serve hot with cheese, sugar, cinnamon, and if you wish to have lasagne, when the pasta is on the pasta roller, divide it across in two pieces, and then cut these into squares, and cook them in hare or crane both, or any meat broth, and serve hot with cheese, sugar, and cinnamon.

The Renaissance genius for mechanics made moving a vast cauldron easy.

TO MAKE NOODLES

Serves 6
10 oz/2½ cups/300 g flour
½ tsp salt
3 eggs, beaten to mix
2-4 fl oz/¼-½ cup/60-125 ml water
4⅔ pints/3 quarts/3 liters meat or chicken stock, or the same quantity of milk with 1 oz/2 tbsp/30 g butter
FOR SERVING:
2 tbsp butter
4 oz/1 cup/125 g grated Parmesan or Romano cheese
3¼ oz/½ cup/100 g sugar
1 tbsp ground cinnamon

1. Sift the flour with the salt on to a board or marble slab, make a well in the center, and add the eggs and most of the water. Start to draw the flour into the center, working the mixture with the fingers of one hand; if necessary add more water to make a smooth dough that is soft and fairly dry. Knead the dough thoroughly until very smooth and elastic, about 5 minutes. Cover it with an upturned bowl and let stand 1 hour to lose some of its elasticity.
2. Roll out the dough as thinly as possible on a floured board, trim the edges and leave until slightly dry but still pliable, about 15 minutes. Sprinkle the top with flour, roll up the dough loosely and cut it crosswise into ½ inch/1.25 cm strips. Alternatively, roll

and cut the noodles with a pasta machine. Spread out the strips on wax/greaseproof paper or paper towels and leave to dry at least 3 hours.
3. Bring the stock or milk and butter to a boil, add the noodles and simmer until the noodles are *al dente*, 2-3 minutes. Drain them, rinse with hot water and reheat in a pan with the butter. Serve with bowls of grated cheese and the sugar mixed with the cinnamon for sprinkling.

Per fare crostate, cioe pan ghiotto con rognon di vitella arrostito nello spedo

Crostate are crisp little morsels often on a base of fried or toasted bread or sometimes pastry; and they are the ancestors of the crisp French croustades made of bread or pastry. As crostini (crostate has come to mean a sweet open pie), they are still a favorite Italian first course, often made with chicken livers or cheese; here Scappi uses veal kidneys in a spicy sauce. Pomegranate juice, with its fruity tartness, was a seasoning the Italians picked up from the Arabs. Burnet is an herb used to flavor butter sauces and cooling drinks, or its slightly bitter leaves can be served in salad.

Take slices of day-old bread cut knife-thick, and toast them on the grill, and spit-roast veal kidneys with a little of the loin, then let them cool a while, and then chop finely with mint, marjoram, burnet, fresh fennel, or if you have none, use dried fennel, pepper, cloves, cinnamon, nutmeg, sugar, egg yolks, pomegranate juice or clear vinegar, and plenty of salt, and when mixed spread on the toasted slices of bread, and arrange in a pie pan so the slices do not overlap, and cover the dish and heat from above, with a few hot cinders below, and leave until the bread has absorbed some of the fat and the mixture is set, and serve hot with pomegranate juice, sugar, and cinnamon. And you can also put fresh butter or melted lard in the pie pan to make the bread richer. The crostate can also be cooked with a slow fire on the grill.

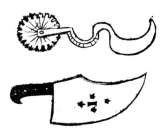

Kidney toast

Serves 8 as first course, 4 as main dish
2 veal kidneys, if possible wrapped in their fat
8 oz/250 g piece lean veal
1 tsp chopped mint
1 tsp chopped marjoram
1 tsp ground fennel seeds
½ tsp ground cloves
½ tsp ground cinnamon
½ tsp ground nutmeg
1 tsp sugar
3 tbsp pomegranate juice or red wine vinegar
salt and pepper
8 egg yolks
8 thick slices white bread
FOR SERVING:
2-3 tbsp pomegranate juice or lemon juice
1-2 tsp ground cinnamon
1-2 tsp sugar

1. Cut all but a thin layer of fat from the kidneys, tie some of the discarded fat around the veal, and roast the kidneys and meat on a spit or in an oven heated to No 6/400°F/200°C until they are browned but still rare in the center, 30-40 minutes. Turn down the oven to No 4/350°F/175°C.

2. Let the kidneys cool, then coarsely chop them with the fat, discarding the white core. Chop the veal and add it. Add the mint, marjoram, fennel, cloves, cinnamon, nutmeg, sugar and pomegranate juice or vinegar and season the mixture highly with salt and pepper. Stir in the egg yolks.

3. Toast the bread and spread the kidney mixture on it, pressing it down well. Put the toasts on a baking sheet and bake in the heated oven until some

of the fat from the kidneys has melted into the toast and the mixture holds together, about 15 minutes. Sprinkle the toasts with pomegranate juice or lemon juice, cinnamon, and sugar and serve at once. The toast can be prepared ahead and baked just before serving.

PER FRIGGERE,
ACCOMMODARE IN AGRESTA LE RANE

This is the recipe for the frogs so beloved of Pope Pius IV. They are sautéed with parsley and garlic, or plainly fried and served with *agresto* (tart grape juice) thickened with egg yolks. Frogs are still a speciality of Pius IV's native Lombardy, where they live in the flooded rice fields of the Po valley.

Remove the head with its big mouth, and cut off the feet up to the first joint, and leave to soak in cold water, changing the water in the course of eight hours, so that the frogs cleanse themselves and plump up, and whiten, and then take them from the water and fry them, either with the legs tucked under the body, or cut off at the joint, removing the bone; sprinkle them with flour and fry them in oil and serve with a little ground salt, and above all do not cover them after frying as they become hard and shrivel and lose their goodness. You can also fry them with cloves of garlic and parsley, and serve them with the garlic and parsley and pepper and ground salt as a sauce, which is the way Pope Pius IV used to eat them in 1564 when I served him. When they have been fried just like this, with flour, you can keep them hot in *agresto* sauce made with fresh *agresto*, and egg yolks.

OPPOSITE: A sixteenth-century artist delights in depicting produce at its very best. Little account is taken of the seasons; here we see spring peas and cherries, summer apricots and melons, autumn figs, pears, blackberries and almonds, and a solitary winter cabbage.

SAUTÉED FROGS' LEGS

Serves 4 as a main course
12-14 pairs frogs' legs (about 3 lb/1.4 kg)
3 oz/²⁄₃ cup/90 g flour
¹⁄₂ tsp salt
large pinch of pepper
2¹⁄₂ fl oz/¹⁄₃ cup/75 ml olive oil
1-2 cloves garlic, crushed
3 tbsp chopped parsley
FOR SERVING:
crushed sea salt
freshly ground black pepper

1. Soak the frogs' legs in cold water for 1-2 hours to plump and whiten them, drain and dry them on paper towels. Mix the flour with the salt and pepper and coat the frogs' legs with it, tossing them to discard the excess.
2. Heat the oil in a pan or skillet and fry the frogs' legs over medium heat until lightly browned and tender, allowing 3-4 minutes on each side. Add the garlic half way through cooking and the pars-ley just before serving. Serve the frogs' legs as soon as possible with mills of sea salt and black peppercorns for grinding.

PER ARROSTIR NELLO SPEDO, E CUOCERE IN PIU MODI ANATRE SELVAGGIE

This survey of the kinds of wild duck and how to cook them gives a good idea of Scappi's encyclopedic knowledge. *Brodo lardiero* is a sweet-sour sauce made from toasted breadcrumbs, red wine, tart flavorings, spices like cinnamon and cloves, and a variety of fruits including wild cherries, prunes, and raisins.

I find that there are different varieties of wild duck – big ones, little ones, ones with variegated feathers and feet, but the best have red feet and bills and they feed in the open countryside, while those that have black bills and feet feed in the valleys and are not so good, but all have the same season from October through to the end of

February, and these birds are best during the coldest months, and all like damp and marshy country, and can be spit-roast like cranes, or cooked in *brodo lardiero*, or cooked in this other way. Pluck and draw the duck and remove the neck and feet and place the duck in a pan with red wine and a little vinegar to cover, and chopped ham, pepper, cinnamon, cloves, nutmeg, ginger, sage leaves and raisins, and close the pan so that the steam does not escpae, and cook for 1½ hours, more or less depending on the age and size of the duck, and when cooked serve with this sauce, and you can cook whole large onions with the duck, and prunes and dried wild cherries.

The cook dismembers a roast duck while his kitchen boy extracts the remaining flavor from the bones with a duck press.

WILD DUCK WITH PIQUANT SAUCE

Serves 4
2 wild ducks, with their giblets
8 oz/250 g cooked lean ham, finely chopped
1¼ pints/3 cups/750 ml red wine
4 fl oz/½ cup/125 ml red wine vinegar
½ tsp pepper
½ tsp ground cinnamon
¼ tsp ground cloves
¼ tsp ground nutmeg
¼ tsp ground ginger
2 tbsp sugar
1 tbsp chopped sage
3¼ oz/¾ cup/100 g raisins
4 medium onions, halved, or 6 oz/175 g pitted prunes (optional)

1. Put the ducks with their giblets in a casserole and add the ham, wine, vinegar, pepper, cinnamon, cloves, nutmeg, ginger, sugar, sage, raisins, and onions or prunes (if using). Cover the pan, bring to a boil, and simmer on top of the stove or cook in an oven heated to No 4/350°F/175°C until tender, ¾-1¼ hours. The cooking time depends very much on the age and size of the ducks.

2. Arrange the ducks on a platter, spoon around the onions or prunes and keep warm. Discard the giblets. If necessary, boil the sauce to reduce it until fairly thick. Taste it for seasoning and serve it in a separate sauceboat.

PER FARE TORTIGLIONE RIPIENO

Scappi's varied recipes for tortiglioni show how advanced his pastries had become. This particular recipe closely resembles a coffee or tea cake. Scappi's instructions are rather hard to follow, but his aim is obviously to produce a rich, spiced mixture between layers of thin yeast dough.

Knead together 2 pounds flour, 6 egg yolks, 2 ounces rose water, 1 ounce yeast dissolved in lukewarm water, and 4 ounces fresh butter or lard that does not smell bad, and quite a bit of salt, for half an hour so that the dough is well worked, and then roll it out thinly and cover with melted butter, that is not too hot, or lard, and with the pastry wheel cut all round the edges of the dough that are always thicker than the rest; sprinkle the dough with 4 ounces sugar, and 1 ounce cinnamon, and then have a pound of raisins that have been boiled in wine, and 1 pound of dates also cooked in wine and finely chopped, and 1 pound of seedless raisins boiled in wine, all mixed together with sugar, cinnamon, cloves and nutmeg, and then spread on the dough with pieces of butter, and roll up the dough lengthwise like crêpes, being careful not to break the dough, and this tortiglione must not be rolled up more than three turns so it cooks better, nor handled too much, but then basted with melted butter that is not too hot, then beginning from one end roll it up lightly like a snail or maze; and have a pie pan prepared with a sheet of the same dough, of the same thickness, basted with butter, and put it lightly over the tortiglione without pressing it down, and cook in the oven in a moderate heat, basting with butter from time to time, and when it is cooked sprinkle with sugar, rose water, and serve hot. The pie pan used for the tortiglione should be open and with low sides.

YEAST CAKE STUFFED WITH RAISINS

Serves 8

FOR THE DOUGH:
½ oz/15 g compressed yeast, or ¼ oz/7 g dry yeast
4 fl oz/½ cup/125 ml lukewarm water
14 oz/3½ cups/450 g flour
½ tsp salt
3 egg yolks
2 tbsp rosewater
2 oz/¼ cup/60 g butter or lard, melted
FOR THE FILLING:
4½ oz/1 cup/140 g raisins
4½ oz/1 cup/140 g currants
8 oz/1½ cups/250 g pitted dates, chopped
8 fl oz/1 cup/250 ml sweet white wine
2½ oz/⅓ cup/75 g butter or lard, melted
   (for brushing)
3¼ oz/½ cup/100 g sugar
1 tbsp ground cinnamon
1 tsp ground nutmeg
½ tsp ground cloves
2 oz/¼ cup/60 g butter, cut in pieces
TO FINISH:
1 egg, beaten with ½ tsp salt (for glaze –
   optional)
1 tbsp rosewater
confectioners'/icing sugar (for sprinkling)
9 inch/22 cm cake pan/tin

1. For the dough: crumble or sprinkle the yeast over the water and let stand until dissolved, about 5 minutes. Sift the flour into a bowl with the salt and make a well in the center. Add the egg yolks, rosewater, melted butter or lard, and yeast mixture and stir to form to smooth dough. Turn out on to a lightly floured board and knead until the dough is smooth and elastic, about 5 minutes.

2. Put the dough in a warm lightly oiled bowl, turn it over so the top is oiled, cover with a damp cloth and leave in a warm place to rise until doubled in bulk, about 1½ hours. Meanwhile, simmer the raisins, currants and dates in the wine until they are plump and the wine is absorbed, 8-10 minutes; let them cool. Butter the cake pan/tin.

3. When the dough is risen, knead it lightly to knock out the air and set aside about a sixth of it. Roll out the remaining dough to a thin rectangle, about 12 × 18 inches/30 × 45 cm. Trim the edges, reserving the trimmings. Brush the dough with melted butter or lard and sprinkle with half the sugar mixed with 1 teaspoon of the cinnamon. Mix the cooled raisin mixture with the remaining sugar and cinnamon, the nutmeg and cloves and spread them on the dough. Dot the filling with the pieces of butter and fold the dough lengthwise to make three layers. Brush the top with melted butter. Curl the dough in the prepared cake pan/tin in a loose spiral, with the original folds at the edges, taking care not to break the dough.

4. Roll out the reserved dough with the trimmings to a very thin round about 12 inches/30 cm in diameter. Cover the dough spiral with the round, tucking down the edges so the spiral is completely covered. Roll out any scraps to make petals, leaves and a stem for a flower decoration on top. Brush the top with melted butter and put in a warm place to rise until the dough has almost doubled in bulk, about 40 minutes. Heat the oven to No 5/375°F/190°C. Brush the dough with the egg glaze, if you like.

5. Bake the yeast cake in the heated oven for 30 minutes, turn down the heat to No 3/325°F/160°C and continue baking until well browned, 30-45 minutes longer, basting from time to time with melted butter. If the cake browns too much during cooking, cover it with foil. When cooked, sprinkle while still hot with rosewater, followed by confectioners'/icing sugar, and serve hot.

LA VARENNE

about 1615–1678

FRANCOIS PIERRE DE LA VARENNE is the founder of French classical cooking. Ever since it appeared in 1651, critics have both acclaimed and belittled his book *Le Cuisinier françois*, but no one has questioned its importance. Very few new cookbooks appeared in France in the 1500's and *Le Cuisinier françois* was the first work of lasting influence since the times of Taillevent. As André Simon noted, the book ran to 30 editions in 75 years and became "the treasured possession of most French households of any distinction for close on a century." The reason for its success is simple: *Le Cuisinier françois* was the first book to record the immense advance which French cooking had made under the civilizing influence of Renaissance values and court styles.

News of the transalpine revolution in cooking probably began to reach France towards the end of the fifteenth century when King Charles VII is said to have introduced his subjects to Parmesan cheese and macaroni. In 1505, the first French edition of *De honesta voluptate* appeared in Lyons, then Europe's banking capital and home to a thriving Italian community. Italy was powerful in politics as well as in the arts and it was natural that François I of France should have chosen an Italian princess, Catherine de Medici, to marry his second son, the future King Henri

OPPOSITE: *The Palace of Versailles was built by Louis XIII in 1631. Louis XIV eventually moved his entire court there, by which time cooking was a fashionable hobby among many noblemen.*

ABOVE: *Frontispiece from the celebrated Elzevir Press edition of* Le Pastissier françois, *1655.*

II. Catherine was only 14 at her marriage in 1533, but as the wife of one French King and the mother of three others, she was destined to dominate France for over half a century. Catherine's greed was proverbial and on one occasion she overate so grossly of her favorite ragoût of cockscombs, kidneys and artichoke hearts that she almost burst. Her son, Charles IX, had a similarly dangerous partiality for *salemigondis*, an Italian stew which inspired the French *salmis*.

In keeping with the Medici love of magnificence, Catherine was accompanied by a retinue of courtiers accustomed to precisely the kind of dishes and table service later described by Bartolomeo Scappi. However, to say that Catherine brought Renaissance cooking to France is an over-simplification. Undoubtedly with her marriage, the vogue in France for all things Italian took off, not least in the design of châteaux and the lifestyle they epitomized. Italian cooks became persons of influence in a princely household, as we know from the encounter which the French essayist Michel de Montaigne had with the master cook of Cardinal Caraffa: "With magisterial gravity, he delivered me a discourse on this science of food – first about the general composition of the sauces, and then describing in detail the nature of their ingredients and their effects; then about differences in

A realistic glimpse of seventeenth-century
French fare shows the tough meats of the time
larded with strips of pork fat, and a plump
suckling pig stretched out beside one of the
pâtés, or raised pies, so beloved by La Varenne.

salads according to the season: what should be heated
and what should be served cold, and the way to garnish
and embellish them to please the eye. After that he came
to describing the order of service, full of fine and
important considerations; the whole overlaid with rich
and high-sounding words that are generally used to
report upon the government of an empire."

Montaigne had summed up the essence of the new
cuisine. It was precisely such attention to detail, balance,
and harmony that made the Renaissance arts so great. As
applied to cooking, it meant the demise of the inflated
banquets of medieval times, with their great displays of
meat and fowl and their feckless use of costly spices.

Le Cuisinier françois belongs to another world. Gone
are the exotic birds and multi-flavored purées. Cuts of
meat are easily identifiable, with the best reserved for
roasting and the rest cooked more slowly in liquid to
break down the tough fibers. Both meat and fowl are
simmered in subtly blended ragoûts, and La Varenne
recognizes the importance of reducing cooking juice to
concentrate the flavor. His very first recipe is for the
all-important bouillon which is often called *fonds* (base)
in French. He has several interesting liaisons flavored
with mushrooms, almonds, or truffles. La Varenne is also
the first French cook to add the classic thickening *roux* (of
fat and flour) to bouillon to make velouté sauce.

Asparagus, as depicted by Louise Morillon,
one of the first great women painters. She was
a contemporary of La Varenne and an
outstanding still-life artist. The long white
stems of the asparagus show that bleaching
vegetables by burying them underground was
a technique already in practice.

An astonishing number of modern dishes are mentioned in *Le Cuisinier françois*, including *boeuf à la mode, oeufs à la neige*, omelettes, beignets, and even pumpkin pie. La Varenne gives special attention to the preparation of vegetables, he uses a bouquet garni to flavor stocks and sauces, and he introduces such techniques as using egg whites to clarify a *gelée*. La Varenne also introduced the French to new ways of cooking tail, feet, tongue, and other variety meats that had long been popular in Italy. Sea fish (especially lobsters and oysters) begin to rival freshwater fish in his repertoire, showing how communications with Paris, 100 miles from the sea, had improved. The difficulties of transporting provisions gave rise to the greatest drama in the annals of cooking, the suicide of the Prince de Condé's cook, Vatel, in 1671. Madame de Sévigné describes how Vatel went unhappily to bed after the roast meat had run short at a dinner for the king. Determined that all should go well the next day, he rose early to take stock of his provisions. Only two carts of fish had arrived instead of the dozen he had ordered. The missing fish turned up fifteen minutes later, but Vatel knew nothing of it; in despair, unable to face

This fish market by Franz Snyders, another
contemporary artist, forms an almost
encyclopedic guide to fish and shellfish. Far
more species are shown than would ever
appear on a market stall – turtle, seal, beaver
and riggling live eels.

the disgrace, he had run upon his sword. The court was overwhelmed by the news: "People said it was because his honor had meant so much to him; his courage was both praised and condemned."

At the court of Louis XIV it was a point of pride to be interested in cooking, and in the years that followed the publication of *Le Cuisinier françois* many nobles gaily turned their hands to the stove. The Duchess of Burgundy invented a sweet-sour sauce of vinegar and sugar for meat, and the indolent Duke of Nevers bestirred himself to do his own marketing. The queen, Maria Theresa of Spain, tried to introduce the dishes of her homeland, but the French did not take to them kindly and only drinking chocolate and *olla podrida* (the catchall stew of beef, game, poultry, and vegetables that is served with its cooking broth) survived beyond her reign. To the king's mistress, Madame de Maintenon, goes the credit for *cotelettes à la Maintenon*, which were pared of their fat

and baked in paper when the royal digestion was in a delicate state.

This was not often; Louis XIV was a voracious eater, more glutton than gourmet. He liked his food floating in gravy with double the usual quantity of spice and was accustomed to consume "four plates of different potages, a whole pheasant, a partridge, a big plate of salad, lamb cut up in its gravy and seasoned with garlic, two good pieces of ham, a plateful of pastries, fruit, preserves, and hard eggs" at a regular meal. Potages (which then meant anything cooked in a pot) are featured prominently by La Varenne. Some resemble a stew of meat and vegetables (such as partridge with cabbage and duck with turnips) served with the reduced cooking liquid as gravy. Others are a purée of vegetables, often thickened with bread, resembling a modern soup.

During the seventeenth century the range of fruit and vegetables in France was transformed, not only by

In this illustration from Le Jardinier françois *by Nicholas de Bonnefons (1651), cooks are peeling fruit, boiling preserves and skimming jam. At the back a cook rolls fruit cheese, a confection of fruit and sugar worked until candied. Behind her hang molds and a jelly bag.*

In this illustration from Le Jardinier françois *by Nicholas de Bonnefons (1651), cooks are peeling fruit, boiling preserves and skimming jam. At the back a cook rolls fruit cheese, a confection of fruit and sugar worked until candied. Behind her hang molds and a jelly bag.*

imports from the Far East and the Americas, but also by more extensive cultivation of plants. Henri IV had planted the first orangery at the Tuileries Palace at the turn of the century, and 50 years later La Varenne could take seasonal supplies of oranges and lemons for granted, not to mention plums, apricots, peaches, and cultivated strawberries. Among vegetables, leeks and onions lost their monopoly to cucumbers, kale, carrots, and cauliflower. Spinach was well established, having become fashionable at the time of Catherine de Médicis (hence *florentine* for a spinach garnish), and the variety of salad greens was much greater – chicory dates from this time, as does romaine lettuce, the seeds of which were reputedly sent from Rome by Rabelais in 1537. Globe artichokes, credited with aphrodisiac properties, were unfailingly popular.

From the New World came potatoes and tomatoes, though the former were not widely grown until the 1750s, and tomatoes were long suspected of being poisonous. However, Jerusalem artichokes were adopted more quickly and La Varenne suggests braising them, then sautéing them with onions and a grate of nutmeg. They came from North America, but the French named them *taupinambours* because their introduction coincided with the arrival in Paris of some Brazilian Indians of the Topinambour tribe. Their English name is equally misleading; the early American colonists called them artichokes because they tasted like the globe variety, while the Italians realized that they belonged to the family of the sunflower or *girasole*, a word which became anglicized to Jerusalem.

The inspiration these new ingredients offered to an inventive cook can be imagined. La Varenne eagerly proposes such recipes as asparagus or cauliflower soup, fricasee of cucumber and artichokes *à la poivrade*. He delights in green peas, a new arrival from Italy, putting them in soups and serving them with chicken. Later, green peas became a craze at court, as Madame de Sévigné noted in 1696: "There is no end to this interest in peas . . . Some ladies sup with the king, and sup well at that, only to return home to eat peas before retiring, without any care for their digestion."

La Varenne was scarcely 35 when *Le Cuisinier françois* first appeared. At that point he had already been

master cook for ten years to the Marquis d'Uxelles, for whom he named his most famous creation, the duxelles of mushrooms seasoned with herbs and shallots, which is still a favorite flavoring for fish and vegetables. Beyond that, little is known about La Varenne himself, except that his name was a pseudonym, taken for some reason from a disreputable cook of an earlier generation who did a little pimping business for his master, Henri IV, and "gained more by carrying the *poulets* (love letters) of the king than by larding them in the kitchen." La Varenne died in 1678 in relative obscurity, having benefited little from his success as a bestselling author.

La Varenne is also credited with the authorship of *Le Pastissier françois*, the first comprehensive French work on pastry-making and one of the most remarkable cookbooks of all time. Although a comparatively large printing was made by the illustrious Elzevir Press in 1655 (two years after the book first appeared), very few copies

Habit de Rôtisseur

Habit de Pescheur.

Habit de Fruitiere

survive, no doubt because the *Pastissier* was a working cookbook, intended for use in the kitchen. Many modern cookbooks could take a lesson from *Le Pastissier*, with its step-by-step directions, accurate measurements, and instructions for temperature control. The book is surely inspired by Italian works such as Scappi's *Opera* that were most detailed and sophisticated in their treatment of pastry. The methods in *Le Pastissier* for making pie pastry, puff pastry, macaroons, and waffles, for instance, are precisely the same today, and it is the first book to mention the small baking ovens known as *petits fours*, soon to become the name for an entire family of little cakes and cookies.

La Varenne's name did not appear on any of the early editions of *Le Pastissier françois*, and there is some reason to doubt that he wrote it. The profession of *pâtissier* was completely separate from that of *cuisinier*, and it is hard to believe that two years after writing *Le Cuisinier françois*, the same author could turn out a second book so different in style and content. Several of the same recipes appear in both books, but *Le Pastissier* is much more detailed, while La Varenne writes in a shorthand that assumes a thorough knowledge of cooking. If La Varenne did write the book, he must have worked closely with an Italian pastry cook.

French cooking developed so rapidly in the wake of *Le Cuisinier françois* that even before his death, La Varenne was criticized as old-fashioned. In 1674, for example, an unidentified Sieur Roland upbraided La Varenne for "such a prodigious superfluity of dishes, such a quantity of stew and hotchpotch, such a singular compilation of viands. . . ."

It is certainly true that some medieval traits linger in *Le Cuisinier françois*. La Varenne has a tendency

ABOVE: *These surrealist figures from the late seventeenth century by Nicholas de Larmessin are composed of the tools and ingredients of their trade.*
OPPOSITE: *This French feast of 1707 with its horseshoe table and great* pièces montées, *or subtleties, shows how medieval banqueting habits still lingered among the fruits, rich gâteaux and pastries of a more sophisticated age.*

to use archaic flavorings like musk and ambergris (believed to be an aphrodisiac) and he recommends some very medieval pies and hashes containing, to modern tastes, an inordinate number of ingredients. Some of his garnishes are lavish in the extreme, like *béatilles* made of cockscombs, chicken wingtips, and livers sautéed and served in a sauce thickened with egg yolk. French writers have also accused La Varenne of the reactionary habit of sweetening savory dishes with sugar, but here they may be mistaken. His intention was probably to achieve with delicate meats like chicken the same kind of sweet-sour effect that we still enjoy with cheesecake. Such combinations have all but disappeared from the French repertoire but are still very much alive in the cooking of northern Europe, particularly Germany and Scandinavia.

Le Cuisinier françois is a seminal work; it marks the end of medieval cooking and the beginning of *haute cuisine*. As such, it contains elements of both. When it was written, France was entering a period of prosperity as the memory of the bitter religious wars of the previous century receded and the reign of Louis XIV, the Sun King, assumed all its glory. La Varenne opened the way to this new era, sharing the limelight with only one other cook, Massialot, who wrote *Le Cuisinier royal et bourgeois* in 1691. Fifty years later both books had been superseded by an outpouring of new works, or at least of works that purported to be new, for on close examination it is clear that many writers were congenital plagiarists. La Varenne's books were pillaged and his name disparaged, then forgotten. Yet he was the first cook to bring order to an undisciplined art that had been developing in France, virtually undocumented, for three centuries. Without him French cooking might never have reached its full flower.

LA VARENNE RECIPES

LE
**CVISINIER
FRANÇOIS,**
ENSEIGNANT LA MANIERE
de bien apprester & assaisonner
toutes sortes de Viandes grasses
& maigres, Legumes, Patisseries,
& autres mets qui se seruent tant
sur les Tables des Grands que des
particuliers.

*Par le Sieur de LA VARENNE
Escuyer de Cuisine de Monsieur le
Marquis d'VXELLES.*

A PARIS,
Chez PIERRE DAVID, au Palais,
à l'entrée de la Gallerie des Prisonniers.

M. DC. LI.
Auec Priuilege du Roy.

LEFT: Pasté d'Anguilles.
ABOVE: This first 1651 edition of Le Cuisinier
françois *displays the name of La Varenne's
patron, the Marquis d'Uxelles.*

Brilliant cook though he was, La Varenne's ability to express his ideas in writing leaves a good deal to be desired. He gives few quantities in his recipes and his instructions are much less detailed than those of his Italian predecessors. His use of spices is restrained and the omission of salt much more noticeable than it was earlier, when food tended to be saturated with spices. Salt and pepper have therefore been added to the following recipes.

POTAGE DE POULETS AUX POIS VERTS

Fresh green peas were new to France in the time of La Varenne, but he had already developed the classic combination of peas with lettuce found today in *petits pois à la française*. His *potages* are not soups but substantial stews.

When your chickens are well cleaned and trussed, put them in a pot with good stock, and skim them well, then put your peas into a frying pan with butter or lard, and cook them gently with lettuces, that you have blanched (that is, put in cold water); also simmer your bread, and then garnish it with your chickens, peas and lettuces, then serve it.

These seventeenth-century cupboard doors show a spring garden and opposite, an autumn outdoor feast. The garden is still in the Renaissance tradition of tiny ornamental beds hedged with box.

CHICKEN CASSEROLE WITH GREEN PEAS

Serves 4
4 lb/1.8 kg roasting chicken, trussed
1¼ pints/3 cups/750 ml well-flavored chicken stock
1 large romaine lettuce, cut in 2 inch/5 cm pieces
2 tbsp butter
14 oz/4 cups/450 g shelled fresh green peas
4 fl oz/½ cup/125 ml water
1 tsp sugar
salt and pepper
2½ oz/¾ cup/75 g fresh white breadcrumbs

1. Put the chicken, breast up, in a large deep saucepan, pour in about three-quarters of the stock to half cover it. The breast will cook in steam while the tougher thighs simmer in stock. Bring slowly to a boil, skim well, cover and simmer until the chicken is tender and no pink juice runs out when the thigh is pierced with a skewer; ¾-1 hour. Take out the chicken and keep warm. Boil the stock until it is reduced to 8 fl oz/1 cup/250 ml.
2. Wash the lettuce thoroughly in cold water and drain it. In a casserole heat the butter and sauté the peas gently for 1-2 minutes without allowing them to brown. Add the water with the sugar, salt and pepper and lay the lettuce on top. Cover and simmer, stirring occasionally, until the peas are just tender, about 15 minutes.
3. Bring the remaining stock to a boil, add the breadcrumbs and simmer gently until the mixture is the consistency of cooked cereal.
4. When the chicken is cooked, discard the trussing strings and set it on top of the peas and lettuce. Stir the reduced chicken stock into the breadcrumb mixture, bring this sauce to a boil, and taste it for seasoning. Spoon it over the chicken and serve.

CHAMPIGNONS FARCIS

Fairy ring mushrooms, morels, truffles and fungi of all kinds were enormously popular in the seventeenth century. Louis XIII loved them so much that as he lay on his deathbed he insisted on stringing morels to dry for the summer. A *bard* is a thin sheet of pork fat.

Choose the largest mushrooms to hold the stuffing, which you will make of several meats or good herbs, so that it is delicate, and bind it with egg yolks, then your mushrooms being stuffed and seasoned, set them on a *bard* or on a little butter; cook them and serve with lemon juice.

STUFFED MUSHROOMS

Serves 4 as first course or accompaniment

1 lb/500 g large mushrooms
8 oz/250 g uncooked veal or breast of chicken
2 tbsp chopped chives
salt and pepper
2 egg yolks
3 tbsp butter
a squeeze of lemon juice

1. Heat the oven to No 4/350°F/175°C. Take the stems from the mushrooms and chop the stems. Finely chop the veal or chicken meat in a food processor or work twice through the fine plate of a grinder/mincer. Add the chopped mushroom stems and the chives with plenty of salt and pepper. Stir in the egg yolks to bind the mixture.

2. Spoon the mixture into the mushroom caps, mounding it well. Spread the butter in a heatproof baking dish, set the mushrooms on top and bake them in the heated oven, basting often, until they are tender and the stuffing is browned, 25-30 minutes. Sprinkle with lemon juice and serve hot.

PASTÉ D'ANGUILLES

This eel pâté is remarkably like *coulibiac*, a Russian dish which is popular in France today. *Coulibiac* consists of layers of sturgeon, hard-boiled/cooked eggs, chopped mushrooms, and rice, all enclosed in pastry. Even the accompanying sauces are similar; modern chefs would serve both melted butter (La Varenne puts butter inside the pâté) and hollandaise, which closely resembles La Varenne's sauce, which he refers to as white. It is possible that he whisked the egg yolks and verjuice together over very low heat to form a pale, mousselike sauce, as described below. For fish pâtés like this one, La Varenne suggests a "garnish from the garden, such as mushrooms, truffles, asparagus, hard-cooked egg yolks, artichoke bottoms, capers, chard, pistachios," but a simple bunch of watercress is acceptable. Salmon is an excellent alternative to eel.

Dress the eels, cut them in rounds and season them; prepare your pastry, and fill it with eel, hard-cooked egg yolks, mushrooms, truffles, if you have them, artichoke bottoms, and good fresh butter. Serve the pâté uncovered, with a white sauce made of egg yolks thinned with verjuice; in case it collapses, fasten it together with buttered paper and string; when cooked, discard the paper.

EEL PÂTÉ EN CROÛTE

Serves 6

FOR THE PASTRY:

12 oz/3 cups/375 g flour
½ tsp salt
5 oz/⅔ cup/150 g butter
2½ oz/⅓ cup/75 g lard or shortening
3 fl oz/6 tbsp/90 ml cold water, more if needed

FOR THE FILLING:

1½ lb/750 g fresh eel, skinned
4 cooked artichoke bottoms
salt and pepper
6 hard-boiled/cooked egg yolks
8 oz/250 g small mushrooms, stems trimmed level with caps
small can truffles, drained and thinly sliced (optional)
5 oz/⅔ cup/150 g butter
1 egg, beaten to mix with ½ tsp salt (for glaze)

FOR THE SAUCE:

3 egg yolks
2 fl oz/¼ cup/60 ml verjuice (see page 17)
2 fl oz/¼ cup/60 ml water
salt and pepper

1. To make the pastry: sift the flour with the salt on to a marble slab or board and make a well in the center. Add the butter, lard or shortening and water. Gradually draw in the flour, working with the fingertips until the mixture resembles crumbs. Add more water if necessary, until the crumbs begin to stick together. Knead the dough lightly to form a ball, then work it with the heel of the hand, pushing it away and bringing it together until it is as pliable as putty, about 1 minute. Cover and chill.

2. For the filling: cut the eel into fillets, discarding the bone; cut each artichoke bottom into 3 rounds. Heat the oven to No 6/400°F/200°C. Roll out the pastry dough on a floured board to a 15 × 10 inch/38 × 25 cm rectangle. Arrange half the eel fillets in a 10 × 3½ inch/25 × 9 cm strip in the center and sprinkle with salt and pepper. Add the hard-boiled/cooked egg yolks, mushroom caps, truffles if used, artichoke bottoms and remaining eel fillets in layers, sprinkling each layer with salt and pepper, and dotting all but the top layer with butter. The rectangle should be as tall and as neat as possible.

3. Cut a square of excess dough from each corner and brush the edges of the dough rectangle with egg glaze. Lift one long edge of the dough on top of the filling and fold over the opposite edge to enclose it. Press gently to seal the dough and fold over the ends to make a neat package. Roll the package over on to a baking sheet so that the seams of dough are underneath. Brush the pâté with glaze. Roll out the excess dough into a long strip, cut it into narrow bands and lay the bands over the pâté to decorate it. Press one long band around the base to finish the edge. Brush the pâté again with glaze. Make a "collar" of doubled foil about 2 inches/5 cm high, butter it, and tie it around the pâté with string or secure the ends with a pin. Make two small holes in the top of the pâté for steam to escape and insert two "chimneys" of foil to keep the holes open.

4. Bake the pâté in the heated oven until the pastry is firm at the sides, about 15 minutes. Remove the foil collar, brush again with egg glaze, and continue baking until the pastry is lightly browned, about 10 minutes more. Turn down the oven to No 4/350°F/175°C, cover the pâté loosely with foil, and continue baking for 1-1¼ hours, until a skewer inserted in the center for ½ minute is hot to the touch when withdrawn.

5. For the sauce: put the egg yolks, verjuice, and water in a small heavy-based pan or in the top of a double boiler and heat gently, whisking constantly until the mixture forms a light mousse the consistency of hollandaise sauce, 5-7 minutes. Add salt and pepper to taste. Note: the sauce will separate if it is cooked too quickly or becomes too hot.

6. To serve: La Varenne suggests cutting around the top of the pâté and lifting off a lid of pastry to reveal the contents. A modern chef would cut the pâté like a loaf, so the layers can be seen. Either way the pâté should be served hot, with the sauce separately.

Asperges à la Sauce Blanche

This "white sauce" made with butter and egg yolks, but not a trace of flour, illustrates how the art of making sauces was still in its infancy at the time of La Varenne. It is an early version of hollandaise, which had not yet received its name.

Take stalks of asparagus, scrape them, then cut them equally, cook them with water and some salt and take them out as lightly cooked as possible, it is the best, and let them drain, then make a sauce with fresh butter, a yolk of egg, salt, nutmeg, a trickle of vinegar, and when all is well stirred and the sauce subtly thickened, serve it.

Asparagus has been a favourite of gastronomes from ancient to modern times. "Quicker than asparagus is boiled" was a Roman proverb meaning "in a flash".

Asparagus with Cream Sauce

Serves 2
1-1½ lb/500-750 g fresh asparagus
FOR THE SAUCE:
1 egg yolk
1½ tsp white wine vinegar
pinch of salt
pinch of nutmeg
2 oz/¼ cup/60 g butter

1. Trim the white part from the asparagus so the stalks are the same length. Rinse them in cold water and with a vegetable peeler remove the tough skin from the lower ends of the stems. Tie the stalks in two bundles and stand them, stems down, in about 2 inches/ 5 cm boiling salted water in an asparagus cooker or a tall pan such as the bottom of a double boiler. Cover and simmer until the green tips are just tender, 8-10 minutes. Lift the asparagus carefully from the pan, drain on paper towels, discard the strings, and keep warm.

2. Meanwhile, make the sauce: put the egg yolk, vinegar, salt, nutmeg and a nut of the butter in a heavy-based pan or in the top of a double boiler and heat gently, whisking to a light mousse, about 2 minutes. Whisk in the remaining butter piece by piece so the sauce thickens creamily. Do not allow it to become too hot or it will curdle. Taste the sauce for seasoning and pour into a bowl to serve with the asparagus.

LAPEREAUX EN RAGOÛT

Game birds, and young animals like the rabbit called for here, were favorites on the tables of the rich in the seventeenth century. However, the poor were not so lucky; game was reserved for the *seigneur* and in certain periods the penalty for poaching was death. La Varenne seasons this dish with a bouquet garni – one of the first mentions of the term.

You can fricasée rabbits in the same way as chickens or sauté them in a frying pan with a little flour mixed with butter, put them to cook gently with good stock and season them with capers, orange or lemon juice, and a bouquet garni or scallions, then serve.

This famous portrayal of a cook featured in some early editions of Le Cuisinier françois. *Game pies were often dressed in the full plumage of the bird.*

RAGOÛT OF RABBIT

Serves 4
3 lb/1.4 kg rabbit, cut in 8 pieces
1 oz/¼ cup/30 g flour
salt and pepper
2 oz/¼ cup/60 g butter
12 fl oz/1½ cups/375 ml stock
2 tbsp capers
juice of 1 orange or 1 lemon
bouquet garni or 4 scallions/spring onions,
*   chopped*

1. Season the flour with salt and pepper and use it to coat the pieces of rabbit. In a large skillet/pan or shallow casserole melt the butter and brown the rabbit pieces on all sides over medium heat. Add the stock, the capers, orange or lemon juice, and bouquet garni or scallion/spring onion, and bring to the boil.

2. Cover and simmer on top of the stove or cook in an oven heated to No 4/350°F/175°C until the rabbit is very tender, ¾-1 hour. Taste the sauce for seasoning, discard the bouquet garni if using, and serve.

TO MAKE ANOTHER SOFT CAKE OR TART WITHOUT CHEESE, WHICH CAKE THE FLEMMINGS DO CALL BREAD DIPPED IN EGGS

The following recipe comes from *The Perfect Cook*, a translation of *Le Pastissier françois* that was published in London in 1656, making it one of the very first French cookbooks to appear in England. The detailed instructions illustrate clearly the difference in style between *Le Pastissier* and *Le Cuisinier françois* – such precision was not to be equaled until the time of Carême, 150 years later.

Put into a Bason, or upon a Table, two pints of fine flower, break and beat two eggs into it, adde thereunto half a pound of fresh butter which you shall have caused to be melted over the fire, with a quarter of a pint of milk, put also into this mixture a spoonful of good beer yeast which is somewhat thick, and rather more than less, as also salt at discretion. You must well mix and work all these things together with your hands, till you reduce them into a well knitted paste, and in the kneading of this your paste you must now and then powder it with a little flower.

Your paste being thus well powdered will be firm, after which make it up into the form of a Loaf, and placing it upon a sheet of Paper, you must cover it with a hot Napkin.

You must also observe to set your said paste neer unto the fire, but not too high, lest that side which should bee too nigh the fire might become hard. You shall leave this said paste in the said indifferent hot place untill it be sufficiently risen, and it will require at least five quarters of an hours time to rise in and when it shall be sufficiently risen, which you may know by its splitting, and separating it self, you must make it up into the form of a Cake, or Tart, which you must garnish over, and then put it into the Oven to bee baked.

The Ovens hearth must be as hot almost as when you intend to bake indifferent great household Bread. This Tart or Cake will require almost three quarters of an hours baking, or at least a great half hour; and when it is drawn forth of the Oven, you may powder it with some sugar, and sprinkle it with some rose-water before you do serve it up to the Table, which depends of your will.

EGG BREAD

Makes 1 large round loaf
8 oz/1 cup/250 g butter, cut in pieces
14 fl oz/1¾ cups/425 ml milk
1 oz/30 g compressed yeast, or ½ oz/15 g dry yeast
1½ lb/6 cups/750 g flour, more if needed
2 tsp salt
2 eggs, beaten to mix
1 egg, beaten to mix with ½ tsp salt (for glaze)
TO FINISH (OPTIONAL):
confectioners'/icing sugar (for sprinkling)
1 tsp rosewater

1. Heat the butter with the milk until melted and let cool to tepid. Crumble or sprinkle the yeast over it and leave until dissolved, about 5 minutes. Sift the flour with the salt on to a work surface, make a well in the center and add the eggs with the yeast mixture. Stir with the hand, gradually drawing in the flour to make a dough that is soft but not sticky, adding more flour if necessary. Flour the work surface and knead the dough until smooth and elastic, about 5 minutes. Shape the dough into a ball, set it on a floured tray and sprinkle the top with flour. Cover it with a damp cloth and set in a warm place until the surface begins to crack, 1-1½ hours.

2. Knead the dough to knock out the air, shape it into a round loaf, and set it on a buttered baking sheet. Cover it and leave again to rise until almost doubled in bulk, about 1 hour. Heat the oven to No 6/400°F/200°C. When the dough is risen, slash the top with the point of a sharp knife, brush it with egg glaze and bake in the heated oven for 30 minutes. Turn the oven down to No 4/350°F/175°C and continue baking until the loaf is browned and sounds hollow when tapped on the bottom, 50-60 minutes longer. Transfer it to a rack to cool. If you like, while the bread is still hot, sprinkle the top with sugar and spoon over the rosewater.

ROBERT MAY

1588–about 1665

To turn from french to English cooking in 1600 is to step back in many ways a hundred years. The refinements of the Renaissance spreading northward through France, were slow to cross the Channel. The influence of Scappi and the other great Italian chefs was so remote as to be almost imperceptible. Memories of great medieval banquets, with their indiscriminate display of flesh, fish, and fowl, were still very much alive. It was with small success that Henrietta Maria of Spain, who married Charles I in 1625, tried to introduce the dishes of her homeland to the court.

However, the proud independence of the English table was soon to be subverted by far more lasting influences, resulting from the political upheavals of Charles I's reign and the Civil War. For years refugees scuttled to and fro across the Channel and the future King Charles II made France his home for a decade. By the end of the interregnum, when the king was restored in 1660, English cooks finally struck out in new directions, determined at least to try the fancy foreign foods that seemed to be so much enjoyed elsewhere.

A cautious interest in the new cooking of continental Europe, tempered by a truly British determination to stick to tradition, characterize *The Accomplisht Cook* by Robert May, first published in 1660. May opens his book with four pages on the Spanish stew of *olla podrida,* known to the English as olio. Later he describes how to

OPPOSITE: *Charles II served pineapples at his table, imported from Barbados. Here we see his gardener proudly presenting him with the first shriveled specimen grown in Britain.*

make *stoffado* (pot roast) and *quelque shose* (fancy French dishes which the English mockingly called "kickshaws" – and cheerfully labels some very English ways of cooking meat as *à la mode.* A poetic tribute at the front of the book notes:

> *He is so universal, he'l not miss,*
> *The Pudding nor Bolonian Sausages.*
> *Italian, Spaniard, French, he all out-goes,*
> *Refines their kickshaws and Their olios.*

But behind this chic façade, May turns with relief to those quintessentially English dishes: puddings, pies, and roasts. As William Forrest, an Elizabethan chronicler, remarked: "Our English nature cannot live by roots, by water, herbs, or such beggary baggage, that may well serve for vile outlandish quarters; give Englishmen meat after their old usage, beef, mutton, veal, to cheer their courage." By May's time roasting had really come into its own, and large cuts of meat like leg of mutton, loin of pork, chine of beef, and whole lamb added variety to the smaller roasts of the medieval table. For accompaniment May suggests a series of "sauces" that might well have come from a modern English menu. "Mustard," he writes, "is good with brawn, beef, chine of bacon and mutton; verjuyce [tart fruit juice] good to boiled chicken and capons." He also recommends "swan with chaldrons," an essence of entrails probably rather like meat glaze, and "ribs of beef with garlick, mustard, pepper, verjuyce, and ginger."

Large roasts demanded considerable skill in carving, an art graphically summed up in an early sixteenth-century book from which Robert May quotes at length. "Break that deer," he urges, "leach [slice] that brawn," "rear that goose," "lift that swan," and so on through more than three dozen different birds and fishes. Such instructions were of ancient origin, but they were by no means superfluous in a time when meat was cut up before serving because everyone ate with their fingers and a spoon. The fork had been brought to England from

Italy in 1608 by Thomas Coryat, but it remained an object of curiosity, earning its importer the nickname of *Furcifer* – literally fork-bearer, but also meaning a villain who deserves the gallows. It was not until the 1650s that the use of forks became widespread. One ingenious rogue made a small fortune under Parliament by selling knives and forks as souvenirs supposedly made from an imposing bronze statue of Charles I, who had been beheaded only a few years before.

French and Italian influence also acquainted the English with new vegetables. *The Accomplisht Cook* contains recipes for "spinage" tart, buttered "sparagus" and pickled "cowcumbers." In their appreciation of

potatoes and salads, the English were a step ahead of the French; La Varenne has scarcely a salad recipe, but Robert May devotes a whole section to salads of all kinds. According to John Evelyn, who in 1699 wrote a book on salads called *Acetaria*, "sallets are a composition of edule (edible) plants and roots of several kinds, to be eaten raw or green, blanch'd or candied (i.e., pickled)." Robert May's idea of a salad (page 80) is much wider – he adds almost anything and arranges the ingredients lovingly in patterns on the platter. The common bond is a dressing made of "oyl and vinegar beaten together, the best oyl you can get."

These innovations did not dislodge pies from their supremacy on the English table. Cooks vied with each other in baking outsize pies like the one from the diocesan kitchens of Durham cathedral which contained a hundred turkeys. Pies were also a favourite vehicle for practical jokes. *Antiquitates Culinariae*, one of the earliest histories of food dating from 1791, relates how in earlier times dwarfs would be hidden in giant pies, undergoing such "temporary incrustation for the cruel amusement of their owners." On other occasions clowns interrupted banquets by plunging into custard pies "to the unspeakable amusement to those who were far enough from the tumbler not to be bespattered by this active gambol." One famous party trick lives on, at least in the nursery, in this allegorical rhyme which dates back several centuries:

Sing a song of sixpence,
A pocketful of rye,
Four and twenty blackbirds
Baked in a pie.
When the pie was opened,
The birds began to sing.
Oh! wasn't that a dainty dish
To set before a king.

Robert May himself is famous for a truly monstrous "trophy" to which he gives pride of place at the front of his book. "The likeness of a ship of war in pasteboard" is drawn into the dining room on a cart to confront a cardboard and pastry castle with battlements, portcullis, and guns of pasteboard armed with real gunpowder. In between stands a giant pastry stag (full of wine) and to its right and left two great pies, one containing live black-birds, the other live frogs (inserted in the baked pie shells through a hole in the crust). A lady then sets off the frolic by pulling an arrow from the stag. Out gushes its "blood" and while the guns of the ship and the castle fire away, the ladies throw eggshells of sweet water at each other to "sweeten the stinck of powder." Finally, when the fun begins to pall, the lid of a pie is lifted and "out skip some frogs, which make the ladies to skip and shreek." Next come the blackbirds, whose flight extinguishes the candles "so that what with the flying birds and skipping

frogs, the one above, the other beneath, it will cause much delight and pleasure to the whole company."

Such amusements had been common at the court of Queen Elizabeth, under whose reign May was born in 1588. His life spanned four reigns as well as the intervening rule of Parliament, this being one of the most turbulent periods of English history. At the end of his career in the 1660s, when he was in his seventies, May looked back wistfully on the peace and prosperity of Elizabeth's age. "Hospitality," he lamented, "which was once a relique of the gentry and a known cognizance to all ancient houses, hath lost her title through the unhappy and cruel disturbances of these times."

Nonetheless May's career shows that England was more affluent than ever before. By his own account his training began in Paris, where he spent five years as a youth, followed by apprenticeship in London and appointments in 13 different households. All his employers were gentry or minor members of the nobility, an unheard-of possibility a hundred years earlier, before commerce had enriched the merchant oligarchy and when only royalty or the church could have afforded a cook of May's education. Needless to say, the staff he commanded was more modest; in place of the hundreds supervised by a master cook in Taillevent's times, Robert May probably headed a team of 20 to 25. Most would have worked in the kitchen itself. According to an account of an earl's household in 1617, the kitchen staff included several undercooks (May's father, himself a cook, had four), three pastrycooks, three kitchen boys, a buyer, purveyor (supplier), a part-time butcher, and three errand boys. The rest of the staff were assigned to the cellar, pantry, buttery, ewery, and scullery, showing that household organization had remained more or less unchanged since the Middle Ages.

Nor had medieval recipes totally disappeared. Scattered throughout May's book are dishes that belong to an earlier age: *furmety, blamanger,* and *umble pies,* as well as sparrows spiced with cinnamon and bustard served with the same sweet-sour *cameline* sauce used by Taillevent. This is no coincidence, for 300 years earlier there had been little to distinguish English cooking from French. There could be no closer parallel to Taillevent's *Le Viandier* than the contemporary *Forme of Cury* compiled by the cooks of the English king Richard II in the 1380s. Here one finds the same emphasis on spices, with sugar used as a seasoning, like salt; there is the same tendency to mash all food to a purée. Even the language of the two books is alike.

A hundred years later, however, the French struck out in new directions as the nobility eagerly studied Apicius, Taillevent, and Platina and adopted their ideas. In England, on the other hand, cooking as an art was largely ignored and *Forme of Cury* lay forgotten until an eighteenth-century antiquary rescued it as a curiosity. Until Robert May, in fact, English recipe books almost always formed part of general treatises on household management and good husbandry. The most famous was *The English Housewife,* written by Gervase Markham in 1615, with a cookery section that digresses in happy inconsequence from how to recover tainted venison to preserving quinces and making pies. Cooking, like medicine, was considered to be something of a mystery, and as late as May's time book after book appeared revealing the secrets of "the closet." Cookery spilled over into quackery and herbal lore flourished in the still room. Here *eau-de-vie* (then regarded exclusively as a medicine) was distilled and remedies brewed with dried herbs. The technique of distilling had been known since the thirteenth century, but it was only around May's time that it was turned to good account by farmers in the Cognac region of France.

May meddles with none of this domestic pharmacopoeia; he was a professional writing for professionals. "Fellow cooks," he declares in a forthright manner, "that I might give a testimony to my country of the laudableness of our profession, that I might encourage young undertakers to make a progress in the practice of this art, I have laid open these experiences." Nobody was more

At the coronation feast of James II in Westminster Hall in 1685, every inch of the table was covered with dishes arranged in a geometric pattern. Little space was left for serving plates and none for glasses, which were passed by the servers.

qualified to do so; with "above 55 years of service" behind him when he wrote his book, May had a unique sense of what was expected of an English cook. This was not a succession of kickshaws and olios, nor pies filled with blackbirds, though such fantasies were important to the prestige of a chef and his master. Rather, in *The Accomplisht Cook* May is addressing thirfty, middle-class households, assuring them that "in the contrivance of these my labors, I have so managed them for the general good, that those whose purses cannot reach to the cost of rich dishes, I have descended to their meaner expense." Such emphasis on economy is not to be found in French cookbooks for another two centuries, and by no means all Englishmen were in sympathy with it. Anthony Wood, a contemporary historian, complained of the "cold meat, cold entertainment, cold reception and cold clownish woman" to be found at his brothers' house.

In the works of Robert May and La Varenne, the distinction between English and French cooking is already discernible. The English took a strictly functional approach in contrast to the French, who were happy to spend hours perfecting the smallest detail and developed a special cooking vocabulary to describe their new art. Then as now, the French and English ranked the creature comforts differently, the French giving high priority to the pleasures of the table, and the English to the amenities of the home. The French were always in hot pursuit of new ideas, whereas the Englishman's curiosity was limited to a little dabbling in olios. The foreign ways with food that engaged May's interest never became part of the body of English cooking. Samuel Pepy's dinner in 1659 of "a dish of marrow-bones; a leg of mutton; a loin of veal; a dish of fowl, three pullets, and a dozen of larks all in a dish; a great tart, a neat's tongue, a dish of anchovies, a dish of prawns, and cheese," would scarcely have been out of place on Mrs Beeton's table 200 years later.

MAY RECIPES

THE

Accomplisht Cook,

OR THE

ART & MYSTERY

OF

COOKERY.

Wherein the whole A R T is revealed in a
more eafie and perfect Method, than hath
been publifht in any language.

Expert and ready Ways for the Dreffing of all Sorts
of FLESH, FOWL, and FISH, with variety of
SAUCES proper for each of them; and how to
raife all manner of *Paftes*; the beft Directions for
all forts of *Kickfhaws*, alfo the *Terms* of CAR-
VING and SEWING.

An exact account of all *Difhes* for all *Seafons* of the
Year, with other *A-la-mode Curiofities*

The Fifth Edition, with large Additions throughout
the whole work: befides two hundred Figures of
feveral Forms for all manner of bak'd Meats,
(either Flefh, or Fifh) as, Pyes Tarts, Cuftards,
Cheefecakes, and Florentines, placed in Tables,
and directed to the Pages they appertain to.

Approved by the fifty five Years Experience and In-
duftry of *ROBERT MAY*, in his Atten-
dance on feveral Perfons of great Honour.

London, Printed for *Obadiah Blagrave* at the *Bear* and
Star in St. *Pauls Church-Yard*, 1685.

---

*OPPOSITE: To Make a Grand Sallet of Divers
Compounds.*
ABOVE: The ill-designed title page of The
Accomplisht Cook *conveys the
unsophisticated ways of the seventeenth-
century English compared with their neighbors
across the Channel.*

Robert May, like his French contemporary La Varenne,
specifies few quantities in his recipes, but he does
take care with seasoning, invariably adding salt where
appropriate. However, the range of ingredients is much
narrower and the recipes less diverse than La Varenne.
May, for example, includes more than 100 recipes for pies.

TO STEW CRABS

With no inland point further than 100 miles from the coast, the English have always consumed a good deal of shellfish.

Being boil'd take the meat out of the shells, and put it in a pipkin with some claret wine, and wine vinegar, minced tyme, pepper, grated bread, salt, the yolks of two or three hard eggs strained or minced very small, some sweet butter, capers, and some large mace; stew it finely, rub the shells with a clove or two of garlick, then dish the shells, the claws and little legs round about them, put the meat into the shells, and so serve them.

The kitchen was just one of the many departments of a great house involved in catering for a large household. Maids are seen her baking, distiling and preserving.

PIQUANT CRAB MEAT

Serves 4 as main course, 8 as first course

5 oz/²⁄₃ cup/150 g butter
1 lb/500 g crab meat
8 fl oz/1 cup/250 ml red wine
1½ tbsp wine vinegar
1 tsp thyme
4½ oz/1⅓ cups/135 g fresh white breadcrumbs
2 hard-boiled/cooked egg yolks, sieved
1 tbsp capers
¼ tsp ground mace
salt and pepper
1 clove garlic, cut in half
8 oz/250 g crab claws (for garnish)
4 large or 8 small crab shells or individual serving dishes

1. Melt all but 2 tablespoons of the butter in a pan and add the crab meat, wine, vinegar, thyme, breadcrumbs, egg yolks, capers, mace, salt and pepper. Cook gently, stirring occasionally, until most of the liquid has evaporated, about 8 minutes. Rub the crab shells or serving dishes with the cut garlic clove.

2. For the garnish: melt the remaining butter, add the crab claws with a little salt and pepper, and heat gently. When the crab meat mixture is cooked, taste it for seasoning, pile it in the crab shells or dishes and top with the claws.

TO BAKE TURKEY FOR TO BE EATEN COLD

Turkeys, brought from the Americas in the sixteenth century, had become commonplace in England a century later. Pies like this, containing a whole boned bird with stuffing, were still served at Christmas 100 years ago and less elaborate pies of veal, ham, or pork are an English institution. Interestingly, Robert May was well aware that cold food needed more seasoning than hot. The lard used in this recipe as a stuffing was almost certainly bacon (*lard* in French); *skirret* is a root resembling parsnip.

Take a turkey-chicken, bone it, and lard it with pretty big lard, a pound and half will serve, then season it with an ounce of pepper, an ounce of nutmegs, and two ounces of salt, lay some butter in the bottom of the pye, then lay on the fowl, and put in it six or eight whole cloves, then put on all the seasoning with good store of butter, close it up, and baste it over with eggs, bake it, and being baked fill it up with clarified butter.

Thus you may bake them for to be eaten hot, giving them but half the seasoning, and liquor it with gravy and juyce of orange.

Bake this pye in fine paste; for more variety you may make a stuffing for it as followeth; mince some beef-suet and a little veal very fine, some sweet herbs, grated nutmeg, pepper, salt, two or three raw yolks of eggs, some boil'd skirrets or pieces of artichocks, grapes, or gooseberries, etc.

TURKEY PIE

Serves 12

puff pastry made with 12 oz/1½ cups/ 375 g butter, 12 oz/3 cups/375 g flour, ½ tsp salt, 8 fl oz/1 cup/250 ml water
9-10 lb/4–4.5 kg whole turkey, boned
1 tsp white pepper
1 tsp ground nutmeg
1½ tsp salt
2 oz/¼ cup/60 g butter
3–4 whole cloves
1 egg, beaten to mix with ½ tsp salt (for glaze)
FOR THE STUFFING:
8 oz/250 g beef suet, ground/minced
8 oz/250 g veal, ground/minced
1 tbsp chopped parsley
1 tbsp mixed chopped herbs (chives, thyme, marjoram)
1 tsp ground nutmeg
salt and pepper
3 egg yolks
8 oz/250 g cooked parsnips, cut in walnut-sized pieces, or 4 cooked artichoke bottoms, cut in eighths
8 oz/250 g seedless green grapes
FOR SERVING HOT:
turkey bones and giblets
1 tbsp orange juice

FOR SERVING COLD:
2 oz/¼ cup/60 g butter, melted
A deep 14 inch/35 cm oval or round pie dish or shallow baking dish

1. Make the puff pastry and chill thoroughly.
2. For the stuffing: mix the suet, veal, herbs, nutmeg, salt and pepper, adding plenty of seasoning if the pie is to be served cold. Stir in the egg yolks. Spread out the boned turkey, skin side down, on a baking sheet and sprinkle it with white pepper, nutmeg, and salt. Spread the veal stuffing on top and scatter over it the pieces of parsnip or artichoke and grapes. Fold the edges of the turkey skin to the center, overlapping them to make a round or oval that will fit the pie dish. Spread the 2 oz/ ¼ cup/60 g butter in the pie dish and lay the dish upside-down on the folded turkey. Using the baking sheet, turn over the turkey and dish and set right side up; tuck the cloves under the bird.
3. Roll out the pastry 1 inch/2.5 cm larger than the dish and cover the top of the pie, tucking the pastry down into the edges to allow for shrinkage. Cut a small hole in the center for steam to escape. Make a 1 inch/2.5 cm "chimney" from aluminum foil and put it in the hole. Brush the pie with egg glaze. Decorate the top with leaves and flowers made from pastry trimmings and brush them also with glaze. Chill the pie 15 minutes and heat the oven to No 7/425°F/220°C.
4. Bake the pie in the heated oven until the pastry is puffed and lightly browned, 20-25 minutes. Cover the pie with foil, tucking it under the edges. Turn down the oven to No 4/350°F/ 175°C and continue baking until a skewer inserted in the center of the pie for ½ minute is very hot to the touch when withdrawn, about 2 hours longer.
5. If serving hot: simmer the turkey giblets and bones in water to cover for 1-1½ hours. Strain this stock and boil it until reduced to 2 fl oz/¼ cup/60 ml; add the orange juice and season it to taste. When the pie is cooked, heat the orange juice mixture until very hot, but not boiling and pour it into the pie through the steam hole.
6. If serving cold: let the pie cool to tepid. Pour the melted butter into the pie through the steam hole and let it cool and set before serving.

TO ROAST A SHOULDER OF MUTTON WITH ONIONS AND PARSLEY, AND BASTE IT WITH ORANGES

England was famous for wool as early as the second century and by the Middle Ages the mutton from her sheep had become the staple meat. Oranges appear in many of May's recipes – they had been common in England since Elizabethan times, when cheerful crowds were in the habit of throwing oranges and eggs at each other on May Day. Anchovy is excellent with lamb, giving a piquant flavor with no trace of fish.

Stuff [the mutton] with parsley and onions, or sweet herbs, nutmeg, and salt, and in the roasting of it, baste it with the juyce of oranges, save the gravy and clear away the fat; then stew it up with a slice or two of orange and an anchovie, without any fat on the gravy, etc.

LEFT PAGE: The Stuart kitchen still relied heavily on game to supply its meat.

By Robert May's time, citrus fruits began to appear commonly in recipes.

ROAST SHOULDER OF LAMB WITH ORANGE

Serves 4-6
4-5 lb/1.8-2.3 kg shoulder of lamb, blade bone removed to make a pocket
2 tbsp butter
12 fl oz/1½ cups/375 ml orange juice
8 fl oz/1 cup/250 ml boiling water
1-2 slices of orange
2 anchovy fillets, finely chopped
FOR THE STUFFING:
2 oz/¼ cup/60 g butter
5 medium onions, sliced
medium bunch of parsley, chopped with stems discarded
½ tsp ground nutmeg
salt
Trussing needle or poultry pins and string

1. Heat the oven to No 5/375°F/190°C. For the stuffing: in a saucepan melt the butter, add the onions and press a piece of foil on top. Cover with the lid and cook very gently, stirring occasionally, until the onions are very soft, 15-20 minutes; do not brown them. Remove the foil, let cool and stir in the parsley, nutmeg and salt to taste.

2. Fill the pocket in the lamb with the stuffing and sew it up or fasten it with poultry pins and string. Spread the butter over the meat, set it in a roasting pan and spoon over a little of the orange juice. Roast the lamb in the heated oven until a meat thermometer registers 160°F/75°C, allowing 18 minutes per pound (40 minutes per kilo) plus 18 minutes more for medium-done meat. Baste the meat often during cooking with the orange juice, reserving half of it.

3. Transfer the lamb to a platter and keep it warm. Discard all the fat from the pan, add the boiling water, remaining orange juice, orange slices and anchovy and bring the gravy to the boil, stirring to dissolve the pan juices and crushing the orange slices and anchovy. Simmer 5 minutes and taste for seasoning. Meanwhile, discard the trussing string from the lamb and transfer it to a serving dish. Strain the gravy and serve separately with the lamb.

TO MAKE A GRAND SALLET OF DIVERS COMPOUNDS

The *neats tongue* mentioned in this recipe is ox or calf's tongue, and *samphire* is an aromatic salty plant that can be eaten fresh or used for pickling; the identity of *caperons* and *crucifix pease* is uncertain.

Take a cold roast capon and cut it into thin slices square and small (or any other roast meat as chicken, mutton, veal, or neats tongue) mingle with it a little minced taragon and an onion, then mince lettice as small as the capon, mingle all together, and lay it in the middle of a clean scoured dish. Then lay capers by themselves, olives by themselves, samphire by itself, broom buds, pickled mushrooms, pickled oysters, lemon, orange, raisins, almonds, blue-figs, Virginia Potato, caperons, crucifix pease, and the like, more or less, as occasion serves, lay them by themselves in the dish round the meat in partitions. Then garnish the dish sides with quarters of oranges, or lemons, or in slices, oyl and vinegar beaten together, and poured on it over all.
On fish days, a roast, broil'd, or boil'd pike boned, and being cold, slice it as abovesaid.

MIXED SALAD FOR AN ENTRÉE

Serves 4-5
13 oz/3 cups/400 g diced cooked capon,
    chicken, lamb, veal or tongue
1 tbsp chopped tarragon
1 onion, very finely chopped
1 head Boston or romaine lettuce, coarsely
    chopped
1 orange, or 1 lemon (for decoration)
FOR THE GARNISH:
3-4 tbsp capers, drained
3¼ oz/½ cup/100 g green olives
3¼ oz/½ cup/100 g black olives
small bunch watercress, stems discarded
3¼ oz/¾ cup/100 g bean sprouts
3¼ oz/½ cup/100 g pickled mushrooms
3¼ oz/½ cup/100 g pickled oysters
2 lemons, peeled and cut in segments
1 oz/¼ cup/30 g raisins
1½ oz/¼ cup/45 g toasted blanched
    almonds

3-4 fresh figs, sliced, or 3-4 dried figs,
    chopped
1 large potato, cooked and diced
FOR THE DRESSING:
3 tbsp wine vinegar or cider vinegar
½ tsp salt
½ tsp pepper
4 fl oz/½ cup/125 ml olive oil or salad oil

1. Mix the cooked capon or other meat with the tarragon and onion and toss with the lettuce. Pile this mixture in the center of a large platter or deep tray and arrange the garnishes around the edge in neat individual piles, putting ingredients of contrasting colors next to each other.
2. For the dressing: lightly whisk the vinegar with salt and pepper until the salt dissolves. Gradually whisk in the oil until the dressing emulsifies, then taste for seasoning. Spoon the dressing over the salad and garnishes.
3. For decoration: cut "teeth" in the orange or lemon with a lemon zester, cut the fruit in half lengthwise, then slice each half crosswise to show the teeth. Arrange the slices on the border of the platter.

MINCED PIES OF BEEF

Originally mincemeat was made literally of minced (ground) meat, which was mixed with dried fruit and spices to preserve it through the winter. Today the meat is usually omitted, leaving the familiar sweet combination of dried fruits, but the genuine mincemeat made by Robert May has much more body and flavor.

Take of the buttock of beef, cleanse it from the skins, and cut it into small pieces, then take half as much more beef-suet as the beef, mince them together very small, and season them with pepper, cloves, mace, nutmeg, and salt; then have half as much fruit as meat, three pound of raisins, four pound of currans, two pound of prunes, etc. or plain without fruit, but only seasoned with the same spices.

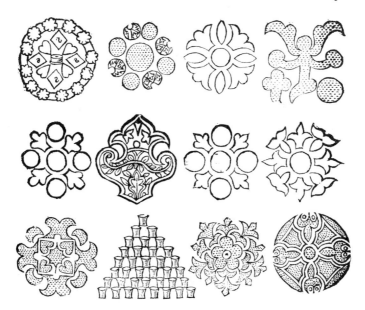

For raised pies the decorated lid and sides of crust often took the place of a dish, rather than being eaten.

MINCEMEAT

Makes about 7 lb/3.2 kg of mincemeat
2 lb/1 kg cooked lean beef, ground/minced
3½ lb/1.6 kg beef suet, ground/minced
1 tbsp salt
2 tsp pepper
2 tsp ground mace
2 tsp ground nutmeg
1 tbsp ground cloves
10 oz/2 cups/300 g raisins
15 oz/3 cups/450 g currants
8 oz/250 g pitted prunes, coarsely chopped
6½-13 oz/1-2 cups/200-400 g sugar
8-16 fl oz/1-2 cups/250-500 ml sherry or
*   white wine*

Mix the ground/minced beef and suet thoroughly with the spices. Add the fruit, with sugar and sherry or wine to taste, and mix well again. Pack in a crock or bowl (not aluminum), cover and store in a cool place for a month or more – it need not be sealed.

QUELQUE SHOSE

As its name suggests, *quelque shose* was a light little dish – this particular recipe resembles a pancake flavored with currants. A *manchet* was a loaf made of the finest quality flour from which most of the bran had been sifted. Coarser loaves were called "cheats" or "cockets," and "trete" – the roughest of all – was almost black and usually made of rye flour. The *tansie* referred to in the recipe was a cross between an omelet and a baked custard, flavored with the herb *tansy*. Until the nineteenth century, sugar was sold in blocks which had to be grated or "scraped" before using.

Take ten eggs, and beat them in a dish with a penny manchet grated, a pint of cream, some beaten cloves, mace, boil'd currans, some rosewater, salt, and sugar; beat all together, and fry it either in a whole form of a tansie, or by spoonfuls in little cakes, being finely fried, serve them on a plate with juyce of orange and scraping sugar.

Printed for Rich: Chifwell

In the 300 years which separate Robert May and Taillevent cooking and baking methods had scarcely changed.

SPICED PANCAKES

Serves 4-6

4½ oz/1 cup/140 g currants or raisins
6½ oz/2 cups/200 g fresh white breadcrumbs
½ tsp ground cloves
½ tsp ground mace
pinch of salt
1¾ oz/¼ cup/50 g sugar
½ pint/1¼ cups/300 ml heavy/double cream
5 eggs, beaten to mix
2 tsp rosewater
4-6 tbsp butter (for frying)
FOR SERVING:
2 oranges, cut in segments
granulated sugar (for sprinkling)

1. Pour boiling water over the currants or raisins, let stand until plump, about 15 minutes, and drain them. Mix the breadcrumbs in a bowl with the cloves, mace, salt and sugar and stir in the cream. Gradually beat in the eggs and continue beating 2 minutes. Let the batter stand 15 minutes for the breadcrumbs to soften, then stir in the rosewater and drained currants or raisins.

2. In a pan or skillet heat about 2 tablespoons butter and pour in the batter with a pitcher to form 3 inch/7.5 cm pancakes. Cook them over medium heat until browned, turn and brown the other side. Keep them warm while frying the remaining batter, adding more butter as necessary.

3. Alternatively, heat 4 tablespoons butter in a 10 or 11 inch/25 or 28 cm pan or skillet. Add all the batter and cook over medium heat until browned on the bottom and still soft on top. Slide the skillet or pan under the broiler/grill and cook until the top is set and browned. Slide the cake out on to a heated platter. Cut it in wedges and serve the cake or the pancakes with orange segments and sugar for sprinkling.

TO MAKE A POSSET SIMPLE

Nourishing pick-me-ups like this posset were once a part of every cook's repertoire. *Sack* is the old word for sherry.

Boil your milk in a clean scowred skillet, and when it boils take it off, and warm in the pot, bowl, or bason some sack, claret, beer, ale, or juyce of orange; pour it into the drink, but let not your milk be too hot, for it will make the curd hard, then sugar it.

Wine, women and song add to the pleasures of such good fare as pies decorated with plumaged birds. The square table is typical of the Stuart period.

SIMPLE POSSET

For each person:
6 fl oz/¾ cup/175 ml milk
3 tbsp sherry, red Bordeaux wine, beer, or orange juice
2 tsp sugar

Scald the milk and heat the sherry, wine, beer, or orange juice in a separate pan until very hot. Heat heavy glasses, mugs or a punch bowl by filling with very hot water, then discarding it. Pour in the milk and gradually stir in the hot sherry, wine, beer, or juice, stirring constantly; the milk will thicken slightly. Note: if too hot, the posset may curdle. Stir in the sugar and serve at once while still very hot.

MENON

LA SCIENCE
DU
MAÎTRE D'HÔTEL
CUISINIER,
Avec
DES OBSERVATIONS
sur la connoissance & proprietés
des Alimens.

A PARIS, AU PALAIS,
Chez PAULUS-DU-MESNIL, Imprimeur-
Libraire , Grand' Salle au Pilier
des Consultations, au Lion d'or.

M. DCC. XLIX.
Avec Approbation & Privilège du Roi.

flourished 1740–1755

Tₕₑ... THE AGE OF LOUIS XV MARKS A high point in the cultural life of France. Cooking was no exception, acquiring all the pomp of a national movement as it came to be valued as a peculiarly French art. Between 1735 and 1755 more great cooks wrote more great cookbooks than in any comparable period before or since, and they enjoyed unprecedented recognition. The most successful member of this prolific generation was Menon, whose many books include the last of the great manuals of court cookery and the first of many cookbooks written for the bourgeoisie.

Almost 100 years separate Menon from La Varenne and during this period French cooking had developed dramatically. In the time of La Varenne, it was still clearly rooted in the traditions of Renaissance Italy and medieval France. By the eighteenth century, this inheritance had been left far behind and it was to the genius of French cooks, working under the patronage of a cultivated aristocracy, that France owed its unquestionable supremacy in the kitchen. Part science, part art, cooking was now a fashionable subject of debate in the self-conscious Parisian salons. Stupefying banquets which dulled the intellect fell into disfavor and the preferred setting for the exercise of wit and gallantry was the supper. The change was less in the number of dishes (which remained copious) than in the number of

OPPOSITE: In the time of Louis XV, intimate suppers took the place of ceremonial meals. Here the guests of Prince de Conti, patron of Jean-Jacques Rousseau, enjoy a little light music as they dine.

guests; ideally not more than twenty people gathered round the table.

When Louis XIV's sixty-eight-year reign came to an end in 1715, even age-old court habits had to change. The new king disdained his great-grandfather's habit of admitting the public to watch the royal meals, preferring to enjoy the company of the queen or of one of his mistresses in private – so much so that he installed a table which sank through the floor to the kitchen, where it was invisibly replenished for the next course.

Naturally Louis XV's hostesses vied for royal approval of the cuisine. Madame du Barry gave her name to a cauliflower soup and Madame de Pompadour, good bourgeoise that she was, was famed for her table where simple country dishes offset the flights of fancy of more aristocratic temperaments. For relaxation, the king himself would often work in the kitchens under the supervision of his friend, the Prince de Dombes, who was the secret author of an attractive little recipe book *Le Cuisinier gascon*. The Duc de Richelieu is said to have brought mayonnaise to France, naming it after his victory at the siege of Mahon in Spain, although some writers have argued that it is of ancient French lineage, descended from *moyeu* meaning egg yolk. It was Bertrand, cook to the Prince de Soubise, who launched the soubise (onion) purée that is still an

In this hunting picnic at Versailles by Charles van Loo costumed ladies and gentlemen dine on the grass attended by their fashionable black servants.

important basic preparation. The two were a colorful pair; the prince is said to have made his omelettes from pheasant and partridge eggs (an extravagance that can hardly have been justified by the results), while Bertrand once shocked his master by ordering fifty hams to make a single sauce. "I will, if you choose, put all the fifty hams into a glass vial no bigger than my thumb," he boasted.

Although the aristocracy took the applause, most culinary invention must have been the work of their chefs, who were in great demand. "It will not be long now before cooks assume the title of artists in cookery," wrote Mercier in 1780 in his fascinating account of city life, *Le Tableau de Paris*. "They are pampered and spoiled, their tantrums are soothed, and it is normal to sacrifice all

other servants for their sake. To entice away the cook from a household is a terrible and unforgivable trick." Madame du Barry went so far as to employ a woman cook. The story goes that after a superb supper, Louis XV asked to talk to the chef. When a woman was presented, the king was so impressed that he awarded her one of the highest decorations in France, the Order of the Holy Ghost, known familiarly as the Cordon Bleu, from the blue sash worn by the members. To this day the term cordon bleu is correctly applied only to a woman.

Menon was almost certainly one of the most sought-after master cooks, but nothing is known about him, not even his first name. He had the luck to be the last in the line of heirs to the traditions of La Varenne,

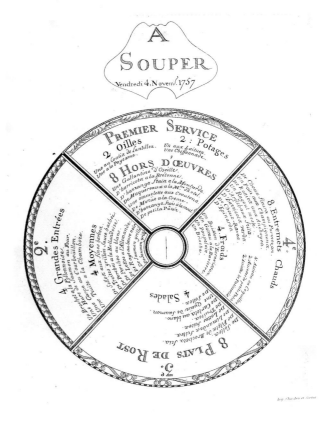

The supper menu served to Louis XV and Madame de Pompadour on Friday, November 4, 1757, shows clearly the four services, each featuring a dozen or more dishes set on the table in a geometric pattern.

and by the time his first book *Le nouveau traité de la cuisine* appeared in 1739, Menon had a head start of which he took full advantage. He also took full advantage of the work of another master cook, Marin, who complained that Menon had poached ideas from his book, *Dons de Comus*. The supplementary volume entitled *La nouvelle Cuisine* which Menon had boldly added to his *Traité* in 1742, continued the movement toward a simpler style of cooking first launched by Marin in *Dons de Comus*.

Marin's book begins with a pedantic essay criticizing *la cuisine ancienne* for its "extraordinary complexity and detail" and promises that in *la cuisine moderne* cooks will find "less trouble, fewer mixtures yet as much variety; a simpler, cleaner, and more knowledgeable kind of chemistry." From today's vantage point of fast food cookery it is a little difficult to credit Marin with simplifying the art. But he certainly did organize it. *Dons de Comus* is a logically planned catalogue of recipes and menus, embracing many of today's classic garnishes (some created by Marin) and almost 100 sauces, few of which would be strange to today's chef.

For some reason Marin's polished work did not enjoy a lasting success and it was a similar three-volume book written by Menon in 1755, *Les Soupers de la cour*, which held the stage until the French Revolution swept away all demand for such lavish productions. To modern tastes the profusion of dishes Menon describes is overwhelming – a typical menu for thirty lists well over a hundred dishes, served in five courses. After the first and third courses, the whole table was cleared and a completely fresh set of dishes laid out in an established geometric design. The second and fourth courses were smaller, complementing the twenty to thirty dishes already on the table. The appointments of the table were just as elaborate as the food. Centerpieces such as china soup tureens, branched candelabra, and bonbonnières proliferated. Instead of the single glass or goblet and knife and spoon used a century before, there was an array of cutlery and crystal for each place setting. Plates were changed between each course – even, remarked a bewildered observer, when they were not dirty.

In *Soupers de la cour* the sauces which have made French cuisine famous are highly developed, and Menon adds them to everything, from hors d'oeuvres through dessert. Most savory sauces were based on a *coulis* of meat and ham which was sliced and cooked very gently in a little fat so the juices were extracted and browned lightly on the bottom of the pan. Then flour was added and the *coulis* was completed with stock, wine, vegetables, and seasonings in much the same way a sauce is made now. The ham was a vital ingredient; those from Montánchez in central Spain (from pigs said to be fattened on a diet of vipers and acorns) had the highest reputation, as evidenced by *sauce espagnole*, the present-day descendant of the original *coulis*. A *coulis* was thick, concentrated, and very extravagant. According to Vincent La Chapelle, another of the great eighteenth-century master cooks, "If you treat about ten or twelve persons, you can take no less than a whole leg of veal to make your *coulis* with, and the nut of a ham to make it good."

White sauce was supposed to be the creation of the chef to the Marquis de Béchamel, private secretary to Louis XIV and a noted food connoisseur, but this was disputed by a Duc d'Escars who exclaimed, "That fellow

Menon was the first writer to consciously distinguish the haute cuisine *of the court from the* cuisine bourgeoise *produced in country kitchens like this one, where the mistress of the house and her child are helping with the cooking.*

Béchamel has all the luck. I was serving breast of chicken *à la crème* twenty years before he was born, yet, as you can see, I have never had the chance of giving my name to the most insignificant of sauces."

The French court went to almost any lengths for the sake of novelty. Menon's imagination stretched on occasion to 100-dish dinners in a single color (white was considered the most elegant) or based on a single meat. For the latest in fruits and vegetables, the court turned to the kitchen garden planted at Versailles by Louis XIV. In this venture the king had been aided by a gardener of genius, La Quintinie, who laid out the prototype *potager* (a name that nicely anticipates the destination of its contents) with neat rows of vegetables and fruit trees espaliered against a high wall for protection against the wind. Louis XIV had taken a personal interest in the propagation of new stock, and many of France's superlative fruit and vegetable varieties originated at Versailles. Louis XV maintained the tradition by importing the latest plants from Holland and England, and by establishing state nurseries in every province, from which cuttings were distributed free.

However, no amount of coaxing would persuade the French to change their attitude to the potato, which although common in England by the 1750s was still regarded in France as pig food. Not until prodded by a fanatical doctor named Parmentier, who once cooked a whole dinner – soup, entrée, entremet, salad, cake, cookies, and even bread – using potatoes, did the French begin to appreciate this cheap, nourishing staple. Parmentier was a clever publicist. He persuaded the king to place a field of potatoes under armed guard. The courtiers so valued its crop that the fashion for buttonholes became the shape of a potato flower. Parmentier, appropriately, has given his name to potato soup.

Soupers de la cour, successful though it was, presented little that was new to the readers of Marin and La Chapelle. The reason Menon's renown outlived theirs was the lasting success of his earlier book *La Cuisinière bourgeoise*, which struck quite a different note, claiming to "reduce expenses, simplify methods, and go some way towards bringing what has seemed the preserve of opulent kitchens within the range of the bourgeoisie." Addressed, significantly, to the female cook, the hearty country recipes it contains such as *andouilles*, calf's feet *à la Sainte Menehoulde*, and leg of lamb *à la persillade* are still the backbone of much household cooking in France.

Written in 1746, *La Cuisinière bourgeoise* was reprinted more often than any other French cookbook until modern times. It became the bible of a new class of cook, the restaurateur (the name comes from the restorative bouillon they invariably served).

The first restaurant (as we would understand the term) opened in 1765 and was an instant success. During the troubled years following the revolution, restaurants became a way of life for town dwellers, and by the close of the century there were around 500 of them in Paris alone. Hitherto, no one had eaten out except of necessity (when traveling, for example) though for centuries "carry out"

food had been sold by the different guilds – the *pâtissiers* (with their savory pies, cakes, and pastries), the *chaircuitiers* (cooked meat sellers specializing in pork), the *oubliers* (baking waffles and wafers) and the *rôtisseurs* (offering roast meat and fowl). The senior of these guilds, the *boulangers*, originally made their loaves round in *boules*, but the French soon realized that by making them elongated they could enjoy more crust.

For liquid refreshment in Paris there was little but taverns to choose from until 1686, when an enterprising Sicilian called Procopio opened the first café. Parisians found a new way of life; in its heyday, the Café Procope was the literary and political meeting place of Paris (it still exists as a restaurant) and imitations quickly followed, each with its own coterie. As well as coffee, Procopio dispensed Sicilian ices – the first to be commonly available in France. By our standards they were primitive concoctions of frozen fruit juice, with a coarse texture more like granité than sorbet, but they were immensely popular. In Menon's time the Orangerie at the Tuileries was surrounded by icehouses for the use of court officials, and he devotes a whole chapter of *Soupers de la cour* to sorbets and ice creams.

Menon wrote for both the old order and the new, and therein lies his distinction. *Soupers de la cour*, with its casual assumption of unlimited time and ingredients, places Menon firmly in the Old World where everything was done in the grand manner, as described by Carême: "Within the households of the King, and of the Princes de Condé, d'Orléans, and de Soubise, the maîtres d'hotel were famous for the excellence of their tables; the men who ran these noble households were truly outstanding both as great chefs and as great administrators; their under-cooks benefited from their teaching, and with the added encouragement they received from the honor and benevolence extended to them by great princes, French cooking was daily enriched and enhanced by their renown." Yet in *La Cuisinière bourgeoise* Menon was writing for the new order – for a world in which the great households had surrendered the initiative to restaurateurs who were forced to work within economic limits, but who enjoyed an independence unknown to their predecessors. In catering to such an audience, Menon began a cookbook tradition that is still flourishing today.

LA
CUISINIERE
BOURGEOISE.
SUIVIE DE L'OFFICE
A L'USAGE
De tous ceux qui se mêlent de dépenses de Maisons.

Nouvelle Edition corrigée & considerablement augmentée, à laquelle l'on a joint la maniere de dissequer, connoître & servir toutes sortes de Viandes.

A PARIS,
Chez GUILLYN, Quay des Augustins, entre les rues Pavée & Gît-le-cœur, au Lys d'or.

M. DCC. XLVIII.
Avec Approbation & Privilége du Roy.

OPPOSITE: *Pot Pourri.*
ABOVE: *The most influential of Menon's many books was* La Cuisinière bourgeoise.

In the hundred years since La Varenne, the advances made in drafting recipes were considerable. Menon's instructions are detailed and he has a wide variety of technical terms such as *braiser* and *blanchir* at his command. A recipe is no longer a sketchy expression of ideas but is well on its way to the precise blueprint we expect today.

PETITS PÂTÉS DE POISSON

The continuous refinement of French cooking during the eighteenth century is clearly seen by comparing this recipe from *Soupers de la cour* with La Varenne's eel pâté (page 64), written a hundred years earlier. An *écu* was a French coin.

Chop the flesh of whatever fish you like and mix it with dried breadcrumbs, cream, salt, pepper, nutmeg, shallots, parsley, chopped spring onion, two egg yolks and a piece of good butter; pound all together. Take puff pastry and roll it out a little thicker than an *écu*, and cut it with a pastry cutter according to the size of the molds; line a mold; put stuffing in the middle and cover with another piece of pastry; press your finger lightly all around just to give it shape; glaze the pastries and cook half an hour; serve them fresh from the oven.

The example set by Louis XIV's gardener, La Quintinie, led to the development of the superb fruits and vegetables of Menon's time. Fruit trees are espaliered against the wall and vegetables are planted in rows as today.

LITTLE FISH PASTRIES

Makes 16-18 medium-sized pastries

puff pastry made with 8 oz/1 cup/250 g butter, 8 oz/2 cups/250 g flour, pinch of salt, and 4 fl oz/½ cup/125 ml ice water, more if needed

4 slices white bread, crusts removed

1 lb/500 g salmon, whiting, pike, haddock or other well flavored fish

8 fl oz/1 cup/250 ml heavy/double cream

2 tsp salt

½ tsp pepper

¼ tsp grated nutmeg

2 shallots, finely chopped

3 tbsp chopped parsley

2 scallions/spring onions finely chopped

2 egg yolks

2 tbsp butter, creamed

1 egg beaten to mix with ½ tsp salt (for glaze)

3 inch/7.5 cm and 3½ inch/9 cm pastry cutters

1. Make the puff pastry and chill for 15 minutes.

2. Heat the oven to No 2/300°F/150°C. Bake the bread in the heated oven until dry but not browned. Work it to crumbs in a food processor or blender. Chop the fish, discarding all skin and bones. Mix the fish with the breadcrumbs, cream, salt, pepper, nutmeg, shallots, parsley, and scallions/spring onions. Purée the mixture in a food processor or blender a little at a time until smooth and transfer it to bowl. Beat in the egg yolks and butter. Taste the mixture – it should be highly seasoned. Heat the oven to No 6/400°F/200°C.

3. Roll out the pastry to ¼ inch/6 mm thickness and stamp out 16-18 3 inch/7.5 cm rounds and an equal number of 3½ inch/9 cm rounds. Set the smaller rounds on a dampened baking sheet and spoon the filling on top, leaving a border. Brush the border with egg glaze, cover with the larger rounds and press the edges together. Brush the tops with glaze and chill 15 minutes. Bake the pies in the heated oven until a skewer inserted in the center for half a minute is hot to the touch when withdrawn, 25-35 minutes. The pastries may be served hot or cold but they are best eaten the same day.

Filet de Boeuf à l'Italienne

Fillet of beef, simply roasted without a marinade, is one of Menon's favorite dishes, showing how much the quality of meat had improved by the mid-eighteenth century. To *lard* means to thread the meat with strips of pork fat to make it more tender.

Lard the upper surface of a fillet of beef, after trimming it well; make cuts in the other side and insert a mixture of parsley, scallion, mushrooms and half a clove of garlic, all finely chopped, basil and powdered bay leaf, kneaded together with grated bacon and seasoned with salt and pepper; wrap the fillet in paper and cook it on a spit; when cooked, coat the side that was not larded with breadcrumbs; brown it in front of the fire and serve a *sauce italienne* **on top.**

Though entitled "La Cuisinière", this well-dressed lady by Engelbrecht can hardly have been a working cook.

Fillet of Beef Italienne

Serves 6–8

4-5 lb/1.8-2.3 kg fillet of beef
2 oz/60 g fat bacon, cut in ¼ inch/6 mm strips (for larding)
1½ oz/½ cup/50 g fresh white breadcrumbs (to finish)
FOR THE STUFFING:
2 tbsp chopped parsley
1 scallion/spring onion, finely chopped
3 large mushrooms, finely chopped
1 clove garlic, crushed
1 tsp chopped basil
½ tsp crushed bay leaf
2 oz/60 g fat bacon, very finely chopped
salt and pepper
larding needle (optional)

1. For the stuffing: mix the parsley, scallion/spring onion, mushrooms, garlic, basil, bay leaf, and bacon with salt and pepper (add no extra salt if the bacon is salty) and work the mixture in a food processor until the bacon fat softens and binds the stuffing together.
2. If roasting in the oven: heat the oven to No 6/400°F/200°C. Lard the underside of the meat with the bacon using a larding needle or poke holes with the point of a knife and insert a strip of bacon in each one. Slash the top of the meat lengthwise with a series of cuts about ¾ inch/2 cm deep and press the stuffing into them; spread any remaining stuffing on top. Tie the meat with string in a firm roll and set it, larded side down, on a rack in a roasting pan. Roast it in the heated oven until a meat thermometer inserted in the center registers 140°F/60°C for rare beef, allowing 15 minutes per pound or 30 minutes per kilogram; baste the meat often during cooking.
3. If roasting on a spit: light the fire or barbecue/broiler. Slash the meat lengthwise about ½ inch/1.25 cm deep on all sides and press the stuffing into the cuts; lard the meat, tie it firmly in a roll with string, and spear on the spit. Roast the beef fairly close to the heat until a meat thermometer inserted in the center registers 140°F/60°C for rare beef, allowing 15 minutes per pound or 30 minutes per kilogram – cooking time varies very much with the heat of the fire; baste during cooking.
4. When the beef is done, sprinkle the top with the breadcrumbs, baste well with drippings and brown under the broiler/grill or over the barbecue. Serve sauce italienne separately, or spoon a little over the meat.

SAUCE PETITE ITALIENNE

Like most of Menon's sauces, this is thickened with a *coulis* – a purée that could be based on concentrated meat essences thickened with a roux of fat and flour, or on vegetables like dried peas or lentils. *Sauce italienne* foreshadows today's classic brown sauces, based on espagnole sauce instead of a *coulis*.

In a casserole put a slice of ham, three or four mushrooms, two or three shallots, half a clove of garlic, a quarter of a bay leaf, and a good tablespoon of oil; cook the mixture over medium heat, moisten it with consommé, a little *coulis* and half a glass of champagne and simmer it over low heat half an hour; skim off any fat and strain.

Tea taken outdoors has long held its charms for those not forced to work in the open. Queen Marie Antoinette went so far as to play milkmaid in the "petit hameau" in Versailles.

SAUCE ITALIENNE

Makes 16 fl oz/2 cups/500 ml sauce
8 oz/250 g slice country ham, diced
4 oz/125 g mushrooms, sliced
2-3 shallots, sliced
½ clove garlic, crushed
small piece bay leaf
1½ tbsp oil
pepper
16 fl oz/2 cups/500 ml brown stock
2½ fl oz/⅓ cup/75 ml dry white wine
salt (optional)
FOR THE COULIS:
1¼ pints/3 cups/750 ml brown stock
3 tbsp butter
3 tbsp flour

1. To make the *coulis*: boil the stock until it is reduced by half. In a saucepan melt the butter, stir in the flour, and cook, stirring, until the flour is golden brown. At once pour in the reduced stock and cook over low heat for 2-3 minutes.

2. Put the ham, mushrooms, and shallots in a heavy-based pan and add the garlic and bay leaf; sprinkle with oil and pepper. Cook over low heat so that the juices are drawn out of the ham and continue cooking until the juices brown. Add the stock, wine, and *coulis* and bring to a boil. Simmer until the sauce is glossy and the consistency of thin cream, 50-60 minutes. Taste it for seasoning – if the ham was salty, more salt will not be needed. Skim off any fat and strain.

SAUMON EN HATELET

This is a good example of the newly developed hors d'oeuvres (literally, "outside of the work") – simple little side dishes served between the soup and the roast.

Cut the salmon in squares the thickness of a thumb, marinate them with a little oil, two raw egg yolks, salt, pepper, parsley, scallion, shallots, all chopped, coat them with breadcrumbs, broil and serve with remoulade in a sauceboat.

SALMON KEBABS

Serves 4 as a main course, 8 as first course
2 lb/1 kg salmon steaks, cut ¾ inch/2 cm thick
5 oz/1½ cups/150 g dry white breadcrumbs
FOR THE MARINADE:
3 fl oz/6 tbsp/90 ml oil
2 egg yolks
1 tsp salt
½ tsp pepper
2 tbsp chopped parsley
2 scallions/spring onions, finely chopped
4-8 kebab skewers

1. Cut the salmon into ¾ inch/2 cm cubes, discarding skin and bones. For the marinade: in a large bowl beat the oil into the egg yolks and stir in the salt, pepper, parsley, and scallions/spring onions. Add the salmon, toss well, cover and let marinate 1-2 hours.
2. Thread the salmon cubes on skewers and roll them in breadcrumbs. Broil/ grill them 4-5 inches/10-12.5 cm from the heat until browned on both sides, allowing 4 minutes on each side. Serve with remoulade sauce.

SAUCE À LA REMOULADE

Remoulade is just one of the many sauces created in the eighteenth century. Menon's remoulade is regarded today as a classic version, the more common one being based on mayonnaise highly spiced with mustard.

In a pan put a shallot, parsley, scallion, a touch of garlic, an anchovy and some capers, all chopped very finely, salt and pepper; beat with a little mustard, some oil and vinegar.

REMOULADE SAUCE

Makes ½ pint/1¼ cups/300 ml sauce
2 shallots, finely chopped
2 tbsp chopped parsley
1 scallion/spring onion, finely chopped
1 small clove garlic, crushed
2 anchovy fillets, chopped
1½ tbsp capers
1 tbsp Dijon-type mustard
5 tbsp wine vinegar
6 fl oz/¾ cup/175 ml oil
salt and pepper

Put the shallots, parsley, scallion/spring onion, garlic, anchovy and capers in a bowl and stir in the mustard. Stir in the vinegar, then beat in the oil a little at a time so the sauce emulsifies and thickens slightly. Add salt and pepper to taste.

OUILLE DE DIFFÉRENT FAÇONS

Ouille is the Spanish national dish *olla podrida* – a huge stew of many meats and vegetables. The Spanish term translates into English as, literally, "rotten pot" and into French as *pot pourri*. The ancestor of *pot au feu, pot pourri* is mentioned in France as early as 1587 and during the seventeenth and eighteenth centuries its popularity never flagged, possibly because it was such an easy and spectacular dish to serve for large numbers. Here, Menon stays with the Spanish: *olla* has become *ouille* in the same way as, in English, *olla* became "olio." In French and English it means a stew or mixture, but in Spanish, *olla* refers to the earthenware pot in which the stew is made. Menon's recipe is ambiguous in that he does not explain whether the vegetables cooked with the meat are served with it, or whether they are thrown out and other vegetables are prepared separately. He probably discarded the vegetables cooked with the meat, because after 5-6 hours of cooking they would be tasteless. Today the usual method is to add vegetables near the end of preparation, timing their cooking carefully so they are all tender at the same moment.

In a casserole put a partridge, a leg of lamb, five or six pounds of beef round and a shank of beef; brown the meat on the stove, turning it from time to time in the casserole until it is about to stick on the bottom; moisten it with simmering broth or with hot water; boil over a low heat for six or seven hours; after an hour of cooking, add all kinds of blanched vegetables, such as parsley roots, carrots, parsnips, onions, turnips, celery, leeks and a mignonette made by putting in a piece of cloth some pepper, ginger, cinnamon, whole cloves, coriander, mace, a clove of garlic and a little savory. Add only a little salt: this broth should be slightly colored, clear and well flavored; the recipe will do for all kinds of clear *ouilles*, which are distinguished only by the name of the vegetables which are served on top; it will also serve for crayfish and rice *ouilles* and others; simmer the soup a long time with sliced bread or croûtes [pieces of toasted bread]; serve in a *ouille* pot and arrange whatever vegetables you would like on top.

POT POURRI

Serves 12
2-3 tbsp oil
1 partridge or pheasant, trussed
3-4 lb/1.4-1.8 kg leg of lamb, on the bone
3-4 lb/1.4-1.8 kg round of beef, preferably on the bone
3-4 lb/1.4-1.8 kg beef shanks, cut in 2 inch/5 cm slices
5-7 pints/3-4 quarts/3-4 liters beef or chicken stock
salt
1 lb/500 g carrots, quartered
8 oz/250 g parsley root/Hamburg parsley
1 lb/500 g baby onions, peeled, or medium onions, peeled and quartered
4-5 baby turnips (1 lb/500 g) peeled and halved
12 oz-1 lb/375-500 g parsnips, peeled and halved lengthwise
1 head celery, cut in 2 inch/5 cm lengths
4-5 medium leeks, halved lengthwise
loaf of French bread, sliced diagonally

FOR THE MIGNONETTE:
2 tsp black peppercorns
2-3 pieces dried ginger root
3 inch/7.5 cm stick of cinnamon
1 tsp whole cloves
1 tsp coriander seeds
2 blades mace
1 clove garlic
2 tsp dried savory

1. In a very large pot such as a ham kettle heat the oil and brown the partridge or pheasant on all sides. Take it out and brown, in turn, the leg of lamb, round of beef and beef shanks. Replace the lamb and beef round in the pot with the shanks and pour over the stock. If the stock does not cover the meat, add enough water to cover.
2. Tie the spices and herbs for the mignonette in cheesecloth and add to the pot. Cover it, bring it slowly to a boil, and skim well. Simmer it, skimming from time to time, until the meat is almost tender, 2-2½ hours depending on the weight and thickness of the

meats. Taste the broth for seasoning and add a little salt if needed.
3. If using pheasant, add it now, and continue simmering 15 minutes. Add the partridge, if using, and carrots and simmer 10 minutes longer. Add the parsley root/Hamburg parsley, if using, onions, turnips, parsnips, celery and leeks and continue simmering until all the meats and vegetables are tender, 15-20 minutes. If you like, toast the bread slices.
4. Transfer the meats to serving platters, arrange the vegetables around them, and keep warm. Add the bread or toast to the soup and boil to reduce until well flavored and thick, 10-15 minutes; discard the mignonette and taste the broth for seasoning. Menon would have served meats, vegetables, and broth together in one great pot, but today the broth is usually served first, followed by the meats and vegetables.

BIGNETS DE FRAISES

Few dishes are simpler or more delicious than fritters – a fact reflected by their constant popularity since the time of Taillevent.

In a casserole put two handfuls of flour with a little oil, a little salt, and three whipped egg whites; moisten with a little white wine, to thin the batter without making it too liquid; take hulled large strawberries, dip them in, fry them and serve glazed with sugar and a hot iron [i.e., a salamander].

The Italian art of making ices was adopted enthusiastically by the French. Here cherubs stir ice cream, freeze it in a churn, pound ice, and fill pots for serving.

STRAWBERRY FRITTERS

Serves 6
1 lb/500 g large strawberries, hulled
deep fat (for frying)
granulated sugar (for sprinkling)
FOR THE BATTER:
4 oz/1 cup/125 g flour
pinch of salt
1 tbsp oil
3 egg whites
6 fl oz/¾ cup/175 ml sweet white wine

1. For the batter: sift the flour into a bowl with the salt. Make a well in the center and add the oil. Beat the egg whites until stiff. Add to the well with the wine. Stir, gradually drawing in the flour to make a smooth batter.

2. Heat the fat to 375°F/190°C, light the broiler/grill. With a fork dip the strawberries one by one in the batter and lower them into the fat. Fry them, a few at a time, until lightly browned, about 2 minutes. Drain them on paper towels and keep hot in a warm oven with the door open while frying the remaining fritters. Sprinkle with granulated sugar and broil/grill until the sugar is caramelized, ½-1 minute. Serve at once.

HANNAH GLASSE

1708–1770

Hannah Glasse wrote the most successful English cookbook of the eighteenth century, but her fame owes more to chance than good cooking. Mrs Glasse was a mystery. When *The Art of Cookery Made Plain and Easy* first appeared anonymously in 1747, the modest "By a Lady" on the flyleaf tickled the public fancy; the signature "H. Glasse" which was scrawled in the fourth edition of 1751 only added to the enigma for no one knew whom this could be. The matter became sufficiently intriguing to interest no less a figure than Dr Johnson, who apropos of the book's origins remarked drily that "women can spin very well, but they cannot make a good book of cookery."

Mrs Glasse remained a mystery until the twentieth century when she was tracked down by methods worthy of the most tortuous detective novel. The sleuth was local historian Madeleine Hope Dodds, and the plot turned on the list of subscribers printed in the first edition of *The Art of Cookery*. Several of these subscribers came from Northumberland and were connected with a family called Allgood. It then emerged that the head of the family, Sir Lancelot Allgood, had had a sister called Hannah who was born in 1708 and had married one John Glasse. Ingenious proof of Miss Dodd's discovery was provided by a curious contemporary work called *Professed Cookery*, written by a certain Ann Cook. The third edition of 1760 opens with an unexplained attack on "A Lady," expressed in painful doggerel:

She steals from ev'ry Author to her Book,
Infamously branding the pillag'd Cook,
With Trick, Booby, Juggler, Legerdemain . . .
and later:
Yet Criticisers Sentiments may pass,
What title can be due to broken Glass . . . .

What did Ann Cook have against Hannah Glasse? Since *The Art of Cookery* was the older of the two books, Hannah could hardly have stolen her recipes. No, the wound went much deeper than that and was apparently inflicted by Hannah's brother Lancelot. The Cooks kept an inn at Hexham near the Allgood family seat and blamed their misfortunes (and ultimate ruin) on Sir Lancelot, who had publicly impugned their honesty.

It was presumably the signature in the 1751 edition of *The Art of Cookery* that alerted Ann Cook to its authorship. From other unflattering allusions in *Professed Cookery*, it seems likely that Ann Cook knew more about her rival than was comfortable for the Allgoods, for recent research in family papers reveals that Hannah was only the half-sister of Lancelot, being the child of a liaison between her father and a local woman. Her father was already married when Hannah was born, and she was taken into his household as part of the family – she later told Lancelot (the only legitimate child) that her real mother was "a wicked witch."

OPPOSITE: *Covent Garden in 1737, ten years before* The Art of Cookery *was published. Hannah Glasse lived in nearby Tavistock Street.*

The staple British ingredients – cauliflower
and a leg of lamb – have changed little since
Hannah Glasse's day.

Hannah was obviously an impulsive girl; in 1724, when only sixteen, she eloped from her grandmother's house in London with a penniless adventurer, John Glasse. A spate of family letters followed: "I am sorry at what I have done, but only at the manner of doing it," she maintained stoutly. After the accusations and recriminations usual on such occasions had died down, Hannah was left married to a thirty-year-old widower, a subaltern officer on half pay whose precarious financial situation was scarcely improved by the annuity of £30 left to Hannah when her father died the following year. However John Glasse seems to have done well enough; for the next twenty years he and Hannah lived a not unprosperous life, partly at Broomfield in Essex (where John Glasse was buried) and partly in London. Eight children were born but Hannah outlived most of them and her family line petered out.

In a letter of November 1744, Hannah shows the first signs of independent enterprise, suggesting she might market Dr Lower's tincture – a patent medicine which later had great success as Daffy's Elixir. No more

was heard of this project but a year later comes her first mention of *The Art of Cookery*. By January 1746 she could report, "My book goes on very well and everybody is pleased with it, it is now in the press."

The Art of Cookery finally appeared the following year and ran to over twenty editions in half a century. Hannah wrote more clearly and precisely than her contemporaries and she seems to have experimented with recipes rather than just copying them, untested, from another book. However *The Art of Cookery* can never have been very easy to use. The book lacks an alphabetical index and no fewer than nine repetitive recipes for gravy are scattered throughout four different chapters. Her treatment of fish is equally confusing and whole sections of the book are not original. Her chapter on creams is taken word for word from the first (1727) edition of *The Compleat Housewife* by Eliza Smith. Later editions of both books borrowed material from each other, so that by the time Hannah died, *The Art of Cookery* was about twice as long as the slim folio volume she had originally written. However it is unlikely she was to

Rabbits were just one of the dozens of foodstuffs peddled by street criers in the heart of eighteenth-century London.

Rabbits O! – Rabbits.

A. Cruickshank Fecit

blame for this plagiarism; recipes were not considered the property of the writer, as defined by the 1709 copyright act. Samuel Johnson regarded cookbooks as "made by transcription," i.e. copied out, one from the other. Whatever the limitations of *The Art of Cookery* as a book, the typical English fare that Hannah somewhat confusedly describes has much to recommend it. The pies, particularly the savory ones of veal, ham, chicken, and the like are outstanding; they come in all varieties – Hannah's savory veal pie is flavored with oysters, sweetbreads, asparagus tips, and wine, while medieval traces linger in the sweet veal pie with raisins, currants, grapes, white wine, and Spanish (sweet) potatoes. When it comes to preserving, great versatility is shown in the bevy of pickles and relishes which the English still love to serve with cold meats; pickled barberries, pickled walnuts, and anchovy catchup would all be viewed with astonishment in France, as would the English wines made of gooseberries, elderflowers, and even turnips, born of necessity in a climate unsuited to grapes.

John Glasse died in 1747, the year *The Art of Cookery* was published. He had never been a reliable earner of money but after his death Hannah's financial problems worsened. She set up as a dressmaker with her daughter Margaret (trained as a milliner) and apparently attracted some distinguished customers. Her brother Lancelot, who stayed with her in London in 1749 when he was a member of parliament, wrote: "Hannah has so many coaches at her door that, to judge from appearances, she must succeed in her business . . . She has grand visitors with her, no less than the Prince and Princess of Wales, to see her masquerade dresses." But Hannah was no businesswoman; her husband had lamented that "she does not calculate well as I could wish in many things," and soon she was cashing in her only reliable source of income, the family annuity. In May 1754 the crash came, and Hannah was declared bankrupt to the tune of £10,000 – in today's money, a considerable fortune. After this debacle, Hannah lost touch with her Northumberland relations, so much so that when the death of "Hannah Glasse" was briefly reported in 1770, no one connected her with the "H. Glasse" of *The Art of Cookery*. So began the mystery of her identity.

Little is known about her last years, but she

certainly continued to write books, first *The Servant's Directory* (1760) and then *The Complete Confectioner*, probably published in the year of her death. The English had long excelled at cakes and pastries, which became much more common once supplies of cheap sugar were assured from the West Indian colonies. Hannah shows a remarkable grasp of how to boil syrup to different degrees of concentration (the foundation of the art of confectionery), and she gives one of the first English recipes for ice cream. The results must have been unpredictable: her only instructions are to take "cream and mix with what you think proper to give it flavour and colour" and then to freeze it over ice and salt. Here she lags far behind her French counterparts, as ices had been popular in France for close on a century.

As in France, cookery writers flourished in England in the eighteenth century but there was a striking difference between the two schools. In England all the most famous writers were women – a phenomenon virtually unknown to the French until the twentieth century. Women cooks had been accepted in England as far back as the late 1600s (when Hannah Woolley's *Queene-like Closet* ran to several editions) and in the 1700s Elizabeth Moxon, Mrs Smith, Mrs Raffald, and (at the close of the century) Mrs Rundell all shared the bandwagon with Hannah Glasse. These women wrote for families with servants. Mrs Glasse might be speaking for

The British taste for tea was firmly established
by Hannah Glasse's day, though it was still
expensive. Here the mistress of the house
measures tea from an unlocked caddy. The
table is set with the delicate china especially
made for such a luxury.

them all when she observes: "If I have not wrote in the high polite style I hope I shall be forgiven; for my intention is to instruct the lower sort, and therefore must treat them in their own way." The French would have considered few of these manuals as cookbooks. When *The Art of Cookery* is compared with *Soupers de la cour* the difference is clear – one exemplifies domestic economy and the other *haute cuisine.*

The odd man out on the English scene was Vincent La Chapelle, who worked for Lord Chesterfield and brought out his *Modern Cook* in 1733. He himself was French, a precursor of the chefs who emigrated to England after the revolution. Lord Chesterfield grew melons, grapes, and pineapples in his hothouses – "the growth, the education and the perfection of these vegetable children," he wrote, "engage my care and my attention next to my corporal one" – and he moved among friends whose palates had been educated on the Grand Tour. Hannah Glasse and her fellows had a rooted dislike of such foreign nonsense. "Such is the blind folly of this age," she exclaims, "that they would rather be imposed on by a French booby than give encouragement to a good English cook."

The chief target of Hannah's wrath is that foundation of French cuisine, the *coulis.* "Read this chapter and you will find how expensive a French cook's sauce is," she says, and she suggests a scaled-down version using only a pound of veal and half a pound of bacon instead of the whole leg of veal and whole ham called for in classic French books. Mrs Raffald even insists that "lemon pickle and browning answers both for beauty and taste (at trifling expense) better than *coulis.*" Such parsimony with ingredients, totally absent from French *haute cuisine*, is at least partly responsible for the depressing reputation of English food. As Voltaire reportedly said, "In England there are sixty different religions, but only one sauce."

The simpler English approach to eating was equally evident in their menus; only two courses were the rule (compared with up to five in France), the first of soup and "made" dishes (often in a sauce) and the second of more substantial roasts with side dishes of vegetables and sweet and savory pies. This lighter English diet was fortified by a cooked breakfast and eternal cups of tea. By

"The Milk Seller" by Thomas Rowlandson (1756-1827). Fresh milk in central London was a rare luxury. Cows were kept in St. James' Park so that passersby could treat themselves to a frothing fresh pint.

Hannah Glasse's time, the Englishman's love of afternoon tea was already legendary. A Swiss pastor, Carl Philipp Moritz, when vacationing in England was indelibly impressed by bread and butter "as thin as poppy leaves" and "by another bread and butter, usually eaten with tea, which is toasted by the fire and is incomparably good. This is called toast."

It is no accident that the most memorable feature of English food was the bread and butter. The outstanding characteristic of the cooking described by Hannah Glasse is its wholesome plainness, still found today in English country cooking. Many of her recipes remain in the British repertoire, but it is not for these that she is remembered. Rather her fame rests on the most popular cookery catchphrase of all time, "First catch your hare," which originated in her innocent instruction, "Take your hare when it is cas'd [skinned] . . ." The image of the cook racing out to catch a hare before putting it in the kitchen pot has amused countless generations.

GLASSE RECIPES

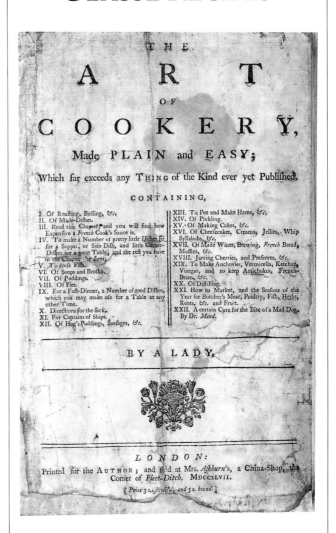

THE

ART

OF

COOKERY,

Made PLAIN and EASY;

Which far exceeds any THING of the Kind ever yet Published.

CONTAINING,

I. Of Roasting, Boiling, &c.
II. Of Made-Dishes.
III. Read this Chapter, and you will find how Expensive a French Cook's Sauce is.
IV. To make a Number of pretty little Dishes fit for a Supper, or Side Dish, and little Corner-Dishes for a great Table; and the rest you have in the Chapter for Lent.
V. To dress Fish.
VI. Of Soops and Broths.
VII. Of Puddings.
VIII. Of Pies.
IX. For a Fast-Dinner, a Number of good Dishes, which you may make use for a Table at any other Time.
X. Directions for the Sick.
XI. For Captains of Ships.
XII. Of Hog's Puddings, Sausages, &c.

XIII. To Pot and Make Hams, &c.
XIV. Of Pickling.
XV. Of Making Cakes, &c.
XVI. Of Cheesecakes, Creams, Jellies, Whip Syllabubs, &c.
XVII. Of Made Wines, Brewing, French Bread, Muffins, &c.
XVIII. Jarring Cherries, and Preserves, &c.
XIX. To Make Anchovies, Vermicella, Ketchup, Vinegar, and to keep Artichokes, French-Beans, &c.
XX. Of Distilling.
XXI. How to Market, and the Seasons of the Year for Butcher's Meat, Poultry, Fish, Herbs, Roots, &c. and Fruit.
XXII. A certain Cure for the Bite of a Mad Dog. By Dr. Mead.

BY A LADY.

LONDON:
Printed for the AUTHOR; and sold at Mrs. Ashburn's, a China-Shop, the Corner of Fleet-Ditch. MDCCXLVII.
[Price 3 s. stitch'd, and 5 s. bound.]

LEFT: How to Make Chocolate Cream.
ABOVE: The title page of the first edition of Hannah Glasse's The Art of Cookery Made Plain and Easy. *The list of subscribers gives the clue to Hannah's adventurous, not to say romantic, career.*

In her recipes, Hannah Glasse takes a more practical line than her French contemporaries; she concentrates on specific instructions for each recipe and usually ignores the more general principles that may lie behind them. Already she takes some of her cooking terms from the French, and the richness of the Gallic cooking vocabulary continues.

TO POT SALMON

To pot means to pack thoroughly cooked meat or fish so as to exclude all the air, then to seal the top with butter. For potted dishes, butter must be clarified, for the milky liquid in regular butter makes food spoil more quickly. When properly done, the mixture can be kept for several months – a necessity in the days before refrigeration. *Jamaica pepper* is allspice, one of the only spices native to the Western Hemisphere. *Salprunella* is a type of saltpetre.

Take a Piece of fresh Salmon, scale it, and wipe it clean (let your Piece, or Pieces, be as big as will lye cleverly in your Pot) season it with *Jamaica* Pepper, black Pepper, Mace and Cloves beat fine, mixed with Salt, a little Salprunella beat fine, and rub the Bone with; season with a little of the Spice, pour clarified Butter over it, and bake it well; then take it out carefully, and lay it to drain; when cold, season it well, lay it in your Pot close, and cover it with clarified Butter as above.

Thus you may do Carp, Trench, Trout, and several Sorts of Fish.

The eighteenth-century kitchen fireplace was a miniature of the medieval one with all cooking done in front of, or over, the open flames. In this frontispiece from a contemporary manual a cookbook lies self-consciously open on the table.

POTTED SALMON

Serves 6
1¼ lb/2½ cups/625 g butter
2 lb/1 kg piece of salmon
2 tsp ground allspice
2 tsp pepper
1 tsp ground mace
½ tsp ground cloves
2½ tsp salt
1⅔ pint/1 quart/1 liter crock, or 8 individual ramekins

1. To clarify the butter: heat it gently until melted and skim foam from the surface. Pour the butter into a bowl and chill it until set. Discard the milky liquid at the bottom of the cake of butter.

2. Heat the oven to No 4/350°F/175°C. Wash the salmon and pat it dry with paper towels. Cut it in half horizontally along the backbone. Mix the allspice, pepper, mace, cloves and salt and rub them into the cut surfaces of the fish. Lay it in a casserole so the pieces are tightly packed together. Melt about a quarter of the clarified butter, pour it over the salmon, and cover tightly. Bake the salmon in the heated oven until no longer transparent in the center, 35-45 minutes depending on the thickness of the fish.

3. Transfer the salmon to a plate to drain and cool. Divide it into pieces, discarding skin and bone. Pack it tightly in a crock or individual ramekins, taking care to exclude all air. Melt the remaining clarified butter and pour it over the salmon to seal it. It can be kept for up to two weeks in the refrigerator.

A RAGOÛT OF OYSTERS

Mrs Glasse might rail against Frenchified cooking, but like all her contemporaries, she did not go so far as to exclude fricassées, ragoûts, and other French-inspired recipes from her book. She was not familiar with a French roux and invariably thickens her sauces by a more laborious method such as the one below. *Raspings* are crumbs "rasped" or grated from a dry loaf of bread.

Open twenty large Oysters, take them out of their Liquor, save the Liquor, and dip the Oysters in a Batter made thus: Take two Eggs, beat them well, a little Lemon-peel grated, a little Nutmeg grated, a Blade of Mace pounded fine, a little Parsley chopped fine; beat all together with a little Flour, have ready some Butter or Dripping in a Stew-pan, when it boils, dip in your Oysters, one by one, into the Batter, and fry them of a fine brown; then with an Egg-slice take them out, and lay them in a Dish before the Fire. Pour the Fat out of the Pan, and shake a little Flour over the Bottom of the Pan, then rub a little Piece of Butter, as big as a small Walnut, all over with your Knife, whilst it is over the Fire; then pour in three Spoonfuls of the Oyster-liquor strained, one Spoonful of White Wine, and a Quarter of a Pint of Gravy; grate a little Nutmeg, stir all together, throw in the Oysters, give the Pan a Toss round, and when the Sauce is of a good Thickness, pour all into the Dish, and garnish with Raspings.

RAGOÛT OF OYSTERS

Serves 4 as first course
FOR THE BATTER:
2 oz/¹⁄₂ cup/60 g flour
3 eggs
grated rind of ¹⁄₂ lemon
¹⁄₄ tsp ground nutmeg
¹⁄₄ tsp grated mace
1 tbsp chopped parsley
FOR THE RAGOÛT:
4 oz/¹⁄₂ cup/125 g butter (for frying)
1²⁄₃ pints/1 quart/1 liter (about 2 dozen) shucked/shelled oysters, with their liquor/liquid
1 tbsp flour
2 tbsp butter
2 tbsp white wine
6 fl oz/³⁄₄ cup/175 ml gravy (see page 108)
pinch of nutmeg
salt and pepper (optional)
2-3 tbsp browned breadcrumbs (for garnish)

1. For the batter: sift the flour into a bowl, make a well in the center and add 2 eggs. Beat to make a smooth paste, add the remaining egg with the lemon rind, nutmeg, mace and parsley and beat 1 minute. Drain the oysters, reserving the liquor/liquid.
2. In a frying pan, melt a little of the butter, dip several of the oysters into the batter, drain them slightly and fry them over brisk heat until brown, 1-2 minutes on each side; remove them and keep warm. Fry the remaining oysters in the same way, using more butter as necessary.

3. Sprinkle the tablespoon of flour into the pan, set it over low heat, and rub over the 2 tablespoons of butter until melted. Stir in the oyster liquor/liquid with the wine, gravy and nutmeg and bring to a boil, stirring. Add the oysters and heat gently, shaking the pan to mix them with the sauce, until very hot.
Note: do not overcook them or they will be tough. Taste the ragoût for seasoning, transfer it to a serving dish, sprinkle with browned breadcrumbs, and serve at once.

TO MAKE GRAVY

Hannah Glasse's gravy may not be as concentrated as French *coulis* but by our standards it is certainly a rich basic sauce.

If you live in the Country, where you can't always have Gravy Meat, when your Meat comes from the Butcher take a Piece of Beef, a Piece of Veal, and a Piece of Mutton; cut them into as small Pieces as you can, and take a large deep Sauce-pan with a Cover, lay your Beef at Bottom, then your Mutton, then a very little Piece of Bacon, a Slice or two of Carrot, some Mace, Cloves, Whole Pepper Black and White, a large Onion cut in Slices, a Bundle of Sweet Herbs, and then lay in your Veal. Cover it close over a very slow Fire for six or seven Minutes, shaking the Sauce-pan now and then; then shake some Flour in, and have ready some boiling Water, pour it in till you cover the Meat and something more: Cover it close, and let it stew till it is quite rich and good; then season it to your Taste with Salt, and strain it off. This will do for most Things.

The BRITISH-BUTCHER.

Despite the British reputation for eating beef, in Hannah Glasse's time meat was not within the reach of all pockets. "A crown, take it or leave it!" sniffs a supercilious butcher to an impecunious customer.

GRAVY

Makes about 16 fl oz/2 cups/500 ml of gravy

8 oz/250 g stewing beef, diced
8 oz/250 g boned shoulder or breast of lamb, diced
3-4 slices bacon
1 carrot, sliced
blade of mace
4-5 whole cloves
½ tsp black peppercorns
½ tsp white peppercorns
1 large onion, sliced
bouquet garni
8 oz/250 g stewing veal, diced
2 tbsp flour
1 pint/2½ cups/600 ml boiling water
salt

1. In a heavy-based pan spread the beef and lamb and top with the bacon, carrot, mace, cloves, peppercorns, onion, bouquet garni and veal. Cover and cook over low heat, shaking the pan from time to time until the juices run from the meat, 5-7 minutes.
2. Sprinkle over the flour, stir to mix, and pour in the boiling water. Bring to a boil, stirring, then cover and simmer the gravy over low heat until it is rich and well flavored, 1-1½ hours. At the end of cooking it should be the consistency of thin cream. Season it to taste with salt and strain.

TO PICKLE LARGE CUCUMBERS IN SLICES

As any gardener knows, cucumbers have the annoying habit of ripening all at the same time. Eighteenth-century cooks, particularly the English, preserved them as pickles to serve over the winter with cold meats. A *race of ginger* is a root. A *crown* was a coin.

Take the large Cucumbers before they are too ripe, slice them the Thickness of Crown-pieces into a Pewter-dish: To every dozen of Cucumbers, slice two large Onions thin, so on till you have filled your Dish; with a Handful of Salt between every Row; then cover them with another Pewter-dish, and let them stand twenty-four Hours; then put them in a Cullender, let them drain very well, then put them into a jar, and cover them over with White Wine Vinegar, and let them stand for Hours; then pour the Vinegar from them into a Copper Sauce-pan, and boil it with a little Salt. Put to the Cucumbers a little Mace, a little whole Pepper, a large Race of Ginger sliced, and then pour the boiling Vinegar on. Cover them close, and when they are cold, tye them down; they will be fit to eat in two or three Days.

Pickles have long been a mainstay of the English table, most of them flavored by at least one member of the onion family.

CUCUMBER PICKLES

Makes 9⅓ pints/6 quarts/6 liters of crisp not-too-sweet pickles

12 cucumbers, cut in ⅛ inch/3 mm slices
2 large onions, thinly sliced
3¼ oz/½ cup/100 g salt
1⅔ pints/1 quart/1 liter white wine
    vinegar
3 blades mace
1 tsp black peppercorns
1½ inch/4 cm piece dried ginger root, or
    3 inches/7.5 cm piece fresh ginger root,
    peeled and sliced
Heatproof jars; paraffin wax

1. In a large non-aluminum bowl, layer the cucumbers and onions, sprinkling the layers with all but 1 teaspoon of the salt. Cover and let stand 24 hours.
2. Drain the cucumbers in a colander, stirring once or twice so they drain thoroughly. Put them in a bowl, pour over enough white wine vinegar to cover them, and let stand 4 hours.

3. Drain the vinegar into a non-aluminum pan and bring to a boil. Pack the cucumbers in a crock or jars with an equal amount of the mace, peppercorns, ginger root, and remaining salt. Pour over the boiling vinegar. Let them cool slightly before sealing with a layer of paraffin wax. Despite Mrs Glasse's advice that the pickles can be eaten within two days, they are much better if kept for at least a month.

HOW TO MAKE CHOCOLATE CREAM

Cocoa beans were brought back by Cortes from Mexico in the sixteenth century, and chocolate became so popular as a drink that the Catholic Church divided in heated debate on whether drinking chocolate on a fast day constituted mortal sin. However, chocolate flavoring did not catch on until much later and Mrs Glasse was one of the first English cooks to use it.

Take a Quart of Cream, a Pint of white Wine, and a little Juice of Lemon; sweeten it very well, lay in a Sprig of Rosemary, grate some Chocolate, and mix all together; stir them over the Fire till it is thick, and pour it into your Cups.

CHOCOLATE CREAM

Serves 8

5 oz/¾ cup/150 g sugar
8 fl oz/1 cup/250 ml sweet white wine
juice of ½ lemon
16 fl oz/2 cups/500 ml heavy/double cream
sprig of fresh rosemary, or 1 tsp dried rosemary
4 oz/125 g semisweet chocolate, grated
8 mousse pots, stemmed glasses or custard cups

In a heavy-based pan stir the sugar into the wine and lemon juice until dissolved. Stir in the cream – it will thicken slightly and be full of bubbles. Add the rosemary and grated chocolate and cook over low heat, stirring until the chocolate melts. Bring to a boil and boil, stirring, until the mixture is the consistency of thick cream, about 5 minutes. Take from the heat, let cool slightly, then strain into mousse pots, glasses, or custard cups. Serve cold.

To Make Whipt Syllabubs

Syllabub is an ancient English dessert dating from medieval times. It is made of cream beaten with fruit juice or wine until thick. The origin of the name is obscure; it may come from *sille* (white wine from the Champagne region of France) and *bub*, meaning a bubbling drink. Mrs Glasse gives several recipes; this one has a base of wine or fruit juice tinted green, orange, or pink with the syllabub spooned on top. Another less practical version calls for milking the cow directly into the syllabub mixture. *Sack* is an old word for sherry and Seville oranges are the bitter oranges used for marmalade.

Take a Quart of thick Cream, and half a Pint of Sack, the Juice of two Seville Oranges, or Lemons, grate in the Peel of two Lemons, half a Pound of double-refined Sugar, pour it into a broad earthen Pan, and whisk it well; but first sweeten some Red Wine or Sack, and fill your Glasses as full as you chuse, then as the Froth rises, take it off with a Spoon, and lay it carefully into your Glasses till they are as full as they will hold. Don't make these long before you use them. You may use Cyder sweetened, or any Wine you please, or Lemon, or Orange-whey made thus; squeeze the Juice of a Lemon or Orange into a quarter of a Pint of Milk, when the Curd is hard, pour the Whey clear off, and sweeten it to your Palate. You may colour some with the Juice of Spinach, some with Saffron, and some with Cochineal, just as you fancy.

Syllabub

Serves 6
FOR THE COLORED LAYER:
8 fl oz/1 cup/250 ml red wine or cider, or 4 fl oz/½ cup/125 ml sweet or medium sherry, or whey made with 12 fl oz/ 1½ cups/375 ml milk with the juice of 1½ lemons or 1½ oranges and a few drops of edible food coloring
2-3 tbsp sugar, or to taste
FOR THE SYLLABUB:
4 fl oz/½ cup/125 ml sweet or medium sherry
grated rind and juice of 1 lemon or 1 orange
3¼ oz/½ cup/100 g sugar
16 fl oz/2 cups/500 ml heavy/double cream
6 stemmed glasses

1. For the colored layer, if using whey: beat the lemon or orange juice into the milk, let stand 30 minutes so the milk curdles thoroughly, and strain the whey through cheesecloth, discarding the curd. Color the whey with green, yellow, or red food coloring. Sweeten the colored whey, red wine, cider or sherry with sugar to taste and spoon it into stemmed glasses.

2. For the syllabub: in a bowl stir the sherry, lemon or orange rind and juice, and the sugar until the sugar is dissolved. Beat in the cream and continue beating until thick froth rises to the surface. Skim off the froth with a metal spoon and spoon carefully into the stemmed glasses to form a layer on top of the liquid. Continue beating and skimming off the froth until only a little thin liquid is left in the bowl; the glasses should be full to the brim. Chill and serve within 4 hours.

FRANCESCO LEONARDI

flourished 1750–1790

I N THE MIDDLE OF THE EIGHT-
eenth century, Europe idled in a halcyon age. Intermittent famines, and the military skirmishes of the great powers as they jockeyed for political dominance, scarcely disturbed the golden prosperity that in England produced the great country houses of the classical revival, and in France the escapist Fragonard paintings of silk-clad shepherdesses gamboling in a fairytale landscape. This was the age of the Grand Tour, when scions of wealthy families pursued the cultural path of Paris, Heidelberg, Rome, Naples, and Venice, with a brief glimpse of the Matterhorn and the ruins of Pompeii along the way.

Into this self-assured cosmopolitan world was born the first Italian cook of any importance since the Renaissance – Francesco Leonardi. "In this world it is not your nationality that makes you what you are, but your talent," declares Leonardi with prescience in his most important cookbook, *L'Apicio moderno*. He certainly put his own talents to good use. By his own account, Leonardi's long career stretches from the 1740s to the 1800s, from the elegance of Naples (then at its apogee), through royalist France and the St Petersburg of Catherine the Great to the French Revolution and the Napoleonic Wars.

L'Apicio moderno was first published in 1790, and its title is significant. Apicius compiled the famous cookbook of ancient Rome and Leonardi intended his work to

OPPOSITE: *Music and masked balls were a highlight of eighteenth-century Italian society. The Venetian artist Pietro Longhi captures the hedonistic spirit of these occasions.*

be both Italian and "modern" in the sense of international and scientific. Given the supremacy of French cuisine in the fashionable kitchens of the time, any "international" work on cooking was bound to be based on French techniques and recipes. (Astonishingly, La Varenne's *Le Cuisinier françois* was still being reprinted in Italian as late as 1815.)

L'Apicio is more than a mere imitation of its French counterparts; with its 3,000 recipes culled from half a dozen countries and its sections of general culinary interest describing, for example, the wines of Europe or new methods of preserving food, it is more like an encyclopedia. There is a Russian nettle soup flavored with onion and garnished with pieces of chicken and hard-cooked eggs (page 120) and a chicken *alla tartara* marinated in oil, onion, garlic, and lemon, then spit-roasted. From Germany and Poland come soups containing "chenedel," Leonardi's rendering of the German *knoedel* or dumpling. There are recipes for sauerkraut and gnocchi *alla tedesca* containing breadcrumbs, pounded rice, butter, nutmeg, Parmesan, egg yolks, and liver – a dish still to be found in the Dolomites. Leonardi also has a good grasp of English cooking as described by Hannah Glasse – he notes their gravy thickened with flour in the roasting pan and is shocked by the vulgarity of their traditional roasts of meat. He remarks that the English make

good sweet pastry for pies, but his boiled suet pudding can hardly have transplanted well to an Italian climate.

For all his international airs, however, Leonardi is an Italian writing for Italians. With fifty years' experience in and out of Italy, he freely adapts foreign recipes, using Italian ingredients like ricotta, and adding Parmesan cheese like a salt for seasoning. He emphasizes the excellence of Italian ingredients – the mussels from the Bay of Taranto, the beef of Tuscany, and the fresh fish which is available everywhere, so that cooks need never rely on salted fish, as in other countries. He uses copious quantities of the white truffles of Piedmont, he stuffs suckling pig with macaroni, and he shares the native partiality for little birds that was to shock English travelers. "They frequently eat kites, hawks, magpies, jackdaws, and other lesser birds," reports a contemporary guidebook. "Between Rome and Naples travellers are sometimes regaled with buffaloes and crows."

Leonardi's experience of Italian cooking was acquired in a princely household. In the early 1750s (after an apprenticeship in France with the epicurean Maréchal de Richelieu) he joined Michele Imperiali, Prince of Francavilla, the *cher amour* of Queen Amelia of Naples and a friend of Casanova. After centuries of foreign domination, Naples, as capital of the newly independent Kingdom of the Two Sicilies, had become renowned for the virtuosity of its music and the gaiety of its masked balls. Where Versailles was wanton, Naples was openly

licentious. "The dissipation of the Neapolitans is really disgusting," complained Lady Orford, Sir Horace Walpole's daughter-in-law. "All ranks seem to live only for tawdry show and idleness. Every day there are fireworks and music . . ." John Moore, an English visitor who attended one of Prince Francavilla's parties, remarked on their luxury even on a fast day: "There were forty people . . . it was the most magnificent entertainment I ever saw, comprehending an infinite variety of dishes, a vast profusion of fruit, and the wines of every country."

Leonardi was apparently less impressed by his patron. He deplored the slovenly habit of serving made dishes, cold dishes, and roasts all at the same time; the practice is acceptable on a military campaign, he says, but not when entertaining princes. Throughout his works, Leonardi upbraids Italians for their naiveté, and the best hope he holds out for them is that "in time" they may be capable of organizing a really grand dinner.

If Italian society was more "provincial" than French, it took correspondingly greater pride in regional cooking traditions. Like Martino and Scappi before him. Leonardi clearly had his own regional allegiances. He recommends zucchini *alla milanese* stuffed with breadcrumbs and béchamel, and a cassata *palermitana* made (as today) with ricotta (page 127). Naturally with his Neapolitan background Leonardi is keen on pasta, and he often bases his recipes on ready-made kinds, showing that the local pasta makers were already highly esteemed. But like

OPPOSITE: Poor fishermen consume a hasty meal of pasta in this 1801 view of the Bay of Naples, the city where Leonardi began and ended his career.
BELOW: A feast at the Teatro San Benneto where Venetians flocked for entertainment, listening to arias sung by castrati.

any modern Italian cookbook, Leonardi's also has a recipe for fresh pasta made with four or six eggs. His gnocchi and fettucine are layered with ham, Parmesan, and melted butter with a cream sauce on the side. Tagliolini are to be boiled for only six and a half minutes – an Italian habit that provoked a German traveling in Italy in 1804 to complain about rice and macaroni "too little boiled." Clearly he was not accustomed to *al dente* pasta.

Most significantly, Leonardi is the first cook to record how the tomato was being used in southern Italy. He can lay claim to originating that classic Neapolitan combination, pasta and tomato; he cooks meatballs in tomato sauce, gives a recipe for chicken *alla siciliana* cooked with ham, onions, herbs, and tomato sauce, and he stuffs tomatoes and explains how to dry them in the

open air for a purée. His *sugo di pomodoro*, made with seeded tomatoes simmered slowly with onions, celery, garlic, basil, and parsley has not changed one iota today.

By the 1760s Leonardi had tired of Naples and spent the next decade or two on the move. Apart from a spell in Rome with the Cardinal de Bernis (who, as befitted a former French courtier, awarded a prize to the city's best cook, the *rosticciere* of Prince Borghese) Leonardi was abroad, first with Louis XV on his military campaigns and then with two Russian noblemen living in exile, Ivan Ivanovich Schuvalov and Grigori Orlov. Schuvalov (a notable Francophile) had been the lover of Empress Elisabeth of Russia, and Orlov the lover of Empress Catherine; they shared a passion for travel, and Leonardi toured with them, no doubt in the grand Russian style

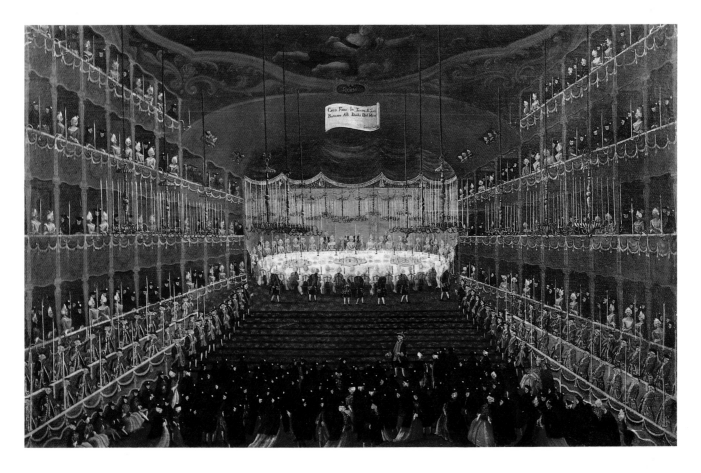

*Many types of cherry, displayed here in a riot
of color by contemporary artist Bimbi.*

with the rest of their household in train. Schuvalov used to remark that the greatest privilege of a rich man was to eat well, and it was certainly through working for these two noblemen that Leonardi acquired his unique international experience. By 1783, when Orlov died, Leonardi was sufficiently distinguished to be called to Russia as steward to the Empress Catherine herself.

Catherine's court had the brilliance of Versailles and Naples but none of their blasé sophistication. The Russians reveled with childlike delight in their great palaces along the Neva, styled after French and Italian models but outdoing them all in splendor. Gold and jewels glittered everywhere; at a celebration for the birth of Catherine's grandchild, the British ambassador reported that "the dessert at supper was set out with jewels to the amount of upwards of two million sterling." This

extravagance was sustained by an army of servants – many nobles kept 500 or more, and as steward of the imperial household Leonardi could have been responsible for double that number. However, far from being trained, most of these "servants" were serfs whose status is conveyed by a stark advertisement from a St Petersburg journal of the time: "To be sold: a girl of 16 of good behavior, and a second-hand, slightly used carriage."

During Leonardi's time at court the lead was taken by Prince Grigori Potemkin, Orlov's successor to Catherine's favors. He thought nothing of spending 20,000 roubles (enough to build a small palace) on a dinner followed by artistic entertainment. At one party the whole of St Petersburg talked about a soup of sterlet (a type of sturgeon) which cost 3,000 roubles and was served in a massive silver bathtub. A grand dinner would begin

Polenta, made with yellow cornmeal, is the traditional accompaniment to calves' liver Venetian style. In this painting the dough is kneaded on a tablecloth to absorb excess moisture, still the best procedure.

with oysters specially imported from Denmark, and in summer Russia's own rivers yielded a superb harvest of fish. In winter, before Christmas, the frozen Neva was the setting for a mile-long market where large quantities of frozen meat were sold. "It would be difficult for even a nice epicure to perceive the difference," remarked an English commentator in 1804, in what must be the first endorsement of frozen foods.

Fresh or frozen, many of the grander ingredients came from afar. "I have frequently seen at the same time sterlet from the Volga, veal from Archangel, mutton from Astrachan, beef from the Ukraine, and pheasants from Hungary and Bohemia," reported William Coxe during a trip through Russia in 1778. Out of season, the cost of a melon in a Moscow market, sent by land carriage from the Caspian, a thousand miles away, could rise fortyfold. The Empress Catherine grew fruits and vegetables in her own hothouses, which must have been extremely expensive to heat during the long Russian winter. One March dinner in St Petersburg was graced by a real cherry tree laden with fruit – "But flavor is lacking from the prodigals of the greenhouse," the great French chef Carême was later to remark of his spell at the Russian court. Catherine herself is said to have had simple tastes, reserving a grand display for formal occasions. In private she kept to cabbage (a taste she shared with Potemkin), rye bread, rusks, and plenty of strong coffee.

Leonardi stayed only a few years in Russia, complaining that he could not stand the climate, then returned to the welcoming sun of Italy, probably reaching Rome in 1787. After the publication of *L'Apicio* in 1790, he spent a few years with the Duke of Gravina in Naples, but he had chosen the wrong moment to abandon the opulence of Russia. When Napoleon's armies invaded Italy, the duke scuttled back hastily to his native Sicily.

The latter days of Leonardi's career are obscure, though he may have had some of the adventures he describes in the preface to his book *Giannina ossia la cuciniera della alpi* (Giannina or the Alpine Cook). Giannina was an innkeeper at Mont Cenis who had married a French cook and traveled with him in Russia, central Europe, and on the high seas, working for the East India Company. The recipes in *Giannina* and in two or three other works produced by Leonardi proved to be no more than adaptations of *L'Apicio*. In deference to the vogue for chinoiserie, one of these books was called *Tonkin*, but disappointingly it treats not of Chinese cooking but of the sweet liqueurs and candied fruits then in fashion on the credenza.

L'Apicio moderno remains his master work. Its ultimate importance for Italian cooking lies not in its French recipes and techniques, much as they added depth and breadth to native traditions, but in its elaboration of cooking as a discipline demanding skill and dedication. Italians had not seen a cookbook of such ambition since the time of Scappi, and in 250 years the indigenous tradition of cooking owed its survival more to its deep roots in Italian homes than to the inspiration of cookbooks. As Leonardi himself wrote, "Pride has been a reason why Italian cooking has deteriorated in the last two centuries; cooks are afraid people would think them ignorant if they were caught consulting a cookbook." Leonardi restored leadership to his "boundless profession" (as he called it), building on the same modest repertoire of meat, pasta, vegetables, and desserts as had featured in Martino and Scappi. The fact that Italian cooking has come so far from there, finding its major expression in 1880 with the classic *La Scienza in cucina* by Pellegrino Artusi, owes much to Francesco Leonardi.

LEONARDI RECIPES

APICIO
MODERNO
DI FRANCESCO LEONARDI

EDIZIONE SECONDA

REVISTA, CORRETTA, ED ACCRESCIUTA
DALL' AUTORE •

*Nec sibi cœnarum quivis temere arroget artem
Ni prius exacta tenui ratione saporum.*
Orat. lib. 2. sat. 4. ver. 35.

TOMO QUINTO.

IN ROMA MDCCCVIII.
Nella Stamperia del Giunchi, presso Carlo
Mordacchini.

Con Approvazione.

LEFT: *Gatto di Lasagne alla Misgrasse and
Pomodoro in Chenef.*
ABOVE: *In this title page Leonardi describes
himself as a Roman and former cook to
Empress Catherine II of Russia, confirming his
credentials in Latin. "No one should speak idly
of cooking without first acquiring some
understanding of flavor."*

Leonardi has an agreeable style; his recipes are as much a
pleasure to read as the results are to eat. If not exemplary
about stating all quantities, he at least gives enough to
indicate the broad outlines of a dish. His comment below
on the Russian love of nettle soup is rare. Normally he
says nothing about the countries he visits, keeping
strictly to the cooking matter in hand; his book is the
more professional, if less lively, because of it.

119

ZUPPA RUSSA DI ORTICA

Leonardi likes to adapt foreign recipes, using Italian ingredients. Here he flavors the soup with Parmesan cheese, and even the eggs for the garnish are stuffed with an Italian cheese – ricotta.

The Russians really love this soup and it is often served in noble households in St Petersburg. To make it take the tips and tender leaves of nettles as fresh as possible, wash well and blanch for a moment in boiling water, then put under cold water, squeeze dry and chop coarsely. Heat a little chopped onion with a piece of butter, then add the nettles and cook a little, sprinkle

with a good pinch of flour, pour over a good white stock made from a capon or good chicken cut in pieces. Cook gently and season with salt. Just before serving thicken the soup with eight egg yolks, stir in cream, pour into the terrine, add the pieces of capon or chicken and eight stuffed eggs fried in butter. It would be good to add a handful of grated Parmesan with the egg yolks and cream. If you want to, add croûtons of bread fried in butter to asparagus soup or this soup; it will depend on the amount of vegetables used and on the soup. Note, however, that if you add bread you won't add either chicken or stuffed eggs.

Leonardi's career was crowned by a spell in St. Petersburg with Catherine the Great. Her residences were awesome but impractical; dishes cooled on their long journey from kitchen to table.

RUSSIAN NETTLE SOUP

Serves 8
1 lb/500 g nettle leaves and tips (spinach or sorrel may be substituted)
1 onion, chopped
2 tbsp butter
2 tbsp flour
2⅓ pints/1½ quarts/1.5 liters chicken stock
salt and pepper
FOR THE LIAISON:
4 egg yolks
4 fl oz/½ cup/125 ml heavy/double cream
1 oz/¼ cup/30 g grated Parmesan cheese (optional)
FOR THE GARNISH I:
3¼ oz/½ cup/100 g cooked chicken breast, diced
8 stuffed fried eggs (see recipe page 121)

FOR THE GARNISH II:
8 slices bread, crusts discarded, diced
4-6 tbsp oil and butter, mixed

1. If using nettles, wash them then blanch them in boiling water for ½ minute and drain thoroughly. Spinach and sorrel need no blanching. Finely chop the leaves of the nettles, spinach or sorrel.
2. In a kettle/large pan fry the onion in butter until soft, add the nettles, spinach or sorrel and cook gently until soft. Stir in the flour, then add the stock and bring to a boil, stirring. Season with salt and pepper, cover and simmer 15-20 minutes.

3. To finish: prepare the garnish of chicken and eggs, or make the croûtons: fry the diced bread in the oil and butter, stirring to brown evenly; drain the croûtons on paper towels and keep warm. Reheat the soup. To add the liaison, mix the egg yolks and cream in a bowl. If using cheese, add it now, beating until smooth. Stir a little of the hot soup into the egg mixture, then stir this mixture back into the remaining soup in the pan. Heat gently until the soup thickens slightly. Note: do not boil or the soup will curdle. Taste for seasoning. If serving with eggs and chicken, divide these among individual bowls and pour the soup on top. If serving with croûtons, pass them separately.

UOVE RIPIENE

Cut the eggs in half, pound the yolks in a mortar, add a piece of butter, a little fresh ricotta or cold panada made very thick by beating three egg yolks, a handful of grated Parmesan, a little salt, ground pepper, nutmeg, powdered cinnamon, 4 raw egg yolks and one white. Mix well and stuff the eggs with this filling, pushing it well in. Roll in flour, dip in beaten egg, sprinkle with breadcrumbs and fry until a nice color.

For centuries cheese makers have relied on wooden rounds to mold fresh curds into cheese.

STUFFED EGGS

8 hard-boiled/cooked eggs, shelled
FOR THE FILLING I:
1 oz/¼ cup/30 g grated Parmesan cheese
salt and pepper
grated nutmeg
cinnamon
3 raw egg yolks and 1 whole raw egg,
    beaten to mix
FOR THE FILLING II:
4 oz/125 g fresh ricotta cheese
salt and pepper
FOR THE COATING:
2 oz/½ cup/60 g flour seasoned with ½ tsp
    salt and pinch of pepper
2 eggs beaten with 1 tbsp oil and ½ tsp salt
2½ oz/¾ cup/75 g dry white breadcrumbs,
    more if needed
deep fat (for frying)

1. Halve the 8 hard-boiled/cooked eggs lengthwise, scoop out the yolks and sieve them. If using the filling of Parmesan cheese, stir in the grated cheese with 3 of the sieved yolks, salt, pepper, nutmeg and cinnamon to taste. Stir in the 3 raw egg yolks and 1 whole egg. Beat in the remaining sieved hard-boiled/cooked yolks. Fill the egg halves and press them back together firmly.
2. If using the filling of ricotta cheese, season the cheese with salt and pepper and beat it until smooth. Beat in the 8 sieved, hard-boiled/cooked yolks. Fill the egg halves as above.

3. Coat the filled eggs first in seasoned flour, then in the egg and oil mixture, then in the breadcrumbs. Let the coated eggs dry at least 15 minutes.
4. To finish: heat the deep fat. Fry the eggs, a few at a time, in hot fat until golden brown. Drain them thoroughly on paper towels. Serve hot or cold.

GATTO DI LASAGNE ALLA MISGRASSE

It has been claimed that this dish was invented in 1799 by a chef of Macerata in honor of the commander of the Austrian forces at Ancona, but the recipe must have a much older tradition as it is clearly familiar to Leonardi writing in 1790. It is a luxurious variation of the usual Bolognese lasagne layered with meat sauce and today is still regarded as a speciality of the region around Ancona.

Entré. **Make dough as for tagliolini with the only difference that you add a nut of butter and do not roll out the dough so thinly. Cut out lasagne in 4 inch or 6 inch squares and cook in boiling salted water, dropping them one at a time at the point where the water is boiling hardest so they do not stick together. When they are** cooked, drain, put in cold salted water then lay out on a clean cloth. Take a well-buttered casserole and sprinkle with breadcrumbs, then make a large star on the bottom with slices of ham, then spread the lasagne on the bottom and round the sides of the casserole so they come right up to the top and overlap the sides, alternating with layers of grated Parmesan, nuts of fresh butter, a little béchamel, a little sweetbread ragù and truffles cooked in very little liquid, powdered cinnamon, ground pepper and nutmeg. When the casserole is almost full, fold inside the lasagne that are hanging over the edge and cover with the same mixture, finishing with just butter and Parmesan; bake until a nice color in a fairly hot oven and then turn out on to a plate and serve immediately.

VERMICELLI.

MACARONI.

BAKED LASAGNE WITH SWEETBREADS AND TRUFFLES

Serves 6
pasta dough (see recipe page 123)
FOR THE FILLING:
2-3 tbsp butter
2½ oz/½ cup/75 g browned breadcrumbs
2 slices cooked ham
sweetbread ragoût (see recipe page 123)
*béchamel sauce made with 2 tbsp butter,
    2 tbsp flour, ½ pint/1¼ cups/300 ml
    milk, salt, pepper and nutmeg*
*small can truffles, sliced, or 2 oz/½ cup/
    60 g cooked pitted prunes, halved*
2-3 tbsp butter
2½ oz/¾ cup/75 g grated Parmesan cheese
½ tsp ground cinnamon
¼ tsp ground nutmeg
salt and pepper
*3¼ pint/2 quart/2 liter capacity moule à
    manqué cake pan/tin, baking dish or
    shallow casserole*

1. Make the pasta dough and roll it out as thinly as possible. Cut it into 4 inch/10 cm squares and leave to dry on paper sprinkled with flour for at least 2 hours.
2. Thickly butter the dish with 2-3 tablespoons butter and sprinkle with breadcrumbs. Cut large diamonds from the ham, discarding any fat, and arrange a star in the base of the dish. Make the sweetbread ragoût and the béchamel sauce for the filling.
3. To cook the pasta: fill a roasting pan with salted water to a depth of 2-3 inches/5-7.5 cm and bring to a boil. Drop in the pasta squares and poach just below boiling point, stirring occasionally so they do not stick, until *al dente*, 3-5 minutes. Transfer them to a bowl of cold water. Note: to avoid sticking, cook the pasta in two batches.
4. To assemble the dish: drain some of the pasta on paper towels and arrange them overlapping in a layer in the bottom of the baking dish. Line the sides of the dish also, letting strips of pasta hang over the edge. Fill with layers of sweetbread ragoût, béchamel sauce, sliced truffles or prunes and drained pasta, dotting the layers with butter and sprinkling with half the cheese, the cinnamon, nutmeg, and salt and pepper to taste. Note: the cheese is already salty, so more salt may not be needed. When the dish is full, fold over the strips of pasta at the edge and cover with a final layer of pasta. Dot the top with butter and sprinkle with the remaining cheese. The lasagne can be prepared up to 24 hours ahead and kept covered in the refrigerator, or it can be frozen. Heat the oven to No 5/375°F/190°C.
5. To finish: bake the lasagne, uncovered, in the heated oven until very hot and golden brown, 35-45 minutes. Let cool slightly, then turn out on to a platter and serve at once.

ZUPPA DI TAGLIOLINI

Make a dough with flour and 4 or 6 eggs and salt, depending on how much pasta you want to make, knead well until not too hard and not too soft; leave to rest a little then roll out paper-thin either in one sheet or separate sheets. Leave to dry a little then roll up and cut into ribbons. Cook for 6½ minutes in boiling, salted water.

PASTA DOUGH

about 1 lb/4 cups/500 g flour
4 eggs
1 tsp salt

Sift the flour on to a marble slab or board, make a well in the center, and add the eggs and salt. Work the eggs with the fingers of one hand, gradually drawing in the flour and adding more flour if necessary to make a smooth dough. Knead the dough thoroughly on a floured marble slab or board until very smooth and elastic, about 5 minutes. Cover it with an upturned bowl and let it rest at least 1 hour.

RAGÙ DI ANIMELLE

Up to the tricks of his trade, Leonardi was aware that prunes make a handy, cheap substitute for truffles. They also add a pleasant touch of sweetness to this dish.

Blanch one or two calves' sweetbreads in boiling water and cut in large pieces, then put in a saucepan with some sliced truffles or prunes, according to the season, or both dried sweetbreads and prunes soaked in water to soften them, a piece of ham, a bit of butter, a bouquet of mixed herbs and cook; when it begins to dry out moisten with ½ glass champagne or other white wine and some coulì and let it reduce by two-thirds, or sprinkle with a pinch of flour and moisten with the wine, and half coulì and half white sauce; season with salt and ground pepper and boil gently. When everything is cooked add some blanched cooked chicken livers, some little stuffing balls or a few small cooked prawns; cook a little longer; remove the fat, and the ham and the bouquet of herbs and serve with lemon juice, either as a Terrine, or as an Entremet or to garnish an Entremet; but in this case use little sauce, no stuffing balls [*chenef*] and prawns, and cut the sweetbreads in large dice.

SWEETBREAD RAGOÛT

1 pair (1 lb/500 g) calves' sweetbreads
2 tbsp butter
1 slice uncooked ham or lean bacon
bouquet garni
4 fl oz/½ cup/125 ml champagne or other dry white wine
about 8 fl oz/1 cup/250 ml brown sauce, made with 1 cup veal stock thickened with 1 tsp arrowroot or potato flour/ starch mixed with 1 tbsp cold water
4 oz/½ cup/125 g chicken livers, or balls of chicken stuffing (see recipe for Stuffed Tomatoes, page 124), or a few shrimps
squeeze of lemon juice

1. Soak the sweetbreads in cold water for 1-2 hours to whiten them. Put them in cold water, bring to a boil and simmer for 5 minutes. Drain and clean them thoroughly, discarding all membrane and skin. Cut them into 1 inch/ 2.5 cm pieces.
2. Butter the base of a heavy saucepan with 1 tbsp butter, set the ham or bacon in the bottom, then the sweetbreads. Add the bouquet garni, champagne and brown sauce and simmer, uncovered, until reduced by two-thirds.

3. Meanwhile, if using chicken livers, blanch them by putting in cold water, bringing to a boil, and simmering 1 minute. Drain and sauté them in butter until brown but still pink in the center. Slice them. If using stuffing balls, cook them in a little stock or fry them in butter until firm.
4. Discard the ham or bacon and the bouquet garni from the sweetbreads and season them to taste, adding a squeeze of lemon juice. Add the chicken livers, stuffing balls or shrimps; continue cooking 1-2 minutes.

POMIDORO IN CHENEF

Leonardi identifies himself with Naples in this recipe – he was obviously proud of the local tomatoes and handles them with affectionate familiarity. Elsewhere he notes that a good· *chenef* (for use in dumplings or stuffing) should be made of equal quantities of chicken, butter, and breadcrumbs, bound with egg yolks. Such simple recipes seem to come more easily to him than the exotica of France and Russia.

Use small Sicilian tomatoes if available, or our own variety, but make sure they are the same size and plunge for a moment in boiling water to remove the skins; **carefully hollow them out from the stalk end and stuff with a good cooked stuffing of chicken breast, not too full, and mix some grated Parmesan. Put slices of onion, carrot on the bottom of a casserole, then cover with bacon and ham, place the tomatoes on this with the hole facing downward, cover with more onion, carrot, bacon and ham. Season with salt and freshly ground pepper, moisten with very little good stock and cook with a quick heat on both sides, but remember they cook very quickly. Let them cool a little then remove without breaking, wipe with a cloth, put on a plate with the hole facing down and serve a little good sauce on top.**

In late eighteenth-century Italy, tomatoes were a novelty often viewed with mistrust and thought to be poisonous.

STUFFED TOMATOES

Serves 4-6 as an appetizer
2 lb/1 kg even-sized medium tomatoes,
*   scalded and peeled*
salt and pepper
2 onions, sliced
2 carrots, sliced
2-3 slices bacon, diced
1 slice cooked ham, diced
6 fl oz/³⁄₄ cup/175 ml white stock
FOR THE STUFFING:
6-8 slices (4 oz/125 g) bread, crusts
*   discarded*
8 fl oz/1 cup/250 ml water
1 cooked chicken breast, ground/minced
*   (4 oz/125 g)*
4 oz/¹⁄₂ cup/125 g butter, softened
2¹⁄₂ oz/¹⁄₂ cup/75 g grated Parmesan cheese
salt and pepper
3 egg yolks

FOR THE TOMATO SAUCE:
2 lb/1 kg tomatoes, seeded and chopped
2 tbsp lard or oil
1 onion thinly sliced
1-2 cloves garlic, crushed
parsley, thyme, bayleaf

1. For the tomato sauce: fry onion in the oil until soft. Add tomato, garlic, herbs, salt and pepper and simmer uncovered, for 15-20 minutes, until the sauce is thick. Strain and taste for seasoning.
2. Cut the core from the tomatoes and scoop out the seeds with a teaspoon, leaving the hole as small as possible. Sprinkle the insides with salt and pepper. Heat the oven to No 6/400°F/200°C.
3. For the stuffing: soak the bread 5 minutes in water, squeeze it dry, then pull it into crumbs. Work the bread

with the chicken in a food processor or grind/mince them together. Beat in the butter and Parmesan cheese with salt and pepper to taste, then stir in the egg yolks. Fill the tomatoes with the stuffing, taking care they do not split.
4. In a heavy-based casserole spread half the onion and carrot slices and sprinkle with half the bacon and ham. Set the tomatoes on top, hole down, and sprinkle with the remaining vegetables, bacon and ham. Sprinkle with salt and pepper and moisten with stock. Bake uncovered in the heated oven until just tender, 20-25 minutes. Note: the tomatoes overcook easily. Transfer the tomatoes to a platter, spoon tomato sauce over them, and serve either hot or at room temperature.

FEGATO DI MONGANA ALLA VENEZIANA

This well-known dish is typical of good Italian cooking, where the flavors of simple ingredients are left to speak for themselves. Leonardi includes it as an "orduvre" but today it is served as a main course, with slices of toasted polenta (baked corn meal).

Finely slice four or five onions and fry in a casserole with a nut of butter, a little oil, chopped scallions or spring onions, add the liver, salt, freshly ground pepper and chopped parsley and cook to perfection, making sure it is very juicy. Serve with its own gravy and plenty of lemon juice.

An eighteenth-century illustration from a poem on the making of salami, for which Italians were already famous. At the back a butcher dismembers a wild boar.

CALVES' LIVER VENETIAN STYLE

Serves 6

2 lb/1 kg calves' liver
2 tbsp olive oil
3 tbsp butter
4-5 onions (about 1½ lb/750 g), thinly sliced
salt and pepper
1 tbsp chopped parsley

Slice the liver as thinly as possible, discarding any skin and membrane. In a frying pan heat the oil and butter and fry the onions gently until soft but not brown, 8-10 minutes. Add the liver, sprinkle with salt and pepper and cook, stirring occasionally until the liver and onions are brown. Note: the speed of cooking is important. If cooked too slowly the liver will stew rather than browning. If cooked too fast it will be dry. Taste for seasoning, sprinkle with parsley and serve at once.

RISSOLE ALLA NAPOLITANA

The Arabs ruled Sicily until the end of the eleventh century and these turnovers, reminiscent of Greek *tiropetas* made with flaky phyllo dough, show the Arab origin of many Italian pastries. Panzarotti filled with local cheese such as provatura (made with buffalo milk), marzolina (made with ewe's milk) and cacio cavallo (made with cow's milk) are popular throughout southern Italy. They are always fried in lard, the common fat of the region, as it is cheaper than oil.

Chop two fresh provatura cheeses, add a little Parmesan, some grated provatura, marzolina and cacio cavallo, a slice of chopped ham sweated for a moment over the heat in a casserole, chopped parsley, no salt, ground pepper, nutmeg, two raw eggs and mix well. Roll out a sheet of pasta brisé made with butter or lard, either will do, about the thickness of a paolo [coin], put little heaps of the cheese mixture around the edge, brush with beaten egg, fold the pasta dough over, press down well and cut out little crescent-shaped ravioli with the pasta wheel. Before serving fry in very hot lard and serve golden brown at once. In Naples these rissoles are called panzarotti.

"The Maccheroni Seller" – by Leonardi's time pasta was established as an Italian staple though still mainly reserved for special occasions.

PANZAROTTI (FRIED CHEESE TURNOVERS)

Makes 25-30 panzarotti
FOR THE PASTRY DOUGH:
1 lb/4 cups/500 g flour
8 oz/1 cup/250 g butter or lard
2 tsp salt
2½ fl oz/⅓ cup/75 ml water, more if needed
FOR THE FILLING:
2 oz/60 g prosciutto or cooked ham, chopped
1 fresh provatura cheese, or 8 oz/250 g mozzarella, diced
1 oz/¼ cup/30 g grated Parmesan cheese
2½ oz/½ cup/75 g grated provolone or Gruyère cheese
1 tbsp chopped parsley
pinch of ground nutmeg
pepper
2 eggs, beaten to mix
deep fat (for frying)

1. For the pastry dough: sift the flour on to a marble slab or board, make a well in the center and add the butter or lard, salt and 2-3 tablespoons of water. Work the central ingredients with the fingertips of one hand until well mixed, then gradually draw in the flour using the whole hand. Add more water if needed to make a dough that is soft but not sticky. Cover it and chill ½-1 hour.
2. For the filling: fry the ham over low heat, stirring, until the fat runs and it browns lightly. Let cool, then mix into the diced provatura or mozzarella, grated Parmesan, grated provolone or Gruyère and parsley. Season to taste with nutmeg and pepper – salt is not needed as the ham and cheeses are already salty. Stir in the beaten eggs to bind the mixture.

3. On a floured board, roll out the dough to ⅛ inch/3 mm thickness. About 1½ inch/4 cm from the edge of the dough, place teaspoonfuls of the filling at 2 inch/5 cm intervals. Brush around the mounds of filling with water, and fold over the edge of the dough to cover them. Press to seal and cut out the turnovers with a ravioli cutter. Repeat with more mounds of filling, gradually working towards the center of the dough.
4. To finish: heat the deep fat to 360°F/ 180°C. Fry the turnovers, a few at a time, in hot fat until brown. Drain them thoroughly on paper towels and serve them as soon as possible.

Cassata palermitana

Instead of being frosted with a glaze, today cassata Palermitana is often macerated in maraschino liqueur, but the ricotta filling flavored with indigenous Sicilian candied fruits and orange flower water is unchanged. Chopped chocolate is often added to the filling instead of being sprinkled on top.

Take some good ricotta and mix with not too much white powdered sugar, a little cinnamon water and the same amount of orange flowers. Some people also mix in strips of candied lemon, orange flowers and chopped pistachio nuts; mix well. Line a casserole or a copper mold on the bottom or sides with sponge cake, put in the ricotta then cover with further slices of sponge cake. After half an hour turn on to a plate with a napkin on it; glaze with a light royal glaze; garnish the cassata with chocolate strands, pistachio nuts or other comfits in an attractive pattern, a few candied pears or other dried fruit; dry the glaze for a minute on the stove and serve cold.

Cassata palermitana

Serves 10-12
9 inch/22 cm diameter sponge cake, weighing about 1 lb/500 g
FOR THE FILLING:
3¼ oz/½ cup/100 g shelled pistachios
2 lb/1 kg ricotta cheese
12 oz/3 cups/375 g confectioners'/icing sugar, sifted
2 tsp ground cinnamon
2 tsp orange flower water
10 oz/1½ cups/300 g candied orange and lemon peel, finely chopped
FOR THE DECORATION:
glacé icing made with 8 oz/2 cups/250 g confectioners'/icing sugar, 2-3 tbsp water and 1 tsp orange flower water
chocolate, pistachios, candied pears, apricots, cherries
9 inch/22 cm springform pan/tin

1. Split the sponge cake into three layers. Set one layer in the bottom of the pan/tin, reserve another layer and cut the third layer into strips to line the side of the mold.

2. For the filling: if necessary, blanch the pistachios for 1 minute in boiling water, drain and skin them; coarsely chop them. Work the ricotta cheese through a sieve, then beat in the confectioners'/icing sugar with the cinnamon and orange flower water. Stir in the candied peel and pistachios and spread the filling in the lined mold, pressing it down well. Set the reserved round of cake on top, cover with a pie pan/tin base or flat plate and set a 1 lb/500 g weight on top. Chill overnight.

3. To finish: remove the plate from the cassata, set it on a rack and remove the springform pan/tin sides. For the icing, sift the confectioners'/icing sugar into a bowl and beat in enough water with the orange flower water to make a stiff paste. Set the bowl in a pan of hot water and stir until the icing is tepid; it should just coat the back of a spoon. If not, add more sifted confectioners'/icing sugar or water until it is the right consistency. Pour the icing over the cake and spread with a metal spatula so the sides of the cake are coated. Note: work quickly as the icing sets fast. Decorate the cake with piped melted chocolate, pistachios and candied fruits, transfer to a platter with a napkin or paper doily and serve.

AMELIA SIMMONS

flourished 1796

THE FIRST COOKBOOK WRITTEN by an American for Americans appeared in Hartford, Connecticut, in 1796 and was entitled quite simply *American Cookery*. It was a modest little volume of some 130 recipes, making none of the extravagant claims to erudition that were customary in Europe, but seeking rather "the improvement of the rising generation of females in America." The book reads like a personal collection of time-honored recipes which had finally made its way into print after passing from hand to hand for several decades. More an aide-memoire for an experienced cook than a manual of instruction for the novice, *American Cookery* skates over everyday techniques to concentrate instead on party dishes like turtle or calf's head, rich cream desserts, and huge fruit cakes. About the author nothing is known except her name, Amelia Simmons, and her disclosure that she was brought up as an orphan.

All the cookbooks then available in America had originated in England and none had the American recipes offered by Amelia Simmons. She uses corn-cobs to smoke bacon and suggests cranberry sauce as an accompaniment to turkey. She gives the first recipes for Indian slapjacks, "johny" or hoe cake, and three versions of Indian pudding (page 139), all using cornmeal, an American staple the English regarded with disdain. Benjamin Franklin, writing in the *London Gazeteer* in 1766, felt compelled to protest:

OPPOSITE: *Detail of "The Residence of David Twining" in Pennsylvania, a typical colonial farm. The artist, David Hicks, was born in 1780 and this painting was done from memory in the 1840s.*

"Pray, let me, an American, inform the gentleman, who seems ignorant of the matter, that Indian corn, take it for all in all, is one of the most agreeable and wholesome grains in the world and that johny cake or hoe cake, hot from the fire is better than a Yorkshire muffin." The contemporary English cook would have found some of Amelia's vocabulary equally unfamiliar; fat for making pastry is "shortening," biscuits have become "cookies" (from the Dutch *koekje*), and scones are called "biscuits". Her cookbook is also the first to use a chemical raising agent called pearl ash – a substance akin to baking soda and derived from potash.

American cookery was such a success that a second edition appeared in the same year. In it Amelia Simmons is at pains to explain that she has had trouble with her publisher – she hopes that "this second edition will appear, in a great measure, free from those egregious blunders, and inaccuracies . . . which were occasioned either by the ignorance, or evil intention of the transcriber for the press." The second edition is indeed very different from the first. Three of the six beef recipes are for steak – a first hint of what was to become an American addiction – and Amelia repairs the almost total omission of fish from the first edition with recipes for bass, shad, codfish, blackfish, and salmon. The greatest innovation is in her cakes. To tea cakes, wiggs (buns flavored with caraway) and gingerbread (page

"Mode of drying fish, wild animals, and other provisions" – the sixteenth-century European artist, Theodore de Bry, tried to visualize an Indian fish-and-alligator barbecue.

141), which are all of obvious English origin, she adds federal pan cake, buckwheat cakes (to be found on many a colonist's breakfast table), and election cake, with its vote-winning flavorings of wine and brandy, known to the future president John Adams as early as 1756. The other uniquely American cake found in Amelia's book is Independence cake (page 140), a fruitcake raised with yeast and grandly decorated with gold leaf. From the recipe's enormous yield (it starts with twenty pounds of flour), it would seem that this cake was made only once a year to crown a town's festivities on the "Glorious Fourth" of July.

At the time Amelia wrote her book, several leaders of the infant Republic – Franklin, Adams and Jefferson for example – had been introduced through their diplomatic missions to a more cosmopolitan diet. Franklin and Jefferson continued to flirt with French cooking but in the year of *American Cookery's* publication, Adams dined with a Massachusetts friend and declared that his "salted Beef and shell beans with a Whortleberry Pudden and Cyder was a Luxurious Treat." The ultimate accolade bestowed on New England cooking came from the French gastronome Brillat-Savarin (exiled from his country by the revolution) who in 1794 was entertained near Hartford, Connecticut. A farmer and his four daughters prepared for him "a superb piece of corned beef, a stewed goose, a magnificent leg of mutton, a vast selection of vegetables, and at either end of the table two huge jugs of cider."

This was just the food familiar to Amelia Simmons, for her book was published in Hartford. As a child, she probably boarded with a respectable family, since in her preface she says that "the orphan, tho' left to the care of virtuous guardians, will find it essentially necessary to have an opinion and a determination of her own." Her determination to produce a cookbook is all the more admirable in view of her probable position as domestic

Pumpkin, corn, apples and squash – four staples of the late American harvest were depicted in all their glowing richness at the turn of the eighteenth century by Jonathan Fisher. They remain classic New England ingredients.

and cook and her semi-literate state – she explains that she lacked "an education sufficient to prepare the work for the press." Her practical education was another matter; at that time in the United States, year-round supplies of household goods were not assured and a knowledge of such basic skills as sewing, brewing, candle-dipping and soap making were important. Since the cold northern climate severely limited the growing season, the life of the family also depended on stores laid down for the winter. Yankee cooks were fiercely proud of their skill with pickles and preserves, a necessity raised to an art. *American Cookery* makes much use of preserved ingredients such as salt pork, dried apples, raisins, and cornmeal. It also includes an attractive selection of fruit jams and jellies as well as the ubiquitous pickled cucumbers.

Further south, on the plantations of Virginia and the Carolinas, the situation was very different. Slave labor meant that cooking could be done on a considerably larger scale, making possible the southern tradition of hospitality. Thomas Jefferson remarked that not once had he been forced to dine alone with his family at Monticello – visitors doubtless craved his ice creams as much as his conversation – and George Washington complained that Mount Vernon was "little better than a well-resorted inn." Few families could afford to entertain on such a scale, but even modest households generally kept a slave or two who could prepare time-consuming southern specialties like beaten biscuits. For Amelia Simmons, quick dishes like pancakes, or the "alamode" beef (page 137) that looked after itself for hours over a low fire, were more practical. When Adams succeeded Washington as president in 1797, the difference in the scale of official entertainment was observed at once.

The remoteness of the southern housewife from the actual business of cooking was reflected in the position of the kitchen, which was often built apart from the main house so that the fire would not add to the oppressive summer heat. In New England, however, the kitchen invariably formed part of the main house. In old farmhouses, it was the principal living room, where all could benefit from the warmth of the great central fireplace whose flues also heated upper and adjacent rooms. A central fire was usually kept going constantly,

and during the day one or two smaller fires would be kindled on each side to boil a kettle of water for washing and cleaning. Controlling the heat was tricky and cooks learned early which logs had a fierce heat that died quickly, and which were steady-burning. All but the most primitive kitchens were equipped with a crane, hinged to swing outward, from which pots and kettles could be suspended at variable heights over the fire. For roasting, meat and fowl were skewered on a spit. Turning the meat was a hot and dull job, assigned to the smaller children and eventually taken over by some crude mechanism such as a string that wound back on itself, or a weighted pulley.

For frying Amelia would have used pans or skillets called spiders, with three feet to hold them firm in the ashes. For browning the tops of puddings there were flat iron salamanders to be heated red-hot. Baking could be done by simply burying a covered pot in hot ashes. This was the original function of the Dutch oven – its base and lid were thoroughly heated before the fire, then the pie, bread, or cake was put inside and the oven surrounded by glowing embers.

Amelia Simmons's recipes assume the use of an oven and most kitchens boasted at least a reflecting oven – a shiny tin box open on the fireside to focus the heat. The best ovens were made of brick, preheated with logs whose ashes were raked out before cooking began. Some brick ovens were constructed at the side of the fire with a

"The Fourth of July picnic at Weymouth Landing", painted by Susan Merrett, shows the kind of communal gathering where Amelia Simmons's vast Independence Day cake, made with twenty pounds of flour and four dozen eggs, would have been appreciated.

door in the fireplace so the wood-smoke went up the chimney; others were built separately, outside the house.

Most housewifes baked their own bread but Frances Trollope, writing in *Domestic Manners of the Americans* in 1832, remarks that despite its excellence, it is not eaten in great quantities; instead, Americans "insist upon eating horrible half-baked hot rolls both morning and evening." Amelia Simmons does not elaborate upon the art; she probably regarded the kneading and baking of bread as a basic technique which children learned at their mother's knees. Where knowledge was required was in choosing ingredients. Grain was often poorly harvested or badly kept – Amelia's one bread recipe is

devoted to the somewhat dubious task of making "good bread with grown flour" (i.e., from sprouted wheat). In extreme cases rye could develop the ergot fungus, thought to be the cause of several early epidemics of hysterical visions known as St Anthony's Fire.

Only in towns could the yeast for bread and coffee cakes he bought at the baker's and even then its strength and freshness varied. Experienced cooks like Amelia made their own at home from "emptins" (another term unknown in England), a type of yeast made from the lees or emptyings of wine or beer. Later, in the West, pioneers relied on sourdough starter, made from mashed potatoes left to ferment, then "fed" from time to time with flour

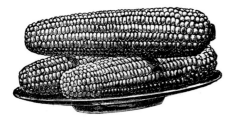

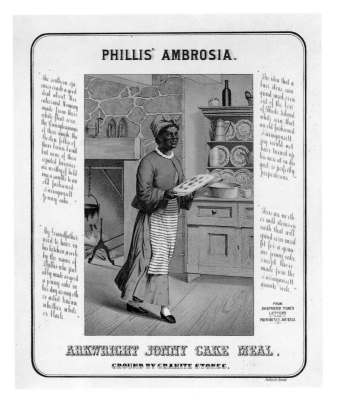

PHILLIS' AMBROSIA.

ARKWRIGHT JONNY CAKE MEAL.
GROUND BY GRANITE STONES.

and water. Good starter was believed to improve with age and a pot of vintage starter was a treasured present to brides. So precious was this means of making bread that the gold rush miners earned the name "sourdoughs" from their habit of taking the pots to bed to prevent the yeast from dying in the icy air.

It is extraordinary to think that when *American Cookery* was printed in 1796, the complex French cuisine described first by La Varenne and then by Menon had been flourishing for 150 years. Recipes for gooseberry tart and bread pudding seem centuries as well as oceans apart from such fancies as Menon's *paupiettes de boeuf à l'estouffade aux capucines confites* (stuffed beef rolls braised and garnished with pickled nasturtium seeds). The contrast with England, however, was not so sharp; familiar "ham and beef-steaks appear morning, noon and night," reported Mrs Trollope, though she found the combinations of dishes very strange. "I have seen eggs and oysters eaten together; the sempiternal ham with apple-sauce; beef-steak with stewed peaches; and salt fish with onions."

The English preoccupation with cake-baking, preserving and cooking codfish – all in an economical fashion – was generally shared by American cooks, as shown by the continuing success in America of established English works like Hannah Glasse's *The Art of Cookery* and Susannah Carter's *The Frugal Housewife*. However, the demand for genuinely American cookbooks is shown by the flood of imitations that followed Amelia's pioneer effort. The first was a special American edition of *The Frugal Housewife* in 1803, in which the publisher changed the original version not a whit but simply tacked on an appendix of thirty recipes. Here we find the first mention of crullers, "whaffles," cornmeal mush, cranberry tarts, doughnuts, and maple syrup. The American publisher of Hannah Glasse's *The Art of Cookery* was not to be outdone; two years later he too brought out an American edition with a special chapter of recipes copied word for word from the appendix to *The Frugal Housewife*. In fact, for the next twenty years, American cookbooks were explicit or furtive adaptations of English classics or of *American Cookery*. Amelia Simmons herself had picked up several of her more English recipes from English writers like Susannah Carter

Phillis, a black Rhode Island cook, was so famous for her Johny cakes that eighty years after her death in 1798 she was portrayed in this advertisement with the comment, "The southern epicures crack a good deal about Hoe cakes and Hominy made from their white flint corn, the Pennsylvania of their mush, the Boston folks of their brown bread, but none of these reputed luxuries are worthy of holding a candle to an old-fashioned Narragansett Jonny cake."

– including the syllabub in which the cow is milked directly into the dessert to froth it.

The popularity of the first American cookbooks (Amelia's recipes continued in print until 1831) shows that a native style of cooking was practised with enthusiasm and pride. Most traditional American dishes, such as hoe cakes, succotash and chowder were well-established; pies were such a passion that the flat wooden boards used as plates in the early days acquired a "pie side" for dessert. While Amelia Simmons described only a very small part of the emerging native tradition, in her modest way she was the first person to give American cooking its own identity. The stilted charm of her books is far more evocative of early American life (often but one step removed from pioneer existence) than many a more professional production.

SIMMONS RECIPES

AMERICAN COOKERY,

OR THE ART OF DRESSING

VIANDS, FISH, POULTRY and VEGETABLES,

AND THE BEST MODES OF MAKING

PASTES, PUFFS, PIES, TARTS, PUDDINGS,
CUSTARDS AND PRESERVES,

AND ALL KINDS OF

C A K E S,

FROM THE IMPERIAL PLUMB TO PLAIN CAKE.

ADAPTED TO THIS COUNTRY,

AND ALL GRADES OF LIFE.

By Amelia Simmons,

AN AMERICAN ORPHAN.

PUBLISHED ACCORDING TO ACT OF CONGRESS.

HARTFORD:
PRINTED BY HUDSON & GOODWIN.
FOR THE AUTHOR.

1796.

LEFT: Chouder.
ABOVE: The title page of American Cookery,
*the first truly American cookbook, sums up the
naiveté of its recipes. The little volume
contained about 130 entries, many of them
only a few lines long.*

Reflecting her heritage, Amelia Simmons's recipes hark
back to an earlier age. Like the first European cooks she
tends to write in note form, and the interpretation of
some of her recipes is a matter of guesswork; those given
here are among the most explicit.

CHOUDER

Amelia Simmons chowder is not the soup we know, but a stew of fish and crackers fried in salt pork with scarcely a trace of liquid – large quantities of water or milk were not added until considerably later. The name almost certainly comes from the Breton expression *faire chaudière*, meaning to make a fish stew in a caldron. Such a stew was taken by Breton fishermen to Nova Scotia and eventually traveled down the coast to New England. By the mid-eighteenth century it had found its way back to England as "chouder." One version similar to this recipe of Amelia Simmons, but baked like a pie with a top crust, appears in the 1770 edition of Hannah Glasse's *Art of Cookery*. The mangoes mentioned here as accompaniment were presumably pickled or in a chutney; perhaps Amelia was thinking of her own optimistic recipe for making so-called mangoes out of green melons.

Take a bass weighing four pounds, boil half an hour; take six slices raw salt pork, fry them till the lard is nearly extracted, one dozen crackers soaked in cold water five minutes; put the bass into the lard, also the pieces of pork and crackers, cover close, and fry for 20 minutes; serve with potatoes, pickles, apple-sauce or mangoes; garnish with green parsley.

FISH CHOWDER

Serves 6
4 lb/1.8 kg whole sea bass, cod, bluefish, haddock, or any firm white fish
1 tsp salt
water
12 (about 2 oz/60 g) unsalted crackers
6 slices (about 8 oz/250 g) salt pork
2 tbsp chopped parsley (for sprinkling)
boiled potatoes, pickles and apple sauce or mango chutney (for serving)

1. Wash the fish, put it in a large saucepan and add the salt and enough cold water to half cover. Cover and simmer until the fish flakes easily, 20-30 minutes; let it cool. Take the fish from the bones, discarding the skin, and divide it into fairly large pieces.

2. Pour cold water over the crackers to cover them and leave 5 minutes to soak. In a large pot fry the salt pork until lightly browned and the fat runs. Add the fish and soaked crackers. Cover tightly and cook over moderate heat until the fish and crackers are lightly browned and all the fat has been absorbed, 10-12 minutes. Taste for seasoning, sprinkle with chopped parsley and serve with boiled potatoes, pickles and apple sauce or mango chutney.

TO ALAMODE A ROUND

By the end of the eighteenth century the original meaning of *à la mode* (fashionable) had become irrevocably associated in cooking with a large cut of beef braised with wine and bones to make a rich gravy. In a primitive kitchen even this basic dish was not easy, hence Amelia Simmons warning to place the meat on top of the bones to avoid scorching on the bottom of the pan. She seals the pot with dough to prevent steam from escaping during cooking, then leaves the meat to marinate overnight in the wine before setting the pot to "hang on" the fireplace crane in the morning. The breadcrumbs added at the end would probably have been browned by holding a shiny tin sheet to reflect the heat of the fire on to the meat.

Take fat pork cut in slices or mince, season it with pepper, salt, sweet marjoram and thyme, cloves, mace and nutmeg, make holes in the beef and stuff it the night before cooked; put some bones across the bottom of the pot to keep from burning, put in one quart Claret wine, one quart water and one onion; lay the round on the bones, cover close and stop it round the top with dough; hang on in the morning and stew gently two hours; turn it, and stop tight and stew two hours more; when done tender, grate a crust of bread on the top and brown it before the fire; scum the gravy and serve in a butter boat, serve it with the residue of the gravy in the dish.

POT ROAST BEEF

Serves 8–10

5 oz/150 g pork fat, ground/minced or finely chopped
2 tsp salt
1 tsp pepper
1 tsp chopped marjoram
1 tsp chopped thyme
½ tsp ground cloves
½ tsp ground nutmeg
½ tsp ground mace
5-6 lb/2.3-2.7 kg boned round or rump of beef, rolled
1½-2 lb/750 g-1 kg beef bones, split
1¼ pints/3 cups/750 ml Bordeaux wine
16 fl oz/2 cups/500 ml water
1 onion, quartered
1½ oz/½ cup/50 g dry white breadcrumbs
FOR THE SEALING DOUGH:
6-7 tbsp water
4 oz/1 cup/125 g flour

1. Mix the pork fat with the salt, pepper, marjoram, thyme and spices. With a pointed knife cut deep incisions in the beef and stuff them with the fat mixture. Put the bones in the bottom of a Dutch oven or heavy casserole, set the beef on top, add the wine, water, and onion and cover.

2. For the sealing dough: stir enough water (about 3 tablespoons) into half the flour to make a soft paste – do not beat or the paste will become elastic. Seal the gap between the casserole and lid with the paste and leave in the refrigerator overnight.

3. The next day, heat the oven to No 3/325°F/160°C. Cook the meat for 2 hours, remove the lid and turn the beef. Make more sealing dough with the remaining flour and water, reseal the lid and continue cooking the meat 1-2 hours longer – a long thin cut will take less time than a thick squat one. Transfer the beef to a heatproof platter on a roasting pan, sprinkle with the breadcrumbs, and baste with a little cooking liquid; broil/grill until browned, then keep hot. Strain the cooking liquid into a saucepan, skim off the fat, and bring it to a boil. Taste it for seasoning and serve separately as gravy with the meat.

POMPKIN

This recipe, labeled simply "pompkin," is in fact a pie, though Amelia Simmons includes it in her section on puddings. Her first version, containing large amounts of cream, must have been for parties and the second, made with milk and molasses, for everyday. Despite its bitterness, blackstrap molasses was often used for sweetening, since outside areas where sugar and maple syrup were produced, it was far cheaper. Molasses (known to the English as treacle) was one of the main bones of contention during the War of Independence, along with rum, for the British insisted on placing a high import duty on the raw product. As John Adams said: "I know not why we should blush to confess that molasses is an essential ingredient in American independence."

No. 1. One quart [pumpkin] stewed and strained, 3 pints cream, 9 beaten eggs, sugar, mace, nutmeg and ginger, laid into paste No. 7 or 3, and with a dough spur, cross and chequer it, and baked in dishes three quarters of an hour.
No. 2. One quart of milk, 1 pint pumpkin, 4 eggs, molasses, allspice and ginger in a crust, bake 1 hour.

PUMPKIN PIE

Makes two 9 inch/22 cm pies
FOR THE PASTRY:
12 oz/3 cups/375 g flour
½ tsp salt
4 oz/½ cup/125 g butter
2½ oz/⅓ cup/75 g shortening or lard
3 fl oz/6 tbsp/90 ml water, more if needed
FOR THE FILLING:
1¼ pints/3 cups/750 ml heavy/double cream
4 eggs, beaten to mix
1¼ pints/3 cups/750 ml cooked, puréed pumpkin
8 oz/1¼ cups/250 g sugar
2 tsp ground ginger
1 tsp ground nutmeg
1 tsp ground mace
Two 9 inch/22 cm pie pans/tins

1. To make the pastry: sift the flour into a bowl with the salt, add the butter and shortening or lard, and cut the fat into small pieces with a pastry cutter or two knives. Rub in with the fingertips until the mixture forms fine crumbs. Stir in the water to form large crumbs, then press them together, adding more water if necessary to make a dough that is soft but not sticky. Chill for 30 minutes.
2. For the filling: beat the cream with the eggs into the cooked pumpkin and stir in the sugar with ginger, nutmeg and mace. Heat the oven to No 4/350°F/175°C.

3. Roll out two-thirds of the pastry, line the pie pans/tins, and fill with the pumpkin mixture. Roll out the remaining pastry and cut two ¾ inch/2 cm bands; reserve them. Cut the remaining pastry into narrow strips and decorate the tops of the pies with a lattice. Lay the reserved pastry bands around the edges of the lattice to hide the lattice edges. Bake the pies in the heated oven until the filling is firm, about 1 hour.

A NICE INDIAN PUDDING

Indian pudding now means a spiced cornmeal pudding sweetened with molasses, but in the early days it referred to any pudding made with Indian meal (i.e., cornmeal). Amelia Simmons gives three versions, the first sweetened with sugar and raisins, the second similar to the modern one, and the third a mixture of milk and meal that was probably only lightly sweetened and intended to be served with meat.

No. 1. 3 pints scalded milk, 7 spoons fine Indian meal, stir well together while hot, let stand till cooled; add 7 eggs, half pound raisins, 4 ounces butter, spice and sugar, bake one and half hour.

No. 2. 3 pints scalded milk to one pint meal salted; cool, add 2 eggs, 4 ounces butter, sugar or molasses and spice q.s. [quantum sufficit; i.e., to taste] it will require two and half hours baking.

No. 3. Salt a pint meal, wet with one quart milk, sweeten and put into a strong cloth, brass or bell metal vessel, stone or earthen pot, secure from wet and boil 12 hours.

Here Indians of early America carry fruit in a dugout canoe to store in a communal granary.

INDIAN PUDDING

Serves 6
1¼ pints/3 cups/750 ml milk
½ tsp salt
1¾ oz/¼ cup/50 g yellow cornmeal
2 tbsp butter
1 egg, beaten to mix
1¾ oz/¼ cup/50 g sugar, or 2 fl oz/
  ¼ cup/60 ml molasses
½ tsp ground cinnamon
½ tsp ground ginger
1⅔ pint/1 quart/1 liter shallow baking
  dish

1. Heat the oven to No 4/350°F/175°C. Scald the milk with the salt. Gradually stir in the cornmeal and cook over low heat until it thickens like cooked cereal, stirring constantly, about 5 minutes. Let cool to tepid, stir in the butter until melted, followed by the egg, sugar or molasses, and spices.

2. Pour into a buttered shallow baking dish and bake in the heated oven until the pudding is set, 1¼-1½ hours. Serve warm.

INDEPENDENCE CAKE

The cryptic instructions for this are typical of many of Amelia Simmons recipes. She gives only some general comments on cake-making, such as "in all cakes where spices are named it is supposed that they be pounded fine and sifted; sugar must be dried and rolled fine; flour, dryed in an oven; eggs well beat or whipped into a raging foam" – surely an exhausting business. The common raising agent was yeast, giving a texture closer to a coffee cake than a modern fruitcake, and the huge quantity of mixture in this recipe must have been baked in several pans. The mention of gold leaf for decorations shows that the cake was intended for a very special occasion; *box* probably refers to the leaves of the shrub used in hedges. The frosting is from another of Amelia Simmons recipes.

Twenty pound flour, 15 pound sugar, 10 pound butter, 4 dozen eggs, one quart wine, 1 quart brandy, 1 ounce nutmeg, cinnamon, cloves, mace, of each three ounces, two pound citron, currants and raisins 5 pound each, 1 quart yeast; when baked, frost with loaf sugar; dress with box and gold loaf.

To frost [the cake]. Whip 6 [egg] whites, during the baking, add 3 pound of sifted loaf-sugar and put on thick, as it comes hot from the oven. Some return the frosted loaf into the oven, it injures and yellows it, if the frosting be put on immediately it does best without being returned into the oven.

INDEPENDENCE CAKE

Serves 12-14

1 oz/30 g compressed yeast, or ½ oz/15 g
   dry yeast
6 fl oz/¾ cup/175 ml lukewarm milk
1 lb/4 cups/500 g flour
8 oz/1 cup/250 g butter
10 oz/1½ cups/300 g sugar
2 eggs, beaten to mix
1 tsp ground cinnamon
1 tsp ground mace
½ tsp ground nutmeg
½ tsp ground cloves
1½ oz/⅓ cup/40 g candied citron peel,
   chopped
3¼ oz/¾ cup/100 g currants
3¼ oz/¾ cup/100 g raisins
2 fl oz/¼ cup/60 ml sweet white wine
2 fl oz/¼ cup/60 ml brandy
FOR THE FROSTING (OPTIONAL):
1 egg white
4 oz/1 cup/125 g confectioners'/icing
   sugar
8 inch/20 cm springform pan/tin

1. Crumble or sprinkle the yeast over the lukewarm milk and let stand until dissolved, about 5 minutes. Sift about a quarter of the flour into a bowl, make a well in the center and add the yeast mixture. Stir, gradually drawing in the flour to make a smooth batter. Cover and leave this sponge in a warm place until bubbles dot the surface, about 40 minutes.

2. Cream the butter, beat in the sugar, and continue beating until the mixture is light and soft. Beat in the eggs, one at a time. Sift the remaining flour with the cinnamon, mace, nutmeg and cloves. Toss the candied peel, currants and raisins with a little of this flour so they are thoroughly coated. Heat the oven to No 5/375°F/190°C and grease the cake pan/tin. Stir the flour into the butter mixture in three batches, alternately with the wine and brandy, adding the candied and dried fruits with the last

addition of flour. Stir in the yeast sponge. Pour the mixture into the prepared cake pan/tin.

3. Bake in the heated oven for ¾ hour, lower the heat to No 3/325°F/160°C and continue cooking until a skewer inserted in the center comes out clean, 1¼-1½ hours longer. If the cake begins to brown too much during cooking, cover the top with foil.

4. While the cake is cooking make the frosting, if using; stiffly beat the egg white and beat in the sifted confectioners'/icing sugar, a tablespoon at a time. When the cake is cooked, turn it out at once on to a wire rack and cover with frosting, letting it drip down the sides; the heat of the cake will cook the frosting slightly and set it.

GINGERBREAD CAKE

Amelia Simmons seems to have been fond of gingerbread as she gives more recipes for it than any other contemporary cookbook. This particular gingerbread is raised with pearl ash (a potash that was the forerunner of baking soda). Potash could be made cheaply from the vast American forests and by the end of the eighteenth century it had become a substantial export, used in the manufacture of soap, cloth, and glass.

Three pounds of flour, a grated nutmeg, two ounces ginger, one pound sugar, three small spoons pearl ash dissolved in cream, one pound butter, four eggs, knead it stiff, shape it to your fancy, bake 15 minutes.

This illustration from the New Economical Housekeeper *(1844) shows how few European amenities had reached the average American kitchen even fifty years after the time of Amelia Simmons.*

GINGERBREAD COOKIES

Makes about thirty 3 inch/7.5 cm cookies
5 oz/²/₃ cup/150 g butter
6 fl oz/³/₄ cup/175 ml light/single cream, more if needed
1 tsp baking soda
1 lb/4 cups/500 g flour
1 tbsp ground ginger
1 tsp ground nutmeg
4½ oz/²/₃ cup/135 g sugar
1 egg, beaten to mix
Cutters for cookies or gingerbread men

1. Heat the butter with the cream until melted and let cool to tepid. Stir in the baking soda. Sift the flour with the ginger and nutmeg into a bowl, stir in the sugar and make a well in the center. Add the cream mixture and egg and stir, gradually working in the flour to make a firm dough. Add a few more spoonsful of cream if necessary. Turn out the dough on a floured board or marble slab and knead until it is smooth and peels easily from the board. Chill for 20 minutes.

2. Heat the oven to No 5/375°F/190°C and grease a baking sheet. Roll out the dough to ³/₈ inch/1 cm thickness and stamp out cookies, gingerbread men or other shapes. Set on the prepared baking sheet and bake in the heated oven until lightly browned around the edges, about 20 minutes. Transfer to a rack to cool. Store in an airtight container.

ANTONIN CARÊME

1783–1833

ANTONIN CARÊME IS PROBABLY the greatest cook of all time. Born in 1783, just before the French Revolution consigned the static elegance of the Versailles court to oblivion, his work reflects the freedom of thought and action that flooded France during the years that followed. He had the intellectual ability to analyze cooking old and new, to simplify methods and menus, and to define every aspect of the art that today is known as *haute cuisine*. He also had a practical brilliance which led him to become the most sought-after chef of his generation, with an international career in the capitals of Europe. Like Napoleon he combined, on his own level, a classic sense of order with romantic ambitions and a flair for self-dramatization.

Carême's achievement is all the more amazing considering that he was totally self-educated, the son of a hard-drinking laborer. At the age of ten, Marie-Antoine (or Antonin as he called himself) was turned out on to the harsh streets of Paris with the words: "Go, my child, and fare well in the world. Leave us to languish; poverty and misery are our lot and we will die as we have lived. But for those like you, with quick wits, there are great fortunes to be made." This paternal confidence was not misplaced; with a touch of the astuteness which was to mark his career, Carême knocked on the door of a modest cookshop where he was

OPPOSITE: *The spacious early nineteenth-century kitchens of the Brighton Pavilion, built for the Prince Regent. Note the splendid array of copper pans (which can still be seen), and the metal covers on the central table for keeping food hot.*

taken in, fed, and engaged to serve a six-year apprentice ship. His ability must have shown early for in 1800, at the age of seventeen, he went to work for Bailly, one of the most famous *pâtissiers* of the day. Carême has nothing but praise for Bailly, a generous man who allowed him to study in the *Cabinet des Gravures*, where he taught himself both to read and to draw.

At the time, the profession of *pâtissier* was at least as prestigious as that of *cuisinier*. Pastrycooks were responsible for *pièces montées*, the great decorative center pieces that were the crowning glory of grand dinners. Carême excelled at these flights of fancy; in his first two books, *Le Pâtissier royal* and *Le Pâtissier pittoresque*, both published in 1815, he produces hundreds of designs for rustic pavilions, ruins, cascades, temples, forts, windmills, and other ornate creations. He insisted that "the fine arts are five in number – painting, sculpture, poetry, music, architecture – whose main branch is confectionery." Such miniature fantasies, their components surrealistically colored and shaped to look anything but themselves, make a mockery of nature, but they cert ainly appealed to Carême's patrons.

His two-year training with Bailly completed, Carême rapidly attracted the attention of the most famous statesman of the time, the Prince de Talleyrand. Talleyrand was a man of many parts; wit and

The presentation of food was one of Carême's greatest enthusiasms. He reduced the motley garnishes that had survived from the Renaissance, topping his dishes with ornamental hâtelets *threaded with colorful ingredients like truffles, cockscombs, and crayfish, then mounted his creation on* socles *or bases.*

bon viveur, he achieved the unusual distinction of acting as foreign minister both to Napoleon and to the restored monarch, Louis XVIII. He kept one of the best tables in Paris; for an hour each morning he conferred on the menu of the day with Carême, who reported that "M. de Talleyrand understands the genius of a cook; he respects it, he is the best judge of subtle improvements, and his expenditure combines wisdom with generosity." Carême had been engaged as *pâtissier*, but he was determined to learn from Boucher, Talleyrand's chef, the art of the *cuisinier*. After twelve years beside Boucher, the pupil had outclassed his master, partly by working in the shadow of all the top chefs of the day as one of the *extras* called in to help on special occasions.

The early 1800s, when France was gripped in the desperate struggle for control of Europe, were hardly the most propitious time for the arts of good living. The great days of the noble households were over, and the deliberately restrained tone of Empire fashions and furniture was carried into the kitchen where provisions and the staff to cook them were greatly reduced. But, forced to economize, cooks made better use of their time and of the ingredients available; the extravagant old *coulis* was abandoned in favor of an espagnole sauce (resembling the one used today) and the huge main dishes of the *ancien régime* were forgotten. Undaunted by this relative austerity, gourmets formed dinner clubs and a new breed of writer appeared – the gastronomic critic. Grimod de la Reynière, for example, wrote the *Almanach des gourmands* (an annual miscellany of food history and gossip) and the most famous gastronome of all, Anthèlme de Brillat-Savarin, regularly visited Talleyrand's table, where he was apparently so preoccupied by the food that he rarely uttered a word.

By the end of the Napoleonic Wars in 1815 both *haute* and *bourgeoise cuisine* would have been recognizable to a modern cook, thanks largely to the influence of Carême and his great rival, Beauvilliers. In contrast to Carême, who was the last of the great chefs in private

service, Beauvilliers made his name as a restaurateur, being the first to "combine an elegant dining-room, smart waiters, and a choice cellar with superior cooking" – all at the cost, Brillat-Savarin reports, of an "inflated bill." Beauvilliers died in 1820, before competition between the two cooks could become bitter – in his last years he was more famous than Carême, having scored a triumph in 1814 with his *L'Art du cuisinier*, regarded as the first worthy successor in seventy years to Menon's *La Cuisinière bourgeoise*. Carême was still known as a *pâtissier* rather than a *cuisinier*, but behind the scenes in the great houses he had already developed the *haute cuisine* so elegantly described in his later books.

The better to establish himself, Carême left Talleyrand's household in 1815 and crossed the Channel to work for the Prince Regent, the eccentric arbiter of England's taste. The prince gave Carême every consideration, remarking graciously on one occasion that the "dinner last night was superb, but you will make me die of indigestion," to which Carême rejoined: "Prince, my duty is to tempt your appetite, not to control it." However, the Prince was not tempted for long; Carême was depressed by the climate and the attitude of his fellow cooks, who resented the attention paid to this foreign interloper. Above all, he found the English generally ignorant of the finer points of good cooking (though the leftovers of Carême's pâtés, offered illicitly after a banquet, commanded a high price). In Carême's opinion the recent influx of French chefs into England had had little effect. "The essentials of English cooking," he wrote, "are the roasts of beef, mutton, and lamb; the various meats cooked in salt water, in the manner of fish and vegetables . . . fruit preserves, puddings of all kinds, chicken and turkey with cauliflower, salt beef, country ham, and several similar ragoûts – that is the sum of English cooking." A more accurate description of old-fashioned English fare could hardly be penned today.

Two years of England were enough for Carême and in 1818 he returned to Paris where further tempting offers awaited him. He joined the staff of Czar Alexander but,

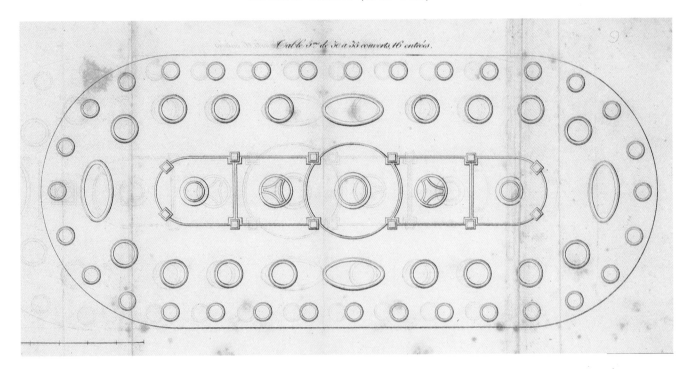

This table arrangement from Le Maître
d'hôtel français *shows service à la français
with a multitude of dishes set out
simultaneously in a grand display.*

predictably, Russia proved no more to Carême's taste than England. Like Leonardi before him, Carême found the climate trying. Fresh produce was available for only four months of the year – an insupportable restriction for one of Carême's talents. So he returned to France and in 1820 went to Vienna to work for the British ambassador. Here Carême was much more at home. He noted with satisfaction that the ingredients and general standard of cooking were second only to Paris. Vienna had been the scene of earlier culinary triumphs when Carême had cooked at the Congress of 1815. Like Talleyrand, he was a veteran of the celebrity-studded international gatherings that determined the political fate of Europe after the Napoleonic Wars.

Returning to Paris in 1823, Carême entered upon the last and most important phase of his life, when through his cookbooks he established himself as the doyen of his profession. The first of these books, *Le Maître d'hôtel français*, had appeared in the previous year; in it Carême describes the hundreds of menus which he personally had created and cooked in the capitals of Europe – eloquent testimony to his boast that he could work faster and more efficiently than anyone else.

Tolerance was never Carême's greatest virtue; he once denounced his colleagues for their "miserable works which degrade our national cooking. Why are you so small in talent and so mean in invention?" The ideal cook, he explains, should have "a discerning and sensitive palate, perfect and exquisite taste, a strong and industrious character; he should be skillful and hardworking and unite delicacy, order, and economy." His strictures would be merely bombastic were it not for the ruthless singleness of mind with which he put them into practice. Carême himself ate little and touched no alcohol. He seems to have had no time for his family, for he makes but one isolated reference to a daughter and does not so much as mention a wife.

In the years that followed the publication of *Le Maître d'hôtel français*, Carême enjoyed an Olympian fame. His dinners were an occasion to remember. One of them, cooked in the summer of 1828, has been recaptured by Lady Morgan (a peripatetic Irish novelist) who reported that Carême was working for a Rothschild "at a salary beyond what any sovereign in Europe might be able to pay, even though assisted by Monsieur Rothschild, without whose aid so many sovereigns would scarcely be able to keep cooks at all." As for the meal: "To do justice to the science and research of a dinner so served would require a knowledge of the art equal to that which produced it . . . every meat presented

145

Grand Buffet de la Cuisine moderne

Carême's fanciful design for a towering, seven-tiered buffet table includes soups, fish, roasts, cold meats, jellies, and blancmanges, as well as some of his favorite pièces montées. *These were usually made of almond paste colored in violet, green, orange, yellow, and brick red, the details picked out in chocolate. The effect must have been stunning, if contrived.*

in its natural aroma; every vegetable in its own shade of verdure." The climax of the meal was a *plombière* "with the hue and odour of fresh gathered nectarines [which] satisfied every sense and dissipated every coarser flavour." Iced bombes such as a *plombière* (based on almond milk and whipped cream, topped with fresh fruit purée) were favorites of Carême's. They offered great scope for his decorative talents and his recipes can hardly be bettered today.

However, it was aspics, with their elaborate molds and garnishes, that gave full rein to his pastrycook's passion for display. The cold buffet, though dating back

to the *credenza* of Renaissance Italy, did not really catch on in France until after the revolution. Carême was its most brilliant exponent. In *Le Cuisinier parisien*, published in 1828, he lays down the principles for making classic *chaudfroids* and aspic dishes, an art which has not significantly developed since then. But even the great can make mistakes and it was with aspic that Carême once had a major disaster. The isinglass (a type of gelatin) failed to arrive and, foolishly, Carême tried to mold his charlottes without it; to his chagrin, they wobbled so dangerously when turned out that they were unusable. He never forgot the disgrace.

His last book was *L'Art de la cuisine française au dix-neuvième siècle*, an exhaustive survey of classic French cooking as perfected by Carême himself and followed with little change until the end of the century. In this book he develops several hundred versions of today's *potages* and institutes the custom of garnishing meat with meat and fish with fish, dispensing with the sweetbreads and cockscombs which had survived from the fifteenth century. The basic sauces – espagnole, béchamel, and velouté – would be familiar to today's chefs, as would Carême's 100 and more variations. Carême has been criticized for extravagance, but in fact it was he who simplified menus; he once described his ideal meal as beginning with vegetable soup, followed by roast or braised fillet of beef served with glazed vegetables or rice and a simple *jus* as gravy. Then would come poached or gratinéed fish, or a fish stew, a roasted fowl with vegetables, pastries, salad, and a dessert. Not until the end of the century did such an admirably classic menu become the rule set by another great chef, Escoffier.

Carême was in poor health while he was writing *L'Art de la cuisine* – the first three volumes appeared in 1833, the year of his death, and two volumes were added later by his friend and colleague Plumérey. Carême had exhausted himself in his dedication to cooking. Rising before dawn to choose the freshest vegetables and fruits from the market, he was on constant duty until ten or eleven at night, and before retiring, no matter how late the hour, he jotted down his progress during the day – notes that doubtless formed the basis of his books. Sometimes he would sleep hardly at all, as the sauces for an important dinner were started at 3 a.m. Added to this, conditions of work were exhausting. "Imagine yourself in a large kitchen at the moment of a great dinner," he relates. "See twenty chefs coming, going, moving with speed in this caldron of heat, look at the great mass of charcoal, a cubic meter for the cooking of entrées, and another mass on the ovens for the cooking of soups, sauces, ragoûts, for frying and the water baths. Add to that a heap of burning wood in front of which four spits are turning, one of which bears a sirloin weighing forty-five to fifty pounds, the other fowl or game. In this furnace everyone moves with speed; not a sound is heard, only the chef has a right to speak, and at the sound of his voice, everyone obeys. Finally the last straw: for

An outdoor sausage vendor peddles his wares. "The pig," wrote Carême in one of his many asides, "so useful a food for man, is indispensable to good cooking."

about half an hour, all windows are closed so that the air does not cool the dishes as they are being served. This is the way we spend the best years of our lives. We must obey even when physical strength fails, but it is the burning charcoal that kills us."

But not for one moment did Carême regret it. "Charcoal kills us, but what does it matter? The shorter the life, the greater the glory," he declared. A man apart, sensitive, egotistical, his personality comes across with a burning intensity that defies criticism. His practical experience was unrivaled; soups, sauces, aspics, pastries, and ices – he was a specialist in them all. Carême's writing covers *haute cuisine* in its entirety – he was interested in anything and everything to do with food. But his observations (unlike those of so many inquisitive minds) never lack acuity; no matter what the subject, Carême has that uncanny knack of reaching the heart of the matter that is the mark of genius.

CARÊME RECIPES

OPPOSITE: *Gâteau Pithiviers.*
ABOVE: *Carême's output of work was
enormous; he died the same year that the first
three volumes of his great* L'Art de la cuisine
française *first appeared.*

Many of Carêmes recipes are of inordinate length, not
because they are complicated, but because he describes
each step in the minutest detail. With the notable
exception of the recipes in *Le Pastissier françois* written in
1653, these are the first old recipes that a novice can follow
with ease.

POTAGE D'AUTOMNE

Almost all Carême's soups are based on well-flavored consommé, which he makes with chicken or beef, veal, and vegetables. For traveling, Carême recommends boiling the consommé until reduced to a thick, sticky juice (meat glaze) then leaving it to set. When cut in cubes it could be diluted with water for use – as with today's bouillon cubes.

Cut as for julienne the white of four leeks, the yellow leaves of two bunches of celery and those of a thinly sliced lettuce; after washing them well, toss them into the boiling consommé; add half a liter of baby peas, a pinch each of sugar and crushed pepper, two large soup spoons of flour, mixed to a soft smooth paste with cold stock; stir the soup with a large spoon, so the consommé thickens smoothly; after an hour and a half of simmering, pour the soup into a tureen containing little croûtons, made according to the rule.

It was Carême's opinion that foreign fruits and vegetables could not compare with French produce. Les Halles was the main food market of Paris, pictured here in 1830.

AUTUMN SOUP

Serves 8
white part of 3 medium leeks, cut in
    julienne strips
leaves of 2 celery hearts, cut in julienne
    strips
½ head romaine lettuce, cut in julienne
    strips
3¼ pints/2 quarts/2 liters well-flavored
    consommé
5 oz/1 cup/150 g fresh green peas
pinch of sugar
pinch of white pepper
salt (optional)
FOR THE LIAISON:
1½ oz/⅓ cup/45 g flour
6 fl oz/¾ cup/175 ml cold consommé

FOR THE CROÛTONS:
6 slices bread, crusts discarded, diced
2 oz/¼ cup/60 g butter
3-4 tbsp oil

1. Wash and drain the leek, celery, and lettuce strips. Bring the consommé to a boil.
2. For the liaison: mix the flour with the 6 fl oz/¾ cup/175 ml cold consommé and blend until smooth. Add to the boiling consommé, stirring constantly, and simmer until the consommé is thickened and smooth, 2-3 minutes. Add the leek, celery and lettuce strips

with the peas, sugar and pepper and simmer, uncovered, until the vegetables are tender, 15-20 minutes. Taste the soup for seasoning, adding more salt and pepper if necessary.
3. For the croûtons: heat the butter and oil and fry the diced bread, stirring, until browned on all sides. Drain the croûtons thoroughly on paper towels and keep warm. If serving in a tureen, put in the croûtons and pour over the soup; if serving in individual bowls, serve the croûtons separately.

SAUCE AU BEURRE À L'ITALIENNE

Most of Carême's sauces take at least twelve hours because they are made step-by-step from basic sauces that are simmered slowly to concentrate their flavor. *Sauce italienne*, based on the comparatively quick *sauce au beurre* which follows, is one of the simplest. Carême recommends serving it with broiled/grilled or poached fish. The olive oil from Aix-en-Provence and the butter from Isigny in Normandy called for here are still reputed to be the best.

After having chopped a little parsley, several mushrooms, a truffle, a touch of garlic, take a fragment of bay leaf and thyme, a whole clove, a little coarsely ground pepper, some grated nutmeg and some salt; after sautéing this seasoning with a little sweet butter over a moderate heat, you add a glass of champagne, then strain out the fragments of herbs and the clove; transfer your mixture into a pan in a water bath containing a large spoonful of butter sauce prepared in the usual way, two spoonfuls of good oil from Aix, some Isigny butter, the juice of a lemon, and serve. The sauce should be highly flavored.

Carême was very conscious of an old and a new style, in mode of dress as well as in cooking. At right he illustrates an embryonic toque – essentially a nightcap with a circular cut-out inserted for coolness.

BUTTER SAUCE À L'ITALIENNE

Makes 16 fl oz/2 cups/500 ml sauce to serve 4-6
½ bay leaf
sprig of thyme, or ½ tsp dried thyme
1 whole clove
2½ tbsp butter
2 tbsp chopped parsley
3 mushrooms, finely chopped
1 truffle, finely chopped (optional)
½ clove garlic, crushed
pinch of grated nutmeg
salt and pepper
4 fl oz/½ cup/125 ml champagne
double quantity of butter sauce (see sauce recipe page 65)
2 tbsp olive oil
juice of ½-1 lemon

1. Tie the bay leaf, thyme and clove with thread or wrap them in a piece of cheesecloth. In a heavy-based pan melt 1 tablespoon of the butter and add the parsley, mushrooms, truffle (if using), garlic, tied herbs, nutmeg, and a little salt and pepper. Sauté over medium heat until the mushrooms are soft, 1-2 minutes. Add the champagne, simmer 5 minutes, and discard the tied herbs.

2. Make the sauce in the top of a double boiler or in a saucepan placed in a water bath. Stir in the champagne and mushroom mixture, then gradually stir in the oil. When the sauce is smooth, add the remaining butter in small pieces and stir until incorporated. Add lemon juice to taste with more salt and pepper if needed. Note: this sauce separates easily and should be made over hot, not boiling, water. The sauce should be served tepid.

POULETS SAUTÉS À LA CASTILLANE

Sautés were invented at the beginning of the nineteenth century, possibly by Carême himself. They involve cooking meat or poultry, either partly or completely, before adding a little liquid, so that a concentrated sauce is obtained without any lengthy reduction at the end of cooking. The heat must be carefully controlled if the meat is to sauté without burning, and this had not been possible before the invention of stoves with flat, evenly-heated tops and the development of a special sauté pan with a heavy base and straight sides, still a standard part of French kitchen equipment. In using tomatoes in this recipe, Carême was ahead of his time as they were not popular in cooking until mid-century.

Take a pound of Bayonne ham or, better still, ham from Malaga, cut in small dice; sauté it in butter so it browns lightly; add to it two chickens, cut in pieces, and cook so that they stiffen without coloring; add four onions, cut in rounds, two boxes of mushrooms, fluted, several stems of parsley, a clove of garlic, and a bouquet garni; let the chickens cook briskly without catching on the bottom of the pan; ten minutes before serving, throw in six tomatoes, cut in two and the seeds discarded; just before serving, deglaze the pan and serve with the garnish and the concentrated cooking liquid from the chickens.

"Gourmands at Table" (1805) shows an all-male Paris dining club – a popular diversion at the time of Grimod de la Reynière and Brillat Savarin.

SAUTÉ OF CHICKEN À LA CASTILLANE

Serves 4
1 tbsp butter
8 oz/250 g raw, lightly smoked ham, diced small
about 3 lb/1.4 kg frying chicken, cut in pieces
2 onions, cut in rounds
8 oz/250 g mushrooms, stems trimmed level with caps
2 stems parsley
½ clove garlic, crushed
bouquet garni
salt and pepper
3 medium tomatoes, peeled, quartered, and seeded
4 fl oz/½ cup/125 ml chicken stock

1. In a sauté pan or large skillet, melt the butter and sauté the ham over medium heat, about 1 minute. Put the pieces of chicken, skin side down, on the ham and sauté until the flesh is firm and white, but not brown, about 5 minutes. Add the onions, mushrooms, parsley, garlic, and bouquet garni and sprinkle with salt and pepper.

2. Cover and cook over medium heat, stirring occasionally and turning the chicken pieces until they are tender and the onions are soft, about 20 minutes. Add the tomatoes, lifting the chicken pieces on top of them, and continue cooking for 10 minutes.

3. Transfer the chicken to a platter and keep warm. Add the stock to the pan and bring to a boil, stirring to dissolve the pan juices. Taste for seasoning, spoon the sauce and garnish over the chicken and serve.

JAMBON BRAISÉ ET GLACÉ À LA PIÉMONTAISE

This braised ham is typical of the splendid *grosses pièces* that formed the centerpieces of grand dinners. *A mirepoix* is a mixture of diced vegetables, used to give flavor to a braise.

Take a good Bayonne or Westphalia ham – it must be lightly cured and of the best quality; trim off some of the fat and put the ham to soak in plenty of water. For a ham of less than a year old, 24 hours is sufficient; then wash it, drain and wrap it in a napkin that you tie tightly. Put it in a large *braisière* [heavy casserole], fill it with water and add four carrots, as many onions, two bouquets garnis of bay leaf, thyme, basil, a whole clove and a little mace. Then start boiling over a very hot stove; skim off a light foam; cover the *braisière* and place it so that the ham just simmers steadily for three hours. Then drain it, peel off the skin and place it on the bottom of a large oval pan in which you simmer it an hour in a *mirepoix* moistened with a large spoonful of consommé, half a bottle of good Chablis, and half a glass of old cognac, all worked through a sieve. It is essential to taste the ham before cooking in this *mirepoix* is finished. If the flesh is slightly salty, it is better to let it cook completely in the first cooking, because the *mirepoix* will firm the flesh, giving it more flavor, but also concentrate the salt it contains. Experience must guide the practitioner in his work: theory can illuminate, but that is all; practice is the heart of the matter. Then glaze the ham in the oven in the heavy oval pan. Set the ham on a platter on a bed of rice *à la piémontaise*, made with 1½ pounds of rice. Decorate the shank of the ham with a frill and serve with it an espagnole sauce, mixed with the *mirepoix* from which all the fat has been skimmed. Serve grated Parmesan cheese separately.

BRAISED HAM À LA PIÉMONTAISE

Serves 12-16

a whole uncooked country ham
    (12-16 lb/5.4-7.2 kg)
rice à la piémontaise (see below)
8 oz/2 cups/250 g grated Parmesan cheese
    (for serving)
FOR SIMMERING:
4 carrots, quartered
4 onions, quartered
large bouquet garni
2 tsp basil
2 whole cloves
2 blades mace
FOR BRAISING:
3 tbsp butter
3 carrots, diced
3 onions, diced
3 stalks celery, diced
16 fl oz/2 cups/500 ml consommé
16 fl oz/2 cups/500 ml Chablis or other
    white wine
4 fl oz/½ cup/125 ml cognac
FOR THE BROWN SAUCE:
3 tbsp oil
2 carrots, diced
2 onions, diced
3 tbsp flour
1¼ pint/3 cups/750 ml beef stock
salt and pepper (optional)
Paper frill (for decoration)

1. Scrub the ham, trim off some of the fat, and soak it for 24 hours in cold water. Drain, wrap it tightly in cheesecloth, put it in a large pot with the carrots, onions, bouquet garni, basil, cloves and mace. Add water to cover, bring quickly to a boil, skim, add the lid and simmer the ham, allowing 15 minutes per pound or 30 minutes per kilo, plus 15 minutes more. Let it cool slightly. Heat the oven to No 4/350°F/175°C.

2. Meanwhile, in a very large oval casserole melt the butter for braising and gently cook the carrots, onions, and celery until soft but not brown, 5-7 minutes. Add the consommé, Chablis and cognac; cover and simmer 30 minutes. Peel the skin from the ham and discard. Put the ham in the casserole, bring to a boil, cover and braise in the heated oven for 1 hour.

3. For the brown sauce: in a heavy-based pan heat the oil and sauté the carrots and onions until soft but not brown. Add the flour and cook over high heat, stirring constantly, until the flour is well browned; do not allow it to burn. At once add three quarters of the stock and bring to a boil, stirring. Skim the sauce and leave it to simmer for half an hour. Add the remaining cold stock, skim again and continue simmering until the sauce is glossy and the consistency of thin cream, 15-20 minutes longer.

4. When the ham is cooked, transfer it to a roasting pan and spoon over enough brown sauce to baste the ham. Turn the oven up to No 7/425°F/220°C. Roast the ham in the heated oven until browned, about 20 minutes, basting again halfway through cooking. Skim all fat from the cooking liquid and taste it; if not too salty, add it to the brown sauce. Bring the sauce to the boil, taste for seasoning and strain it. Spread the rice à la piémontaise in a large serving dish and set the ham on top. Decorate the shank of the ham with a paper frill. Serve the sauce and a bowl of grated Parmesan cheese separately.

RIZ À LA PIÉMONTAISE

The rice of Carolina had already made its mark by Carême's time, but the blanching and washing needed show that its quality was very different from today.

Wash in warm water a pound and a half of Carolina rice several times; after blanching it a few seconds, drain it and simmer three-quarters of an hour in a pan, mixing it with twelve ounces of butter, three large spoonsful of good consommé, a little coarsely ground pepper and two soup spoons of grated Parmesan; when turning it out on the platter, sprinkle it lightly with the same cheese.

RICE À LA PIÉMONTAISE

Serves 12-16
12 oz/1½ cups/375 g butter
1½ lb/3½ cups/750 g long grain rice
1¼ pints/3 cups/750 ml consommé
1¼ pints/3 cups/750 ml water
salt and pepper
4 oz/1 cup/125 g grated Parmesan cheese

In a very large heavy-based pan melt the butter, add the rice, consommé, water and a little salt and pepper and sprinkle with 3-4 tablespoons grated cheese. Cover and simmer until all the liquid is absorbed, 20-25 minutes. Let stand, covered, for 10 minutes, then stir lightly to fluff up the grains and taste for seasoning. Spread the rice in a large hot serving dish and sprinkle with the remaining cheese before placing the ham on top.

GARNITURES DE PETITES CAROTTES À LA FLAMANDE

Carême was famous for his simple ways with vegetables. He insisted that they should never be overcooked and went so far as to cut root vegetables in cylinders so that they cooked evenly.

Cut a bunch of new carrots in little cylinders with a vegetable cutter, then blanch and refresh them and cook them with consommé, a little butter and some sugar. When reduced to a glaze, just before serving add a pinch of chopped, blanched parsley, and serve them mixed together.

BABY CARROTS À LA FLAMANDE

Serves 4
1 lb/500 g baby carrots
12 fl oz/1½ cups/375 ml consommé
1 tbsp butter
2 tsp sugar
1 tbsp chopped parsley

1. With a large apple corer, cut the carrots into cylinders, trimming the tops and roots. Put the carrots in a pan of cold water, bring to the boil, and cook for 2 minutes. Drain and refresh under cold water.
2. Mix the consommé, butter and sugar in a pan, add the carrots and simmer until they are almost tender. Increase the heat and boil until the liquid is reduced to about 1 tablespoon and makes a shiny glaze. Meanwhile twist the parsley in the corner of a piece of cheesecloth, pour boiling water over it, and squeeze it dry; the parsley will be bright green. Add it to the carrots, toss to mix and serve.

Antonin Carême (1783-1833)

155

SOUFFLÉ PARISIEN AUX FRAISES

Classic soufflés were Carême's invention, though puddings made fluffy with meringue had been known for many years. It was thanks to new ovens heated by air draft instead of the old method of filling with hot coals that the constant heat needed for a true soufflé could be maintained. The *croustade* or pastry case was not eaten; it was made with the same straight sides as our soufflé dishes, and in fact inspired them.

After hulling a large basket of good strawberries, crush them. Work them through a fine sieve to obtain a purée; mix a pound and a half of powdered sugar with eighteen stiffly whipped egg whites. When all is well blended, stir in the strawberry purée until thoroughly mixed. Pour the mixture into a *croustade* of eleven inches diameter and three and a half inches in height; surround it with

three buttered sheets of paper. This *croustade* is cooked in advance, as for a *croustade* of hot pâté *à la financière*, but it should be rolled very thin. It can also be cooked at the same time as the soufflé and works just as well, but the soufflé must be cooked a little longer. I prefer the *croustade* to be cooked in advance. Put the soufflé in a moderate oven and give it a good hour's cooking. When it is ready to serve, put red-hot cinders on a large baking sheet. Take the soufflé from the oven and place it on the hot cinders so it stays puffed. Meanwhile, cover it with powdered sugar and glaze it with a red-hot iron; then carry it very quickly to the dining room. Lift it with the help of a pan lid, and set it on a platter, which should be covered with a fine damask napkin. Take off the paper holding up the soufflé and serve it at once. Soufflés of raspberries, gooseberries, and mirabelle or greengage plums are made in the same way.

PREVIOUS PAGE: In 1815 Carême went to England to cook for the Prince Regent, banqueting here in London, but British tastes were too conservative for Carême and three years later he was on his way to Russia.

"Arrival in Paris" – presumably yesterday's travelers, like today's, made haste to one of the city's many fine restaurants.

STRAWBERRY SOUFFLÉ

Serves 4-6
8 oz/1 pint/250 g strawberries, hulled
3¼ oz/½ cup/100 g sugar, more to taste
5 egg whites
confectioners'/icing sugar (for sprinkling)
2⅓ pint/1½ quart/1½ liter soufflé dish

1. Heat the oven to No 4/350°F/175°C. Purée the strawberries in a blender or food processor. Stir in half of the sugar, adding more to taste depending on their sweetness. Butter the soufflé dish.
2. Stiffly whip the egg whites. Add the remaining sugar and continue beating until this meringue mixture is glossy and holds a tall peak, about 1 minute. Stir a little meringue into the strawberry purée, mixing it well, then add

the purée to the remaining meringue; fold them together as lightly as possible. Spoon the soufflé mixture into the prepared mold – it should reach almost to the top. Bake it in the heated oven until puffed and brown, 25-30 minutes. The center should still be slightly concave. Sprinkle the top with confectioners'/icing sugar and serve it at once.

GÂTEAU PITHIVIERS

The origins of puff pastry are obscure; it is thought to have come from Italy or Spain where it may have been inspired by the Arab skill with sweet pastries (their wafer-thin pastry is made quite differently, however). Puff pastry was familiar to La Varenne, who made it more or less by the classic method, and Carême was a master at it, famous for his lightness of hand. He lists a dozen variations of the puff pastry *gâteau pithiviers*, which is still made today. "Turns" refers to the rolling and folding process by which the pastry is made and a *litron* is an old 12-ounce measure. The aveline almonds called for in the filling are regular or sweet almonds, not the bitter almonds occasionally called for in small quantities to add piquancy (as in the macaroons mentioned in this recipe).

Make half a litron of puff pastry dough. When it has had eight turns, divide it in two, giving two-thirds of the volume to one piece, then roll this out large enough to cut a round nine inches in diameter. Pile the trimmings from this round on the remaining pastry, and make with it another round of seven inches diameter; place it on a baking sheet. Then lightly moisten the edges of the round and spoon the filling on top. Spread it evenly to within an inch of the border of the pastry, then carefully cover the filling with the other pastry round, pressing it on the base in order to stick the edges together and prevent the filling from escaping during cooking. Flute the edge of the gâteau, marking the pastry with the point of a knife at half an inch from the filling. Lightly gild the top, then mark a palm leaf, or a rose, or simply some even stripes. Put it in a hot oven. When it is browned, move it nearer the mouth of the oven so that the pastry can dry without browning. After three-quarters of an hour of cooking (the base of the pastry should be very crisp, otherwise this type of gâteau is not good to eat) cover it evenly with sugar so it can be glazed by making a little hot flame at the mouth of the oven.

After pounding eight ounces of aveline almonds (blanched), add six ounces of fine sugar, four of Isigny butter, two of bitter macaroons, four egg yolks, and a tiny pinch of salt. When all is well beaten, add four spoonsful of whipped cream.

GÂTEAU PITHIVIERS

Serves 6
puff pastry made with 6 oz/1½ cups/175 g flour, 6 oz/¾ cup/175 g butter, pinch of salt, and 2½ fl oz/⅓ cup/75 ml ice water, more if needed
1 egg, beaten to mix with ½ tsp salt (for glaze)
granulated sugar (for sprinkling)
FOR THE FILLING:
4 oz/¾ cup/125 g whole blanched almonds
2 oz/⅓ cup/60 g sugar
2 oz/¼ cup/60 g unsalted butter, softened
1 macaroon, crushed
2 egg yolks
tiny pinch of salt
2 fl oz/¼ cup/60 ml heavy/double cream, whipped until it holds a soft peak

1. Make the puff pastry dough and chill for at least 30 minutes. For the filling: grind the almonds in a food processor with 2 tablespoons of the sugar until the oil is released, making them slightly sticky. Add the remaining sugar and the butter, and continue working until very smooth and pastelike. Add the crushed macaroon, egg yolks, and salt, and continue working until the mixture is very smooth and holds together. Gently stir in the whipped cream. Heat the oven to No 6/400°F/200°C.
2. Cut off two-thirds of the dough. Roll out the large piece ¼ inch/6 mm thick into a 10 inch/25 mm round. With a sharp knife cut out a 9 inch/23 cm round and reserve. Pile the trimmings one on top of another and add to the remaining one-third of dough. Roll it out to an 8 inch/20 cm round and cut a 7 inch/18 cm round from it, discarding the trimmings.
3. Set the 7 inch/18 cm round on a baking sheet and brush a 1 inch/2.5 cm strip around the edge of the round with egg glaze. Pile the filling in the center and spread it to within 1 inch/2.5 cm of the edge of the dough. Set the 9 inch/23 cm round on top and press the edges firmly together to seal both rounds so the filling cannot escape. Holding the back of a knife parallel to the board, score the edges of the pastry with horizontal cuts to encourage it to rise and with the knife held vertically pull in the edges at regular intervals to form scallops. Brush the top lightly with glaze, then mark it with curved lines radiating from the center like a flower and make a hole in the center for steam to escape.
4. Set the gâteau in the top of the heated oven and bake it until the pastry is puffed and browned, about 20 minutes. Turn down the heat to No 4/350°F/175°C, set the gâteau in the bottom of the oven and continue baking until very crisp, about 30 minutes longer. Five minutes before the end of cooking, sprinkle the gâteau with sugar and continue baking until it forms a glaze. Transfer the gâteau to a rack to cool and serve warm or cold.

SOYER

1809–1858

Fᴏʀ ꜱʜᴇᴇʀ ɪɴᴠᴇɴᴛɪᴠᴇɴᴇꜱꜱ and love of show, no cook has matched Alexis Soyer, whose first recorded prank (at the age of twelve) was to call out the fire brigade by ringing the church bells at midnight in his home town of Meaux-en-Brie. Expelled from choir school as a result, he gleefully abandoned thoughts of the priesthood for a career in cooking.

Soyer worked in Paris for nine years at a time when French cuisine was rising to new heights. Restaurants and dining clubs flourished; Carême enjoyed a legendary reputation which was the envy of all other chefs; and vicarious pleasure reached its apogee in the gastronomic writings of Brillat-Savarin, whose *Physiologie du Goût* appeared in 1826. Like Carême, Soyer must have been a quick learner – at seventeen he had already taken charge of a considerable restaurant and catering business. However, the recurrent unrest in France was discouraging. Worse still, Soyer was in trouble with a lady who was carrying his child. So in 1831 he left Paris to join his brother in London.

At this time England was the richest country in the world. The aristocracy lavished its wealth on fine houses, art collections, Italian opera, and retinues of servants, including numerous French chefs who were attracted by the security and high wages. In 1813 (just before Carême's brief stay in England) the most famous of these chefs, Ude, had written *The French Cook* especially for the English market, and by the time Soyer arrived the elegant cooking which this book describes was the mark of every gentleman of fashion. Some members of the aristocracy kept as many as four chefs, including a Frenchman for sauces and an Englishman for roasts. When the Duke of Buckingham, deeply in debt, was urged to dismiss his Italian pastry cook, he exclaimed "Good God, may'nt a man even have a biscuit with his glass of sherry!".

This was also the golden age of the London Club – Brook's, White's, the Carlton, and the Athenaeum, each with its own ambience and adherents. In 1837 Liberal members of parliament (the party of social reform) founded a club appropriately called the Reform. Soyer was invited to be its chef and had a unique opportunity to design his own kitchens. His creative genius burgeoned in a series of spendid gadgets including the first mechanical spit run by steam, "refrigerators" cooled by running ice water, and a row of gas ovens whose temperatures could be accurately controlled – a great innovation. He ruled his domain with such precision that "the minute hand did not pass more regularly over the face of the clock than the assistants of Soyer revolved round him as the center planet of their system."

OPPOSITE: During the Irish potato famine Soyer set up soup kitchens in Dublin. His Shilling Cookery for the People *was the first cookbook written for working people.*
ABOVE: Portrait of Alexis Soyer by his wife Emma.

The renown of the Reform Club's kitchens was as great as its cooking, and tours conducted by Soyer were a popular pastime. Every afternoon he would hold court in the kitchens, described by one visitor as "spacious as a ballroom, kept in the finest order and white as a young bride." It was not only the kitchens that were worth seeing. When the prime minister, Lord Melbourne, remarked on the good looks of the kitchen maids, Soyer quipped, "Yes, my Lord, we want no plain cooks here."

Soyer was quite different from the conventional picture of a white-clad chef. A red velvet cap was his trademark, set jauntily to one side, and his flowing clothes were equally distinctive, all cut on the bias (or *à la zoug-zoug*, as he would say). At the beginning of his career at the Reform, Soyer had married Emma Jones, already reputed as a gifted portrait painter. But the marriage was not destined to last; in 1842 Emma died in childbirth. Soyer was heartbroken; he took months to resume his work, and it was another four years before he published his first book, fancifully named *The Gastronomic Regenerator*.

Here is the food of the Reform Club – grouse à la

Rob Roy, ribs of beef à la George the Fourth, and most famous of all, lamb chops Reform (page 166) – breaded chops served with a brown sauce, flavored with pickles and redcurrant jelly. Like other foreign chefs in England, Soyer had to adapt his style to the tastes of his masters, who preferred square meals with plenty of meat and game, culminating in that quintessentially English dish, the savory. Carême himself had returned to France rather than live with the Prince Regent's lack of sensitivity to the finer points of his cooking. Some employers appeared even less appreciative of their French chefs. Felix, chef to the Duke of Wellington, came to his former employer, Lord Seaford, in tears. "My poor fellow," said Lord Seaford, "what is the matter? Has the Duke been finding fault?" "Oh no, my Lord," Felix exclaimed, "I would have stayed with him if he had honored me with a reproof. But he takes no notice of me. He passes over me as if I were a doormat. I serve him a dinner that would make Ude or Francatelli burst with envy and he says nothing. I serve him with a poor dinner, dressed, and badly dressed, by a maid-cook and he says nothing. If he were a hundred times a hero, I could not serve such a master."

While cooking at the Reform Club, Soyer was also

channeling his prolific energies into further inventions. In the commercial food field, he marketed Soyer's Sauce (rapidly bought out by Messrs Crosse and Blackwell), followed by Soyer's Nectar, Ozmazone (a concentrated meat extract) and Soyer's Relish. For the kitchen he developed a household version of the Reform Club ovens, a patent sink stopper, a "magic" coffeepot, and an egg cooking machine. His proudest creation was his "magic stove," a portable device weighing only 3½ pounds, the forerunner of today's chafing dish.

But Soyer also had a more serious side to his personality. For much of the population, this was the hungry forties. Fired by the attention given to his recipes for cheap, nutritive soups, Soyer went to Ireland during the 1847 potato famine to put his ideas into practice. In Dublin he set up soup kitchens and succeeded in feeding some 26,000 people daily at barely half the usual cost.

"The Kitchen Department of the Reform Club" (1841). "To show them at one glance," wrote the Spectator, *"the partition walls are cut away, and a bird's eye view is given of the several kitchens, larders, sculleries, and batterie de cuisine; the different functionaries are at their posts, and the accomplished chef, Monsieur Soyer, is in the act of pointing out to a favoured visitor the various contrivances suggested by his ingenuity and experience."*

Two years later, in 1849, he published *The Modern Housewife*, a family cookbook of the type popular in England since the 1600s. *The Modern Housewife* appears to be a hurriedly composed, unoriginal work and compares poorly with similar books of this period. Yet it signaled Soyer's enduring concern with the food of ordinary people, to which he was to return a few years later with much greater success.

In 1850 Soyer resigned from the Reform over some trifling change in the club rules; always an independent spirit, he had long been disliked by some members for his cheerful assumption of equality. He then made a disastrous foray into the restaurant business, taking the lease of a mansion near the Great Exhibition of 1851. Squandering money on furniture and decoration for what was advertised as a "Gastronomic Symposium of All Nations", Soyer overextended himself, finally losing his licence for allowing rowdiness (the

symposium included an American bar where cocktails made their first public appearance in London). Undaunted, Soyer returned to catering, organized more soup kitchens, and was asked to investigate a meat supply scandal in the Navy.

By 1853 he had also put his name to a history of food called *The Pantropheon*. Thirty-five leaden chapters replete with classical references (almost 3000 from cover to cover) range over topics as varied as sea-hedgehogs and kitchen gardens – hardly the style of Soyer. Most likely the true author was Adolphe Duhart-Fauvet, a scholarly Frenchman teaching in London. His personal copy of *The Pantropheon* was recently found and contained an aggrieved note about Soyer's duplicity in acquiring the manuscript, translating it, then passing it off as his own work. An unreadable monument to pedantic research, *The Pantropheon* can have done little to help Soyer's finances.

However, in 1855 Soyer published a book, undoubtedly his own, on a subject after his own heart. *A Shilling Cookery for the People* is by far his most original and important cookbook, the first to be specifically directed at the new working class. Soyer enlivened its functional recipes with a series of instructive letters passing between Hortense and Eloise. These imaginary characters had already appeared in *The Modern Housewife*, but they were now in "altered circumstances" and forced to practice "the most rigid economy." "It is our duty, Eloise, in this work," writes Hortense, "to bring every wholesome kind of cheap food to the notice of the poor, so that with a little exertion, they may live, and live well, with the few pence they earn, instead of living badly, at times and most extravagantly at others . . . The artisan requires as much nourishment as possible and should not pay extravagantly for fancy joints when lamb's fry is to be had for a trifle."

The letters now make whimsical reading – at one stage poor Hortense is reduced to writing on the back of a frying pan for lack of a table – but the book had a serious educational intent in an age when survival in the cities often presented rural immigrants with a challenge they

had not known on the land. The straightforward cooking advice and down-to-earth recipes are a tribute to Soyer's practical and humane nature. Although some dishes, like baked calves' hearts and sheep's head and feet, may seem more economical than appealing, most of the recipes for such favorites as Irish stew are still appropriate today. The book was an immediate success, selling 110,000 copies in four months.

Soyer now entered upon his last and greatest adventure: he went to war. The full implications of the Crimean War, into which Britain slipped without reflection in May 1854, did not dawn upon the nation until the rigors of the Russian winter set in the following year. The horrors reported by Florence Nightingale were but a small part of a long story of supply shortages, bad communications, and appalling leadership and organization. Impulsively, Soyer volunteered his services to reorganize the hospital and field kitchens "if the government will honour me with their confidence." The offer was eagerly accepted and Soyer at once started experimenting with standard rations and his famous campaign stove.

On arrival at the Scutari hospital in Constantinople, he found a desperate situation. The kitchen (consisting only of eight copper boilers) was run by temporarily assigned soldiers who were apparently so ill-trained that they threw away the broth in which the meat was cooked. The few thousand men in the hospital were far too ill to digest the regular ration of meat, bread, potatoes, tea, and porter (beer). Thanks to his genius for organization, Soyer transformed the hospital diet and so galvanized the kitchen orderlies that he was able to reduce them in number from thirty-four to eight. In England even the sceptical Mr Punch admitted that "too many cooks had spoiled the broth at Scutari and now Mr Soyer has put it all to rights."

Next Soyer crossed to the Crimea, where with the same mastery he produced "army receipts applicable for barracks, in camp or while on the march by the use of the new field stove." His contrivance – still used by the British Army as late as 1935 – needed only twenty pounds

162

English clubs flourished during the nineteenth century and it was Alexis Soyer who established the reputation of their cooking. He must have often presented dinners similar to those at the Thatched House Club (above), featuring a generous spread of dishes and a decanter for each gentleman to quench his thirst.

of wood to cook for a hundred soldiers. In his *Culinary Campaign*, Soyer describes the cheerful field dinners he cooked and shared with the officers and men. Punch celebrated his success in a little ditty entitled "Cordon Bleu":

> *The Cordon Bleu to the War is gone,*
> *In the ranks of death you'll find him.*
> *His snow-white apron girded on*
> *And his magic stove behind him.*
> *"Army beef," says the Cordon Bleu,*
> *"Though a stupid bungler slays thee,*
> *One skillful hand thy steaks shall stew,*
> *One artist's pan shall braise thee."*

When peace was restored in 1857, Soyer returned to England after two years' absence, his health broken by the same Crimean fever that nearly killed Florence Nightingale. However, he refused to give in, and soon he had completed his campaign memoirs and introduced the

British public to his latest inventions – a Scutari teapot and a "sea-going" baking dish.

In 1858 Soyer died at the age of only 48. For over twenty-five years he had worked in England, reaching a wider audience than any cook before him, whether through his books, his bottled sauces, his kitchen gadgets, his soup kitchens for the poor, or his banquets for the famous. Perhaps Soyer was more an impresario than a cook. In the words of a contemporary, he was "a very clever man, of inventive genius and inexhaustible resource; but his execution is hardly on a par with his conception and he is more likely to earn his immortality by his soup-kitchen than by his soup." In many ways Soyer was a modern man. His interest in gadgetry was a portent of automation, and his sympathy for the welfare of the poor in an age when most cooks catered exclusively to the tastes of the rich, foreshadowed the social concerns of a later generation.

SOYER RECIPES

OPPOSITE: *Côtelettes de Mouton à la Reform.*
ABOVE: *Soyer described his experiences in the*
Crimea in A Culinary Campaign. *On the title*
page he is appropriately flanked on one side by
cannon balls and on the other by his campaign
stove – an invention of such efficiency that it
was still used by the British army in the 1930s.

Soyer combines a knowledge of French cooking terms
with a remarkable command of English. However
the presentation of his recipes does not compare in
clarity with those of Mrs Beeton, who was almost his
contemporary.

COTELETTES DE MOUTON À LA *REFORM*

This most famous of all Soyer's recipes is still served at the Reform Club in London.

Chop a quarter of a pound of lean cooked ham very fine, mix it with the same quantity of bread-crumbs, then have ten very nice cotelelettes, lay them flat on your table, season lightly with pepper and salt, egg over with a paste-brush, and throw them into the ham and bread-crumbs, then beat them lightly with a knife, put ten spoonfuls of oil in a sauté-pan, place it over the fire, and when quite hot lay in the cotelettes, fry nearly ten minutes (over a moderate fire) of a light brown color, to ascertain when done, press your knife upon the thick part, if quite done it will feel rather firm; possibly they may not all be done at one time, so take out those that are ready first and lay them on a cloth till the others are done; as they require to be cooked with the gravy in them, dress upon a thin border of mashed potatoes in a crown, with the bones pointing outwards, sauce over with a pint of the sauce Reform and serve.

Soyer was the first chef to market his creations commercially on a large scale. Soyer's Sauce proved immensely profitable for Messrs. Crosse and Blackwell. Never averse to publicity, Soyer splashed his portrait, red velvet cap jauntily askew, on most of his products.

*L*AMB CHOPS REFORM

Serves 4
10 well-trimmed rib or loin lamb chops, cut about ¾ inch/2 cm thick
1 egg, beaten to mix with ½ tsp salt and ¼ tsp pepper
4 oz/½ cup/125 g lean cooked ham, very finely chopped
3¼ oz/1 cup/100 g dry white breadcrumbs
2 fl oz/¼ cup/60 ml oil
mashed potatoes made with 4 medium potatoes, 3-4 tbsp butter, about 4 fl oz/ ½ cup/125 ml milk, salt and pepper
16 fl oz/2 cup/500 ml Reform sauce (see recipe page 167)
a bunch of watercress (for garnish, optional)

1. Brush the chops with the beaten egg until well coated, then dip them in a mixture of the chopped ham and bread-crumbs, pressing with a knife so they are well coated. In a frying pan heat the oil and sauté the chops over medium heat until golden brown, allowing about 4 minutes on each side for pink meat and 1-2 minutes longer per side for well done meat. If the chops are firm when pressed, they are well done.

2. Spread a thin layer of mashed potatoes on the bottom of a platter and arrange the chops in a circle on top, bones pointing up and out like a crown roast. Spoon over the Reform sauce to cover the chops and potato and serve the remaining mashed potatoes separately.

SAUCE À LA REFORM

This sauce appeals to the British love for sharp flavors like pickles and vinegars, softened with a touch of sweetening. Chili vinegar can be made by soaking 2-3 dried hot red peppers in a bottle of malt vinegar for at least a week. A *tamis* is a fine meshed strainer.

Cut up two middling-sized onions into thin slices and put them into a stewpan and two sprigs of parsley, two of thyme, two bayleaves, two ounces of lean uncooked ham, half a clove of garlic, half a blade of mace and an ounce of fresh butter; stir them ten minutes over a sharp fire, then add two tablespoonfuls of Tarragon vinegar, one of Chili vinegar, boil it one minute; then add a pint of brown sauce, or sauce Espagnole, three tablespoonfuls of preserved tomatoes, and eight of consommé; place it over the fire until boiling, then put it at the corner, let it simmer ten minutes, skim it well, then place it again over the fire, keeping it stirred, and reduce until it adheres to the back of the spoon; then add a good tablespoonful of red current jelly, and half do. [dozen] of chopped mushrooms; season a little more if required with pepper and salt; stir it until the jelly is melted, then pass it through a tamis into another stewpan. When ready to serve, make it hot and add the white of a hard-boiled egg cut into strips half an inch long, and thick in proportion, four white blanched mushrooms, one gherkin, two green Indian pickles, and half an ounce of cooked ham, or tongue, all cut in strips like the white of egg; do not let boil afterwards.

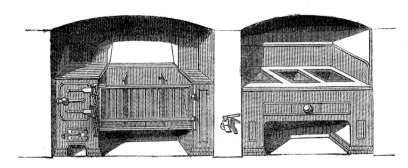

By Soyer's day the choice in cast iron ranges was wide. At left, a family model and at right, a professional stove heated by charcoal.

REFORM SAUCE

Makes about 16 fl oz/2 cups/500 ml sauce
2 tbsp butter
2 onions, thinly sliced
2 oz/¼ cup/60 g uncooked ham, diced
½ clove garlic, crushed
1 large bouquet garni
small blade mace
2 tbsp tarragon vinegar
1 tbsp chili vinegar
one recipe quantity of gravy (see page 108)
2 medium canned tomatoes, drained and chopped
4 fl oz/½ cup/125 ml beef stock
1½ tbsp redcurrant jelly
salt and pepper

FOR THE GARNISH:
4 medium mushrooms
white of 1 hard-boiled/cooked egg
1 gherkin pickle
2 sweet dill pickles
½ slice cooked lean ham or tongue

1. In a saucepan melt the butter, add the onion, ham, garlic, bouquet garni, and mace and cook over high heat, stirring, until the onions and ham are browned, about 10 minutes. Add the tarragon and chili vinegars and cook 1 minute. Add the espagnole sauce, tomatoes, and stock and simmer gently, stirring occasionally for about 30 minutes or until the sauce is of a consistency that coats the back of a spoon.

2. For the garnish: trim the mushroom stems and chop them. Cut the egg white, mushroom caps, pickles, and ham or tongue into thin strips about ½ inch/1.25 cm long.

3. When the sauce is the correct consistency, add the chopped mushroom stems and redcurrant jelly and stir until the jelly is melted. Taste it for seasoning and work the sauce through a tammie or a fine strainer. Just before serving, reheat the sauce, add the garnish, and heat gently for 1 minute without allowing the sauce to boil.

HERRING BROILED, SAUCE DIJON

Fresh herrings contain a volatile oil which rapidly turns rancid. Until Soyer's time, they were a rare delicacy. However, they became quite common once rail transport developed.

The delicacy of these fish prevents their being dressed in any other way than boiled or broiled; they certainly can be breadcrumbed and fried, but scarcely any person would like them; I prefer them dressed in the following way: I wipe them well with a cloth, and cut three incisions slantwise upon each side, dip them in flour, and broil slowly over a moderate fire; when done, sprinkle a little salt over, dress them upon a napkin, garnish with parsley, and serve the following sauce in a boat: put eight tablespoonfuls of melted butter in a stewpan, with two of French mustard, or one of English, three tablespoonfuls of fresh cream, and a little pepper and salt; when upon the point of boiling, serve.

Before the advent of fish farming and all-weather vessels, a fishmonger's slab must have varied enormously from day to day. When full, it would have overflowed with the out-size specimens in this picture.

BROILED/GRILLED HERRING WITH MUSTARD SAUCE

Serves 6
6 large fresh herring (¾-1 lb/375-500 g each)
1 oz/¼ cup/30 g flour
salt
2 tbsp chopped parsley
FOR THE SAUCE:
4 oz/½ cup/125 g butter
2 tbsp Dijon-type mustard, or 1 tbsp prepared mustard
salt and pepper
2 fl oz/¼ cup/60 ml heavy/double cream

1. Wash the fish, pat dry with paper towels, and make three slantwise slashes on each side of them. Coat with flour and broil/grill them 4-5 inches/ 10-13 cm from the heat until the fish flakes easily when tested with a fork, 5-8 minutes on each side.
2. Meanwhile make the sauce by melting the butter and stirring in the mustard with salt and pepper. Add the cream and reheat gently, stirring, until hot. Arrange the fish on a platter, sprinkle with salt and parsley, and serve the sauce separately.

SOUFFLÉ GLACÉ AU CURAÇAO

Soyer liked to climax a meal with a fanciful confection. In *The Gastronomic Regenerator* he gives many recipes for iced desserts disguised as peacocks, baskets of mushrooms, and the like. This iced soufflé is one of the simplest. Sugar syrup *au cassé* has been cooked until it forms a brittle, slightly sticky thread when chilled in water. *Isinglass* is a type of gelatin prepared from fish.

Make a custard of six yolks of eggs as directed for *crème au marasquin*, but omitting three parts of the sugar; put into your freezing-pot, and when half frozen have ready the following preparation: boil a quarter of a pound of sugar *au cassé*, have ready five whites of eggs whipped very stiff, with which mix the sugar by degrees; when quite cold mix with the custard, adding half a pint of whipped cream and three glasses of Curaçao, freeze the whole together, keeping the pot twisted until you have obtained a good consistency; have ready a number of small round paper cases, place a band of paper round each, half an inch above the top, and fill with the above preparation; place them in a flat tin box, sprinkle ratafia crumbs upon the top of each, place the lid upon the top of each, place the lid upon the box, which must close very tight, and bury it in ice and salt for six hours; when ready to serve, take them out of the box, detach the bands of paper from them, dress upon a napkin, and serve. They will have every appearance of having just left the oven.

CUSTARD FOR CRÈME AU MARASQUIN

Put the yolks of five eggs in a stewpan, with six ounces of powdered sugar, beat well together with a wooden spoon; in another stewpan have a pint of milk, in which put an ounce and a quarter of isinglass, boil ten minutes, stirring occasionally to keep it from burning, throw in two sticks of vanilla, take it from the fire, put a cover upon the stewpan till three parts cold, then take out the vanilla, pour the milk in the other stewpan upon the eggs and sugar, mix well together, and stir over the fire until becoming a little thick and adhering to the back of the spoon, but do not let it boil, pass through a tammie into a round bowl.

ICED CURAÇAO SOUFFLÉ

Serves 8

6 fl oz/¾ cup/175 ml Curaçao liqueur
12 fl oz/1½ cups/375 ml heavy/double cream, stiffly whipped
3 large macaroons, crushed to fine crumbs
FOR THE CUSTARD:
1 pint/2½ cups/600 ml milk
1 vanilla bean, split, or 1 tsp vanilla extract/essence
¼ oz/1 tbsp/7 g gelatin
2 fl oz/¼ cup/60 ml water
6 egg yolks
3 tbsp sugar
FOR THE MERINGUE:
3¼ oz/½ cup/100 g sugar
4 fl oz/½ cup/125 ml water
5 egg whites
1 liter soufflé dish or 8 individual ramekins

1. Tie a paper collar around the dishes to reach well above the rim.
2. For the custard: scald the milk. If using vanilla bean, scald the milk with the bean, cover, and leave to infuse for 10-15 minutes. Sprinkle the gelatin over the water and let stand until spongy, about 5 minutes. Beat the egg yolks with the sugar until light and slightly thickened. Stir in the hot milk, return the mixture to the pan and heat gently, stirring, until the custard thickens. Take at once from the heat. Note: do not allow the custard to boil or it will curdle. Discard the vanilla bean; if using vanilla extract, add it now. Let the custard cool slightly, then stir in the softened gelatin. Strain the custard and chill over a bowl of ice water or in the freezer, stirring it occasionally and adding the Curaçao when cool.

3. For the meringue: heat the sugar with the water until dissolved, bring to a boil and cook until the syrup reaches 257°F/125°C on a sugar thermometer. Meanwhile stiffly whip the egg whites. Pour the hot syrup on to the egg whites, beating constantly, and continue beating until the meringue is glossy and cool.
4. Fold the custard into the cool meringue, then gently fold in the whipped cream. Spoon the mixture into the soufflé dishes so it comes well above the edge of the dishes. Sprinkle with macaroon crumbs and freeze until firm, 4-5 hours.
5. If freezing the soufflé for more than 24 hours, transfer them to the refrigerator for 1-2 hours before serving so the consistency softens slightly. Remove the paper collars just before serving.

ISABELLA BEETON

1836–1865

THE MOST SUCCESSFUL EURO-
pean cookbook ever published is *Household Management*
by Isabella Beeton. Always referred to simply as "Mrs
Beeton", the book has been repeatedly updated in succes-
sive editions and is still in print today, more than 100
years after the original was written. Even more astonishingly, though the book packed over 1,500 recipes into an
exhaustive survey of every imaginable household art
from selecting servants to table setting, Mrs Beeton was
only twenty-four when she produced it.

Into that twenty-four years she had crammed more
practical experience than most women have in a lifetime.
Isabella Mary Mayson was born in London in 1836, the
eldest daughter of what was to become a family of
twenty-one children. When she was four her father died
and her mother, left with four small girls, soon remarried.
Bella's stepfather was Henry Dorling, clerk of the racecourse at Epsom and a widower
who also had four children. As the
family expanded, they overflowed
into what must be one of the most
unconventional dwellings on
record – the racecourse grandstand.
In other respects, however, their
upbringing was typical of the
Victorian middle class: Bella was
coached by excellent masters (an
education that was to stand her in
good stead) and as she grew older
she must have been entrusted with
much of the housekeeping. In one
of her letters she complains that no
sooner had one small brother or

sister been nursed back to health, than it was the turn of
another to fall sick.

By the time she met Samuel Beeton at the age of
nineteen, Bella was a self-confident, handsome young
woman with blue eyes, whose humor failed to conceal the
strength of her nose and chin. Sam was Bella's perfect
complement – brilliant, mercurial, and a trifle neurotic,
but with a rising reputation as a young publisher. Alone,
neither would have achieved the success they did. Determined to be a model wife, Bella set herself to learning the
theory of cooking and housewifery, and scarcely was she
married in 1856 than Sam set her to work on *The English-
woman's Domestic Magazine*.

This publication was one of several that appealed to
the new middle class of the industrial age. Thrift and respectability ruled their lives, so the magazine debated
such questions as "Can we live on £300 a year?" and tire-
lessly instructed ladies in dress-
making, bead-work, and the
improvement of their minds. On
this subject Mrs Beeton has surprisingly liberated views, extolling
America, where women can
become "preachers, public speak-
ers, lecturers and medical practi-
tioners." One of the most successful features of *The Domestic
Magazine* was a correspondence
column of readers' letters and
recipes – there was even a "soup *à
la cantatrice*," dubbed "good for the
voice," contributed by the singer
Jenny Lind.

OPPOSITE: *Victorian prosperity shows clearly
in this 1865 picture of Leadenhall meat and
poultry market, whose links with the City of
London dated to 1411.*

TEA TABLE.

*This illustration from a turn-of-the-century
edition of Mrs. Beeton's* Household
Management *shows how the Victorian
custom of loading the dinner table with a
profusion of silver* épergnes, *flowers, and
dishes also extended to tea time.*

Borrowing ideas from other authors such as the respected Eliza Acton, Mrs Beeton was able to embark on her master work. She claimed to have tried all the recipes in *Household Management*, though it is hard to believe that in the midst of constant writing, trips abroad with her husband, and the birth of two children (both of whom died in infancy), she could also have found time to test an average of fifteen recipes a week for two years. The work was overwhelming and Mrs Beeton was the first to admit it. "I must frankly own," she declares in her preface to *Household Management*, "that if I had known beforehand that this book would have cost me the labour it has, I should never have been courageous enough to commence it."

Household Management appeared in installments in 1859 and as a book in 1860. It is a pleasure to read. In contrast to the flowery phrases that were then the fashion, Mrs Beeton writes succinctly and with an enviable fluency. She strikes just the right note of reassuring authority and she has a sense of order which places her far ahead of her competitors. She is the first to list the quantities of ingredients, cooking time, and servings with every recipe.

Much of the generation to whom *Household Management* was addressed had been born and bred in towns, so Mrs Beeton carefully states the approximate season for each recipe (something that any country woman would have known from childhood) and directs her readers how to do their marketing. Naturally she devotes little space to preserving, the pride of the country housewife, as it presupposes a well-stocked kitchen garden. Convenience foods like mushroom ketchup are given Mrs Beeton's

The royal family led the fashion for picnics for which Mrs. Beeton caters with such gusto. Her picnic for forty included a dozen different meats, six pounds of butter, and no fewer than ten dozen bottles of liquid refreshments. No wonder she advised packing three corkscrews.

blessing, as is baking powder, which had been commercially available since about 1850. Before then cooks used an unreliable mixture of baking soda and an acid ingredient like buttermilk or molasses.

Mrs Beeton does her best to anticipate every eventuality, and many a modern hostess would agree with her that "The half-hour before dinner has always been considered as the great ordeal through which the mistress, in giving a dinner-party, will either pass with flying colours, or lose many of her laurels." She is at her best on picnics, a recreation the Victorians pursued with unflagging energy despite the inclement English weather. Mrs Beeton's "bill of fare for a picnic of 40 persons" includes six roasts of lamb and beef, a ham, various roast birds, several assorted pies and salads, and

a collared calf's head, not to mention more than seventeen dozen puddings, cakes, and breads, plus half a pound of tea. That indispensable English accompaniment to lamb, "a bottle of mint sauce, well corked," is not forgotten, nor is a mysterious stick of horseradish – surely not to be grated on the spot. The staggering beverage allowance of ten dozen bottles, both alcoholic and non-alcoholic, certainly necessitated her laconic instruction to "take three corkscrews."

The fact that forty should be considered a normal number for a picnic reflects the size of the average Victorian family; Mrs Beeton's flock of twenty brothers and sisters was unusual even for those days, but several offspring, plus the odd maiden aunt or two, made ten at table a normal occurrence. Mrs Beeton casts a fascinating

OPPOSITE: *Billingsgate fish market in the heart of cockney London. The name is apparently derived from "bawling (bellan) quay". In Mrs. Beeton's time, "That's Billingsgate" denoted vulgar and coarse language.*
BELOW: *No detail of the family Christmas dinner is lost in this sentimental Victorian print: "Christmas comes but once a year."*

light on the life of such households. A family whose income is £1,000 a year, she says, might expect to employ a cook, an upper housemaid, nursemaid, under house-maid and a manservant at a total cost of between £60 and £65 a year. "It is desirable," she cautions, "unless an experienced and confidential housekeeper be kept, that the mistress should herself purchase all provisions and stores for the house."

Youngsters ate in the nursery and Mrs Beeton recommends her simplest cakes as "suitable for children" and even gives them their own Christmas pudding (page 182). The French chef Ude, who worked in England earlier in the century, was convinced that this habit of limiting children to plain food "so they are not intro-duced to their parents' table till their palates have been completely benumbed by the strict diet observed in the Nursery and Boarding-Schools," was responsible for the generally abysmal standard of English cooking. Cocooned in the bourgeois world of the Victorian family, Mrs Beeton would not have agreed. Like her spiritual grandmother, Hannah Glasse, nothing can shake her conviction that "British is Best."

This chauvinism was encouraged by the queen, to judge from the books written by her cook, Charles Francatelli, who favored dishes *à l'anglaise* (plainly boiled). Francatelli's forte was desserts, and in *The Royal Confectioner*, published in 1856, he advocates the curious custom (also described by Mrs Beeton) of setting out dessert before a dinner begins. "Fashion, upheld by good sense, in placing the dessert permanently on the table before the company are seated, has introduced a benefi-cial as well as a charming innovation." Francatelli's cakes, creams, and compotes are by no means as elaborate as Carême's, but one still wonders how they held up in the heat and jostle of a grand dinner which could last for three or four hours.

Grand as these French cooks were, Mrs Beeton far outdid them in scope and to this day none has bettered her thorough grasp of the subject. *Household Management* immediately proved the type of bestseller for which all

publishers yearn. From the first it needed no advertising; sales picked up steadily by word of mouth, then continued year after bumper year. Sam lost no time in making the most of such a hot property. Isabella had a third child, to their joy a healthy son. She revised *Household Management* yet again to appear as a dictionary, completing the work in January 1865. Two weeks later she died of puerperal fever after giving birth to their fourth child.

Samuel Beeton was overwhelmed; his financial affairs went from bad to worse and without his wife's steadying hand he was unable to cope. In 1886 he went bankrupt and was forced to sell his copyright to *Household Management*. Slowly the book began to shed its original contents to suit changing tastes. At the turn of the century, for example, Herman Senn, a professional chef, dropped many of Mrs Beeton's more basic dishes, substituting delicate little Edwardian molds and gar-

nishes. His example has been followed so relentlessly that in today's editions of *"Mrs Beeton"*, virtually the only trace remaining of the original author is her name. Happily a facsimile edition of the original was published on its centenary in 1968.

Written when the "dear Queen" was the proud symbol of British supremacy, *Household Management* reflects both the best and the worst of the Victorian age. Mrs Beeton can sound insufferably priggish when she lets her desire to instruct run away with her. Any housewife who could live up to her standards would be a paragon indeed. But it is impossible not to be interested by her recipes, amused by her anecdotes and happy turns of phrase, and amazed by the sheer overwhelming detail of the book. Nothing is forgotten, nothing left to chance, not even the temperature of the dining room, which (says Mrs Beeton) should be "about 68 degrees" – a directive which most English homes have studiously ignored.

BEETON RECIPES

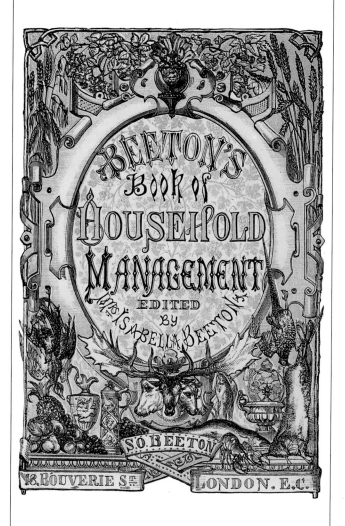

OPPOSITE: Moulded Pears.
ABOVE: The overflowing title page from
Household Management *is typical of the*
following 1,100 pages, each crammed with
forbiddingly tiny type that gives little hint of
Mrs. Beeton's liveliness of mind. Mrs. Beeton
died five years after it was published in 1860,
aged only 29.

Mrs Beeton's recipes, with their carefully listed ingredients, cooking time, servings, and approximate cost, have served as models for many years. She subordinates a very Victorian weakness for italics to the need for clarity – unlike the Queen herself, who peppered her writing with triple underlinings and exclamation marks. Several of her cooking methods may appear unorthodox, but they work perfectly in practice.

OX-TAIL SOUP

All traditional English cookbooks have two recipes for oxtail soup, one thick and the other clarified with egg white to make a consommé for special occasions. This is the thick, everyday version which is almost a meal in itself.

INGREDIENTS. – 2 ox-tails, 2 slices of ham, 1 oz. of butter, 2 carrots, 2 turnips, 3 onions, 1 leek, 1 head of celery, 1 bunch of savoury herbs, 1 bay-leaf, 12 whole peppercorns, 4 cloves, a tablespoonful of salt, 2 table-spoonfuls of ketchup, ½ glass of port wine, 3 quarts of water.

Mode. – Cut up the tails, separating them at the joints; wash them, and put them in a stewpan, with the butter. Cut the vegetables in slices, and add them with the peppercorns and herbs. Put in ½ pint of water, and stir it over a sharp fire till the juices are drawn. Fill up the stewpan with the water, and, when boiling, add the salt. Skim well, and simmer very gently for 4 hours, or until the tails are tender. Take them out, skim and strain the soup, thicken with flour, and flavour with the ketchup and port wine. Put back the tails, simmer for 5 minutes, and serve.

Time. – 4½ hours.

Average cost, *1s. 3d. per quart*.

Seasonable *in winter*

Sufficient *for 10 persons.*

OXTAIL SOUP

Serves 10

2 tbsp butter
2 oxtails (about 2 lb/1 kg each), cut in joints
8 oz/250 g uncooked lean ham, diced
2 carrots, sliced
2 medium white turnips, sliced
3 onions, sliced
1 large leek, sliced
small bunch of celery, sliced
2-3 sprigs parsley
1 tsp thyme
1 bay leaf
12 peppercorns
4 whole cloves
6 pints/3½ quarts/3.5 liters water
1 tbsp salt
2 fl oz/¼ cup/60 ml red port wine
2 tbsp tomato ketchup
FOR THE THICKENING:
2½ oz/⅓ cup/75 g butter
1½ oz/⅓ cup/45 g flour

1. In a large pan/kettle melt the butter and add the oxtails, ham, carrots, turnips, onions, leek, celery, parsley, thyme, bay leaf, peppercorns, cloves and about a quarter of the water. Cook over high heat, stirring, until the juices are drawn from the meat and have evaporated to form a thick brown liquid in the bottom of the pan. Add the remaining water, cover, and bring slowly to a boil. Skim well, add the salt, cover and simmer until the meat is very tender and falling off the bones, 4-5 hours. Skim the soup and stir it from time to time.

2. Take out the oxtails and reserve them. Strain the liquid and if possible chill it overnight so the fat solidifies on top. Skim off the fat; the liquid should measure about 4 pints/2½ quarts/2.5 liters but if it has evaporated too much add more water.

3. To thicken the soup, melt the butter in a saucepan and stir in the flour. Cook until well browned and stir in the liquid. Bring to the boil, stirring until it thickens, then replace the oxtails. Stir in the port. Mix a little of the hot liquid with the ketchup and stir into the soup. Taste for seasoning, simmer 5 minutes and serve.

BEEF-STEAKS AND OYSTER SAUCE

Oysters have long been used to enrich meat and poultry and they have only recently become expensive.

INGREDIENTS. – 3 dozen oysters, ingredients for oyster sauce, 2 lbs. of rump-steak, seasoning to taste of pepper and salt.
Mode. – Make the oyster sauce and when that is ready, put it by the side of the fire, but do not let it keep boiling. Have the steaks cut of an equal thickness, broil them over a very clear fire, turning them often, that the gravy may not escape. In about 8 minutes they will be done, when put them on a very hot dish; smother with the oyster sauce, and the remainder send to table in a tureen. Serve quickly.
Time. – *About 8 to 10 minutes, according to the thickness of the steak.*
Average cost, *1s. per lb.*
Sufficient *for 4 persons.*
Seasonable *from September to April.*

STEAK WITH OYSTER SAUCE

Serves 3
oyster sauce (see below)
3 rump/sirloin steaks, 1 inch/2.5 cm thick
salt and pepper

Make the sauce and keep it hot in a water bath; do not overcook it or the oysters will toughen. Sprinkle the steaks on each side with salt and pepper. Broil them about 4 inches/10 cm from the heat, allowing 3-4 minutes on each side for rare meat; turn them three or four times during cooking. Transfer the steaks to a hot serving dish, coat them with a little of the sauce, and serve the rest separately.

OYSTER SAUCE

It is amusing to find Mrs Beeton subscribing to the ancient fallacy that beating mixtures in one direction makes them lighter.

INGREDIENTS. – 3 dozen oysters, ½ pint of melted butter, made with 1 teaspoonful of flour, 2 oz butter, ⅓ pint of milk, a few grains of salt.
Mode. – Open the oysters carefully, and save their liquor; strain it into a clean saucepan (a lined one is best), put in the oysters, and let them just come to the boiling-point, when they should look plump. Take them off the fire immediately, and put the whole into a basin. Strain the liquor from them, mix with it sufficient milk to make ½ pint altogether, and make the sauce. Mix the butter and flour smoothly together on a plate, put it into a lined saucepan, and pour in the milk. Keep stirring it one way over a sharp fire, let it boil quickly for a minute or two. Put in the oysters, which should be previously bearded, if you wish the sauce to be really nice. Set it by the side of the fire to get thoroughly hot, *but do not allow it to boil,* or the oysters will immediately harden. Using cream instead of milk makes this sauce extremely delicious. When liked add a seasoning of cayenne, or anchovy sauce; but, as we have before stated, a plain sauce *should* be plain, and not be overpowered by highly-flavoured essences; therefore we recommend that the above directions be implicitly followed, and no seasoning added.
Average cost for this quantity, 2s.
Sufficient *for 6 persons. Never allow fewer than 6 oysters to 1 person, unless the party is very large.*
Seasonable *from September to April.*

OYSTER SAUCE

Makes 12 fl oz/1½ cups/375 ml sauce
12 fl oz/1½ cups/375 ml (about 18) shucked/ shelled oysters, with their liquor/liquid
4 fl oz/½ cup/125 ml milk, more if needed
2 tsp flour
2 tbsp butter
salt

Put the oysters with their liquor/liquid in a saucepan, bring them just to a boil – they should look plump – and let cool slightly. Strain off the liquor/liquid and add enough milk to make 6 fl oz/¾ cup/ 175 ml. Discard the rubbery ring (beard) from the oysters. Work the flour and butter on a plate with a fork until smooth. Put in a heavy-based pan with the milk and bring to a boil, stirring constantly. Simmer 2 minutes and take from the heat. Add the oysters and a little salt to taste. Serve at once.

MOULDED PEARS

This is one of the first mentions of commercial gelatin; before Mrs Beeton's time, cooks had to rely on the natural gelatin they could boil from bones, or on *isinglass* (prepared from fish) – a substance similar to gelatin but less easy to use.

INGREDIENTS. – 4 large pears or 6 small ones, 8 cloves, sugar to taste, water, a small piece of cinnamon, ¼ pint of raisin wine, a strip of lemon-peel, the juice of ½ lemon, ½ oz. of gelatine.
Mode. – Peel and cut the pears into quarters; put them into a jar with ¾ pint of water, cloves, cinnamon, and sufficient sugar to sweeten the whole nicely; cover down the top of the jar, and bake the pears in a gentle oven until perfectly tender, but do not allow them to break. When done, lay the pears in a plain mould, which should be well wetted, and boil ½ pint of the liquor the pears were baked in with the wine, lemon-peel, strained juice, and gelatine. Let these ingredients boil quickly for 5 minutes, then strain the liquid warm over the pears; put the mould in a cool place, and when the jelly is firm turn it out on a glass dish.
Time. – *2 hours to bake the pears in a cool oven.*
Average cost, *1s. 3d.*
Sufficient *for a quart mould.*
Seasonable *from August to February.*

Even in the nineteenth century pears were available nine months of the year thanks to early varieties and late-pickers which could be stored a month or two in a cool dry cellar.

PEAR MOLD

Serves 6
16 fl oz/2 cups/500 ml water
3¼ oz/½ cup/100 g sugar, or to taste
8 cloves
2 inch/5 cm piece cinnamon stick
4 large or 6 small firm pears
¼ oz/1 tbsp/7 g gelatin
strip of lemon peel
juice of ½ lemon
6 fl oz/¾ cup/175 ml red port wine
2⅓ pint/1½ quart/1.5 liter plain mold or deep dish

1. Heat the oven to No 2/300°F/150°C. Put the water, sugar (the amount needed depends on the sweetness of the pears), cloves, and cinnamon into a casserole or heatproof pot. Peel, core and halve the pears and put them at once into the syrup so they do not discolor. Cover tightly and bake in the heated oven until the pears are very tender; cooking time depends on their ripeness but will be at least an hour.
2. Let the pears cool slightly, then drain them, reserving the juice. Wet the mold and arrange the pears, rounded side down, in the bottom. Chill 3-4 tablespoons of the pear juice in a bowl, sprinkle over the gelatin, and let stand until spongy, about 5 minutes.

3. Put the remaining pear juice in a pan with the lemon peel, lemon juice, and port and simmer 5 minutes. Pour the hot liquid into the gelatin and stir until dissolved. Let cool to tepid, and strain some of the mixture over the pears to form a layer that just covers them. Chill until set, strain in the remaining liquid, and chill until firmly set.
4. To unmold the pears, dip the mold briefly in warm water. Wipe it dry and pull the mixture gently away from the sides of the mold with your fingers to break the airlock. Set a flat plate upside down on top, and unmold the pears on to the plate.

RHUBARB AND ORANGE JAM
(TO RESEMBLE *SCOTCH* MARMALADE)

Adding inexpensive rhubarb to stretch oranges is an economical ruse typical of Mrs Beeton, and so is the optimistic designation "to resemble Scotch marmalade," considered by many to be the best kind – perhaps because marmalade originated in Dundee. As it turns out, the unorthodox combination is at least as good as any citrus marmalade.

INGREDIENTS. – 1 quart of finely-cut rhubarb, 6 oranges, 1½ lb. of loaf sugar.
Mode. – Peel the oranges; remove as much of the white pith as possible, divide them, and take out the pips; slice the pulp into a preserving-pan, add the rind of half the oranges cut into thin strips, and the loaf sugar, which should be broken small. Peel the rhubarb, cut it into thin pieces, put it to the oranges and stir altogether over a gentle fire until the jam is done. Remove all the scum as it rises, put the preserve into pots, and, when cold, cover down. Should the rhubarb be very old, stew it alone for ¼ hour before the other ingredients are added.

Time. – ¾ to 1 hour.
Average cost, *from 6d. to 8d. per lb. pot.*
Seasonable *from February to April.*

This mid-nineteenth-century kitchen shows some effects of the industrial revolution; it is lighted by gas jets, metal items like the coalshuttle and molds abound, and the fire is enclosed behind bars, anticipating the closed range.

RHUBARB AND ORANGE JAM

Makes about two 16 oz/1 pint/500 ml jars of jam
6 navel oranges
2 lb/1 kg rhubarb, thinly sliced
1¼ lb/3 cups/600 g sugar
Heatproof glasses or jars, and paraffin wax

1. Using a vegetable peeler, remove the rind from 3 of the oranges and reserve. Using a serrated-edge knife and cutting with sawing motion, remove both rind and pith from the remaining 3 oranges and discard.
2. Heat the oven to No ½/250°F/120°C. Cut the reserved rind into thin slices and slice the orange flesh. Put them in a preserving pan with the rhubarb and heat gently, stirring, until the juice runs from the rhubarb. Meanwhile warm the sugar in the heated oven for 5-10 minutes.

3. Add the sugar to the orange and rhubarb mixture and heat gently, stirring until the sugar has dissolved. Bring to a boil and boil rapidly without stirring, skimming occasionally, until the jam gives a gel test.
4. Take from the heat, pour into hot sterilized jars, and let cool. When cold, seal with paraffin wax, cover with paper, and store in a cool, dry place.

CHRISTMAS PLUM-PUDDING (VERY GOOD)

The "few days" suggested by Mrs Beeton is the minimum time the pudding should be made ahead; like fruit cakes, the flavor of plum pudding matures if kept for several months. Mrs Beeton's note about preparing several puddings at once is typical of her practical approach to entertaining. Traditionally every member of the household stirs the mixture and charms are added – a bachelor's button, spinster's thimble, rich man's sovereign, lucky horseshoe, etc. – indicating the fortune of the finder when the pudding is served. Most modern recipes add 4 oz/ ½ cup/125 g sugar and spice to taste.

INGREDIENTS. – 1½ lb. of raisins, ½ lb. of currants, ½ lb. of mixed peel, ¾ lb. of bread crumbs, ¾ lb. of suet, 8 eggs, 1 wineglassful of brandy.
Mode. – Stone and cut the raisins in halves, but do not chop them; wash, pick, and dry the currants, and mince the suet finely; cut the candied peel into thin slices, and grate down the bread into fine crumbs. When all these dry ingredients are prepared, mix them well together; then moisten the mixture with the eggs, which should be well beaten, and the brandy; stir well, that everything may be very thoroughly blended, and *press* the pudding into a buttered mould; tie it down tightly with a floured cloth, and boil for 5 or 6 hours. It may be boiled in a cloth without a mould, and will require the same time allowed for cooking. As Christmas puddings are usually made a few days before they are required for table, when the pudding is taken out of the pot, hang it up immediately, and put a plate or saucer underneath to catch the water, that may drain from it. The day it is to be eaten, plunge it into boiling water, and keep it boiling for at least 2 hours; then turn it out of the mould, and serve with brandy-sauce. On Christmas-day a sprig of holly is usually placed in the middle of the pudding, and about a wineglassful of brandy poured round it, which, at the moment of serving, is lighted, and the pudding thus brought to table encircled in flame.
Time. – *5 or 6 hours the first time of boiling; 2 hours the day it is to be served.*
Average cost, *4s.*
Sufficient *for a quart mould for 7 or 8 persons.*
Seasonable *on the 25th December, and on various festive occasions till March.*
Note. – *Five or six of these puddings should be made at one time, as they will keep good for many weeks, and in cases where unexpected guests arrive, will be found an acceptable, and, as it only requires warming through, a quickly-prepared dish.*

CHRISTMAS PUDDING

Serves 10
8 slices (about 8 oz/250 g) white bread
1¼ lb/4 cups/600 g raisins
6 oz/1⅓ cups/175 g currants
3¼ oz/1 cup/100 g mixed chopped candied peel
12 oz/375 g beef suet, ground/minced
8 eggs, beaten to mix
4 fl oz/½ cup/125 ml brandy
FOR SERVING:
4 fl oz/½ cup/125 ml brandy
sprig of holly (for decoration)
3¼ pint/2 quart/2 liter heatproof ceramic mold or bowl

1. Butter the mold or bowl. Discard the crusts from the bread and work it to crumbs in a food processor or blender. In a large bowl put the raisins, currants, candied peel, suet and breadcrumbs and stir until thoroughly mixed. Add the eggs and brandy and continue stirring until well mixed. Spoon the mixture into the prepared mold, pressing each spoonful down well with the back of a spoon.
2. Cut a round of brown paper and one of foil 4 inches/10 cm larger than the rim of the mold or bowl. Butter the brown paper and put both rounds together, foil up. Make a 1 inch/2.5 cm pleat across the center (this allows for expansion) and lay over the mold or bowl, butter side down. Tie securely with string, leaving a loop for easy removal when cooked.
3. Put the mold on a rack in a deep saucepan, add a generous layer of boiling water and add the lid. Boil steadily for 5-6 hours, adding more water when necessary so the pan is never dry and the pudding cooks in steam. It is important that it should boil constantly. Lift out the pudding and let it cool. Discard the brown paper and foil, replace with freshly buttered paper and foil, and store in a dry place.
4. To serve: steam the pudding over boiling water for 2 hours longer. Turn it out on a hot plate. Heat the brandy, pour it over the pudding at the table, and flame. Top with a sprig of holly and serve at once with brandy sauce.

PLUM-PUDDING SAUCE

As Mrs Beeton says, this is a very rich and excellent sauce, a highly alcoholic version of the usual brandy butter or hard sauce.

INGREDIENTS. – 1 wineglassful of brandy, 2 oz. of very fresh butter, 1 glass of Madeira, pounded sugar to taste. Mode. – Put the pounded sugar in a basin, with part of the brandy and the butter; let it stand by the side of the fire until it is warm and the sugar and butter are dissolved; then add the rest of the brandy, with the Madeira. Either pour it over the pudding, or serve in a tureen. This is a very rich and excellent sauce.
Average cost, 1s. 3d. for this quantity.
Sufficient *for a pudding made for 6 persons.*

BRANDY SAUCE

Makes about 8 fl oz/1 cup/250 ml sauce, to serve 10
4 oz/½ cup/125 g butter
about 3¼ oz/½ cup/100 g sugar
3 fl oz/6 tbsp/90 ml brandy
3 fl oz/6 tbsp/90 ml Madeira

Put the butter and sugar in a saucepan with half the brandy and heat gently in a water bath, stirring constantly, until the sugar has dissolved and the mixture is very soft. Do not let it become too hot or the butter will be oily. Take it from the heat and stir in the remaining brandy and Madeira. Pour the sauce over the pudding or serve it in a separate sauceboat.

SCOTCH SHORTBREAD

Good shortbread, with its high proportion of butter, should have a crumbly, almost granular texture.

INGREDIENTS. – 2 lbs. of flour, 1 lb. of butter, ¼ lb. of pounded loaf sugar, ½ oz. of caraway seeds, 1 oz. of sweet almonds, a few strips of candied orange-peel.
Mode. – Beat the butter to a cream, gradually dredge in the flour, and add the sugar, caraway seeds, and sweet almonds, which should be blanched and cut into small pieces. Work the paste until it is quite smooth, and divide it into six pieces. Put each cake on a separate piece of paper, roll the paste out square to the thickness of about an inch, and pinch it upon all sides. Prick it well, and ornament with one or two strips of candied orange-peel. Put the cakes into a good oven, and bake them from 25 to 30 minutes.
Time. – 25 to 30 minutes.
Average cost, for this quantity, 2s.
Sufficient to make 6 cakes.
Seasonable at any time.
Note. – Where the flavour of caraway seeds is disliked, omit them, and add rather a larger proportion of candied peel.

SCOTCH SHORTBREAD

Makes two 6 inch/15 cm squares
8 oz/1 cup/250 g butter
12 oz/3 cups/375 g flour
1¾ oz/¼ cup/50 g sugar
1½ tsp caraway seeds, or 2 tbsp sliced or chopped candied orange peel
2 tbsp slivered almonds, finely chopped
1 tbsp sliced or chopped candied orange peel (for topping)

1. Heat the oven to No 4/350°F/175°C. Cream the butter, stir in the flour, sugar, caraway seeds if using, and chopped almonds, and work the mixture with your hand to form a ball. Turn it out on a floured marble slab or board and knead it with the heel of your hand until very smooth and it peels in one piece from the board.
2. Divide the mixture in two, set each piece on the baking sheet, and pat or roll it to a 6 inch/15 cm square. Pinch the edges to flute them and mark each square into bars. Press the candied peel lightly into the top. If omitting caraway seeds, add the extra portion of candied peel.
3. Bake the squares in the heated oven until very lightly browned, about 30 minutes. Let cool slightly, then cut along the lines to form bars. Transfer the shortbread to a rack to cool completely. Store it in an airtight container.

ORIGINAL MENUS

FANNIE FARMER

1857–1915

"COOKERY," WROTE FANNIE Merritt Farmer, "is the art of preparing food for the nourishment of the body." To that forthright if somewhat forbidding statement she added: "Progress in civilization has been accompanied by progress in cookery." The year was 1896, the place Boston – a city believed by many of its citizens to be "the hub of the universe" – and the writer a thirty-nine-year-old semi-invalid who had already earned a considerable reputation as the dynamic principal of the Boston Cooking School.

Fannie Farmer's rise to fame can be traced to a chance question about the "heaped" spoons and cups by which cooks had always measured ingredients. "Couldn't they be level?" asked one of her students. The alert Fannie, ever trying to take the guesswork out of cooking, was quick to realize the implications. She also outlawed such traditional measures as butter "the size of an egg" and "wineglasses" of liquid. By vigorous promotion through her school, books, newspaper columns, and lectures, she swept aside the remnants of the cumbersome European system of measuring ingredients by weight and set Americans firmly on the course of level measurement by volume.

Fannie Farmer was born in Boston in 1857, the eldest of the four daughters of John Franklin Farmer, "a stately man of great charm but little practical ability," according to his great-niece, Wilma

OPPOSITE: "Original Menus" from Curtice Brothers Co. of Rochester, New York, who were early into satisfying the American appetite for processed foods. This leaflet advertized sweet corn, "whole boneless ham", and tomato ketchup.

Lord Perkins. The Farmers were of "untainted New England stock, Unitarian and bookish" and the family was warm and close-knit. When she was thirteen, Fannie suffered a paralytic stroke that put an end to all hopes of a college education. For a time she was a paid mother's helper but everyone could see that her ability and determination destined her for a more challenging career. Fannie's married sister discovered a teacher-training school which did not require a high school diploma of its students, and in 1887, at the age of thirty, Fannie enrolled in the Boston Cooking School for a two-year course. After graduation she stayed on as assistant to the principal, who died a year later. The trustees then elected Fannie to replace her.

Despite Fannie's physical handicap – she was permanently lame – she proved an energetic and capable director. She encouraged her students to experiment with new dishes, she was constantly testing new products, and hardly surprising, she was passionately concerned with invalid cookery. "As a teacher," said Mrs Perkins, "Fannie was incomparable, if at times something of a trial to her devoted students. They used to sigh that she would almost always ask, after a recipe had been tested and retested, 'Could it be better?'"

Obsessed with accuracy, Fannie Farmer soon found inadequate the school textbook written by a predecessor, Mrs Lincoln. Not

185

only were the recipes too few to make it a comprehensive work of reference, but by Fannie's standards the instructions were scanty. She worked hard on a replacement, and her nephew Dexter Perkins, then a boy of six, remembers his aunt limping up and down the room as she dictated the manuscript to his mother. Family tradition has it that the day she delivered the manuscript to her chosen Boston publishing house (Little, Brown), Fannie dressed with care for once, even wearing white gloves.

Initially aloof, Little, Brown finally agreed to act as her agent. Fannie was to pay all the costs of producing the book, they were to supervise its production and distribution. According to Mrs Perkins, the book "remained in Fannie Farmer's possession" with royalties going to her. Little, Brown paid dearly for his doubts; when Fannie died in 1915, over half her $161,000 estate was in copyrights. Her cookbook has always been a bestseller; nearly four million copies, in 13 editions, have been published since the first order of 3,000 copies in 1896.

The reasons for the success of *The Boston Cooking-School Cook Book* are plain. Fannie's instructions are simple enough for any novice to follow and the measurements are precision itself. The recipes range from general favorites like doughnuts to such New England specialties as baked beans (page 194) and chowder, with a heavy emphasis on cakes and desserts. Fannie is firm on how to make good bread (a subject "of no small importance"), her instructions on broiling (grilling), boiling, and the like are exhaustive, and she is deeply interested in nutrition and the scientific principles lying behind cooking techniques. To some modern minds, however, Fannie may seem a kill-joy; the nearest she gets to admitting that eating can be a pleasure as well as a necessity is to suggest adding flowers to an invalid's tray.

For 70 years a theme of sobriety and thrift had dominated American household works, ever since Lydia Child had written *The American Frugal Housewife* in 1829 and dedicated it to "those who are not ashamed of economy." Mrs Child's contemporary and equal in influence, Eliza Leslie, was more easy-going, but her half-dozen works are also pervaded by an emphasis on respectability and virtue. Both ladies well knew how the vicissitudes of the American economy – banks that went

under, crops that failed – could fell the middle class. To these sermons on self-help, Catharine Beecher, whose sister wrote *Uncle Tom's Cabin*, added a tone of militancy. The two sisters founded several schools for girls, and in 1845 Catharine published *A Treatise on Domestic Economy for Use in the Home*, a pioneer work in home economics. "Let the young women of this nation find that domestic economy is placed in schools on equal or superior grounds to chemistry, philosophy, and mathematics, and they will blush to be found ignorant of its first principles," she proclaims.

These proselytizing ladies were active at a time of drastic change in the status of American women. Now that the land was tamed, a wife was no longer caught up with her husband in the adventures of settling America. The family, from being a self-contained unit that could, if need be, produce its own food, weave its own cloth, and make its own soap and candles, was in most areas becoming part of a more urban community. Now more intellectual skills were demanded of the housewife, plus the ability to adapt to the exigencies and allurements of town life. Lydia Child and Eliza Leslie deplored idle, spendthrift women. Their tactic was to elevate them to the status of "homemaker" and so emphasize the dignity and importance of their duties. Catharine Beecher was to improve upon this title by labeling the housewife a "domestic scientist." The conviction that household management was a serious subject to be learned in school rather than picked up at home is quite apparent from *The Boston Cooking-School Cook Book*, which is intended to be studied as a text as well as used in the kitchen.

After eleven years of running the Boston Cooking School, the restrictions of training teachers became irksome and Fannie opened her own "Miss Farmer's School of Cookery." She was a striking figure – blue eyes, pince-nez, red hair greying handsomely at the temples, "slender and firmly corseted", a student of 1912 has recalled. Her energy knew no bounds. In an interview to a French visitor, Jules Huret, she explained what her students learnt in 60 lessons.

"In the first course, we show them how to lay a fire, how to use a gas stove, how to cook potatoes and eggs and bake bread and apples, how to filter coffee, and how to make bread dough, simple soups and a few puddings.

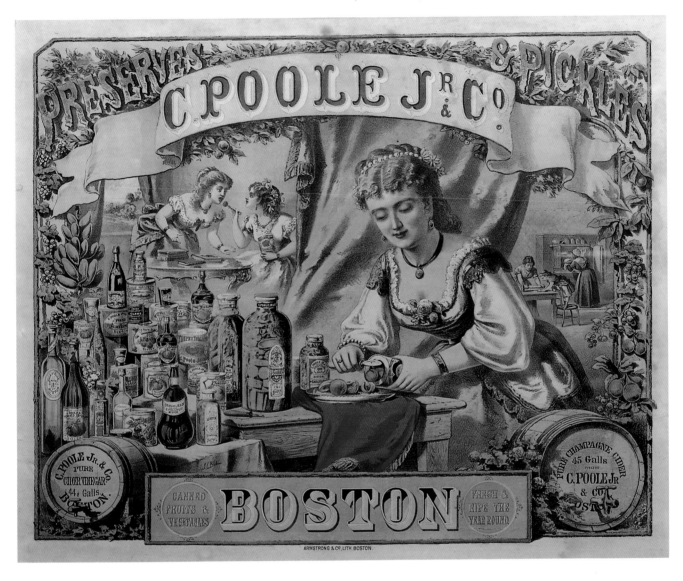

It was Nicolas Appert, a Frenchman, who
invented canning in the early 1800s, but it was
Americans of Fannie Farmer's time that
adopted the technology as their own.

The second and third course is more advanced cooking. The fourth is on pastries, salads and desserts. In the fifth course students learn how to serve, as before giving orders to others one must know how to carry them out oneself. So my students learn how to clean tables, polish floors, sweep up and dust, make butter balls, stack dishes, cups and glasses in cupboards, clean silver, arrange table decorations for all kinds of occasions, make Russian tea, English tea, iced tea, serve guests, make sandwiches, choose different wines and liqueurs – in a word, they learn French-style service.

The sixth course is cooking for nurses. I go with students into a hospital and do a demonstration in the public ward. Then I train them to do shopping, and to buy supplies. So they learn about prices. From time to time, French chefs come and help – those from the the best hotels in Boston, and sometimes from a tansatlantic liner. The chef from the *Touraine*, for instance, has come several times from New York between crossings, and gives lessons to my girls."

Fannie's reputation was by now considerable, and the demonstration lectures she gave twice weekly

By the late nineteenth century every well-equipped kitchen had its closed range, which provided oven and stovetop heat, and hot water. Keeping it clean, however, was an unenviable task.

attracted 200 people. Toward the end, when her illness recurred, she spoke from a wheelchair. Even in her younger days, an assistant did most of the cooking, partly to save Fannie's limited strength and partly, said Mrs Perkins, because "she was too impatient to cook a whole meal." She must often have been too busy; in a letter of 1912, she notes that "Miss Allen has two waitress's classes on Monday. One in the A.M. and one in the P.M. Next week we shall be running sixteen hospital classes, sixteen private-classes and we start our third marketing class. With the special lessons we are more than busy." She wrote regularly for *Woman's Home Companion*, and one year later she lectured in over 30 American cities.

Amid all these activities, which would have overtaxed many a healthier person, Fannie also found time to write half a dozen other cookbooks including her own favorite, *Food and Cookery for the Sick and Convalescent* (the subject of lectures she gave at the Harvard Medical School), and *A New Book of Cookery*, published in 1912. The latter book shows a different, more sophisticated side to her cooking – perhaps the result of the many visits she made with her family to New York restaurants, when each would order a different dish and taste carefully to guess the recipe. Dishes like jellied poached eggs, sweetbreads Lucullus (page 193) and coupe Caruso belong clearly to the French tradition that flourished at Delmonico's, the Astor, the Knickerbocker, and the Waldorf, whose dining room was then ruled by the legendary Oscar.

Turn-of-the-century America was a place of conspicuous consumption, and the more flourishing of Fannie Farmer's local readers put away a lot of food. Her typical family dinner menu called for soup, roast, an "entrée" or composed dish, vegetables, a salad, and dessert. Such abundant fare was typical of middle-class America, although the choice of dishes varied enormous-

ly, depending on local tradition and ethnic tastes. No country has had such a long and rich harvest of regional cookbooks as the United States – a heritage which dates back to 1824 (when Mrs Randolph wrote her classic *The Virginia Housewife*) and which still prospers today in the books and locally printed paperbacks of clubs and church groups. Even Fannie's *Boston Cooking-School Cook Book*, which from its first appearance in 1896 had a general appeal, still belonged unmistakably to New England, no less than Amelia Simmons's *American Cookery* written exactly a century earlier.

During that hundred years the average American kitchen had been transformed. The great open fireplace that was so wasteful of wood had vanished, and in its place stood a castiron range with an oven and space on top for heating pots. In the first edition of *The Boston Cooking-School Cook Book*, Fannie mentions only coal or wood as fuel for these stoves, but the Boston Gas Company had already opened a showroom in 1875. In those days before thermostats, the standard way to test the heat of an oven was with the hand. A student relates how, gold watch at the ready, Miss Farmer would time the moment when the heat forced her hand out of the oven, 20-30 seconds was the allowance for a "quick" oven and 45-60 seconds for a slow one. Into the oven, year round, went chickens raised in incubators and meat from cattle fattened by new feeding methods. Fruit and vegetables, now reaching the great American cities by train, were more likely to come fresh from the grocers than from the housekeeper's "put-up" winter stock of preserves. Ships no longer called at Boston to take ice from Wenham Lake to all corners of the earth; the technique of icemaking had been mastered and the domestic refrigerator was soon to arrive. The great food-processing and canning industries were developing, along with brand names like Knox's gelatin, Quaker rolled oats, and Baker's chocolate.

In England thirty years earlier, Mrs Beeton had been preoccupied with much the same revolution in household management, and there are many parallels between her book and Fannie Farmer's. Both women were writing for a family market where good living had to be combined with economy. Both were concerned with teaching the basics of cooking to a wide audience. But

where Mrs Beeton is chatty and digresses into the past, Fannie sticks firmly to the task immediately before her. In a world of increasing mechanization and uniformity, cooking was becoming an intellectual discipline which it was the duty of a conscientious housewife to assimilate, be she rich or poor. "It is my wish," Fannie wrote in her introduction to *The Boston Cooking-School Cook Book*, "that this book may not only be looked upon as a compilation of tried and tested recipes, but that it may awaken an interest through its condensed scientific knowledge which will lead to deeper thought and broader study of what to eat."

Carême would have applauded the sentiment, but he would have been astonished at the direction in which it led Fannie Farmer. The American insistence on accuracy in cooking is the antithesis of the free-wheeling French spirit in which chefs rarely measure ingredients but rely on experience and flair in putting them together. This contrast persists today; while Americans clamor for cookbooks with step-by-step instructions, the French housewife seems content with a few cursory remarks.

Despite the passage of almost eighty years, Fannie Farmer still commands an enormous following. First revised by Fannie herself to cover the use of gas and electric ranges, her book has been repeatedly updated, most recently by Marion Cunningham in 1979. Fannie Farmer may have had her limitations as a practical cook – ironically, the family considered her cooking talents inferior to those of her sister May and of the family housekeeper – but her gift for organization and for communicating ideas to others was outstanding, as was her business acumen. Today careers for women are taken for granted, but a hundred years ago a woman of Fannie Farmer's high visibility was rare. Her standards of precision have had an incalculable effect on modern American cooking, earning for Fannie Farmer a permanent place in the history of cooking as the "mother of level measurements."

Farmer Recipes

OPPOSITE: *Entire Wheat Bread.*
ABOVE: *The book we know as* Fannie Farmer *started life as the* Boston Cooking-School Cook Book *and remains a classic in millions of American households.*

Fannie Farmer's recipes follow the style we use today. Her instructions are terse and to the point and need little or no adaptation for the modern kitchen. Curiously, for someone so precise about measurements, she seldom says how many servings a recipe yields. Her vagueness about oven heat and baking times may be attributed to the idiosyncracies of the wood or coal burning ranges which required as much care and feeding as a household pet. However, later editions of her books did take into account the advances made in standardizing kitchen appliances, and readers knew if "Fannie" said a cake took thirty minutes to bake at 350°F in Boston, it probably took the same time in Boise, Idaho.

DEVILLED SCALLOPS

The American love of do-it-yourself cooking showed early and Fannie Farmer's *Chafing Dish Possibilities*, published in 1898, had a ready sale. This recipe exemplifies her sparing use of seasonings; seldom in her book does she call for more than salt and pepper, mustard, onions, shallots, and a few herbs such as parsley, thyme, and bay leaf.

Clean one pint scallops, heat to boiling point, drain, and reserve liquor. Melt three tablespoons butter, add two tablespoons flour, mixed with one-half teaspoon salt, one-fourth teaspoon mustard, and a few grains cayenne. Pour on gradually the reserved liquor. When sauce begins to thicken, add the scallops. Serve with brown bread sandwiches.

DEVILLED SCALLOPS

Serves 2
8 oz/1 cup/250 g bay or sea scallops with
    their liquor/liquid
3 tbsp butter
2 tbsp flour
½ tsp salt
¼ tsp dry mustard
pinch of cayenne
8 thin slices buttered whole wheat bread
    (for serving)

1. Add enough water to the scallop liquor/liquid to make 5 fl oz/⅔ cup/150 ml. Put the scallops with the liquor/liquid in a chafing dish or saucepan, heat until almost boiling, and drain, reserving the liquor/liquid.
2. Melt the butter in the pan, stir in the flour, salt, mustard and cayenne and cook until foaming. Add the liquor/liquid, blend well, and heat, stirring, until the sauce thickens. Add the scallops, turning them so they are well coated with sauce, and heat gently until very hot. Serve at once with thinly sliced bread and butter as accompaniment.

GLAZED SWEETBREADS LUCULLUS

Foreign cooking was not Fannie's forte – she cooks pasta to a mush and refers to French-style tournedos steaks as "tornadoes." However, Americans of her day did consume parts of the animal which are ignored today – sweetbreads, tripe, and brains – and in this respect, at least, the diet was closer to the European than it is now. In the following recipe, Fannie takes several shortcuts that would make a French chef shudder, like using canned artichokes, but the results amply justify her methods.

Trim sweetbread and parboil in Sherry wine until plump, the time required being about one-half hour. Keep covered during the cooking, turning twice. Cool and cut in pieces. Put one and one-half tablespoons butter in frying pan, and when melted add one-half teaspoon beef extract. Cook sweetbread in mixture until glazed, turning frequently. Drain canned artichoke bottoms and reheat; then arrange on circular pieces of sautéd bread. Place pieces of sweetbread on each and pour around Lucullus Sauce made by adding one cup chopped sautéd mushrooms to one cup tomato sauce.

Fannie Farmer, the "mother of level measurement", would have approved of this young cook's careful observation of his measuring cup. Note the patent egg beater.

GLAZED SWEETBREADS LUCULLUS

Serves 4
1½ lb/750 g (1½-2 pairs) sweetbreads
6 fl oz/¾ cup/175 ml sherry
2½ tbsp butter
½ tsp meat glaze
4 cooked artichoke bottoms
FOR THE CROÛTES:
4 slices bread
2 tbsp oil
2 tbsp butter
FOR THE LUCULLUS SAUCE:
8 oz/250 g mushrooms, chopped
1 tbsp butter
8 fl oz/1 cup/250 ml tomato sauce
salt and pepper

1. Soak the sweetbreads for 2-3 hours in cold water; drain and rinse them. Blanch them by putting in cold water, bringing to a boil and simmering 2 minutes. Drain them, rinse, and remove any ducts and skin. Put them in a small pan with the sherry, cover, and simmer until very tender, 25-35 minutes. Drain them, reserving the sherry for the sauce if you like. Press them between two plates and let cool. Cut the sweetbreads in thick slices.
2. For the croûtes: cut large rounds from the slices of bread, fry them in the oil and butter until brown on both sides, drain on paper towels and keep warm.

3. For the sauce: sauté the chopped mushrooms in the butter over low heat until all the moisture has evaporated; add the tomato sauce and reserved sherry, if using. Bring to a boil and add salt and pepper to taste.
4. To heat the artichoke bottoms, melt 1 tablespoon of the butter in a pan and heat the artichokes gently without browning. In a frying pan melt the remaining 1½ tablespoons butter, and add the meat glaze. Put in the sliced sweetbreads and sauté over medium heat, turning often, until glazed and golden brown. Set an artichoke bottom on each croûte, top with the sliced sweetbreads and arrange on a deep serving plate. Spoon around the sauce and serve.

BOSTON BAKED BEANS

This dish has survived from colonial days, when beans, pork, and molasses were among the most abundant staples in the kitchen. In Puritan households, the beans were baked all day Saturday to serve fresh in the evening; they were warmed over for Sunday breakfast and served cold for the midday meal, thus enabling the cook to observe the ban against working on the Sabbath.

Pick over one quart pea beans, cover with cold water, and soak over night. In morning, drain, cover with fresh water, heat slowly (keeping water below boiling point), and cook until skins will burst – which is best determined by taking a few beans on the tip of a spoon and blowing on them, when skins will burst if sufficiently cooked. Beans thus tested must, of course, be thrown away. Drain beans, throwing bean-water out of doors, not in sink. Scald rind of one-half pound fat salt pork, scrape, remove one-fourth inch slice and put in bottom of bean-pot. Cut through rind of remaining pork every one-half-inch, **making cuts one inch deep. Put beans in pot and bury pork in beans, leaving rind exposed. Mix one tablespoon salt, one tablespoon molasses, and three tablespoons sugar; add one cup boiling water, and pour over beans; then add enough more boiling water to cover beans. Cover bean-pot, put in oven, and bake slowly six or eight hours, uncovering the last hour of cooking, that rind may become brown and crisp. Add water as needed. Many feel sure that by adding with seasonings one-half tablespoon mustard, the beans are more easily digested.**

If pork mixed with lean is preferred, use less salt.
The fine reputation which Boston Baked Beans have gained, has been attributed to the earthen bean-pot with small top and bulging sides in which they are supposed to be cooked. Equally good beans have often been eaten where a five-pound lard pail was substituted for the broken beanpot.

Yellow-eyed beans are very good when baked.

The springtime sap running in the maple tree has long been cause for celebration. If snow is still on the ground, crystallized maple candy can be made on the spot.

BOSTON BAKED BEANS

Serves 10-12
2 lb/1 kg dried pea beans
8 oz/250 g fat salt pork
3 tbsp sugar
1 tbsp salt
1 tbsp molasses
1½ tsp dry mustard (optional)
1 gallon/5 quart/5 liter bean pot or deep casserole

1. Pick over the beans, cover with cold water, and leave to soak overnight. Drain them, put in a pan with water to cover, add the lid, and bring slowly to a boil. Cook, keeping just below boiling point, until the beans burst when a few are lifted on a spoon and you blow on them, 2-3 hours. Add more water during cooking if the beans get dry.
2. Heat the oven to No ½/250°F/120°C. Blanch the salt pork by bringing it to a boil in cold water. Drain it, score the rind deeply at ½ inch/1.25 cm intervals, and cut a thin slice from the bottom. Drain the beans, discarding the cooking liquid. Put the slice of pork in the bottom of the bean pot or casserole and add the beans – the pot should be almost filled. Bury the piece of pork in the beans, leaving the rind exposed. Mix the sugar, salt, molasses and mustard, if used, with a cup of boiling water and pour it over the beans. Add more boiling water to cover, add the lid and bake the beans in the heated oven for 6-8 hours, uncovering them during the last two hours so the pork rind becomes crisp.

FUDGE

Melt one tablespoon butter, add one-half cup milk and one and one half cups sugar; stir until sugar is dissolved, then add five tablespoons prepared cocoa, or two squares unsweetened chocolate. Stir constantly until chocolate is melted. Heat to boiling point and boil twelve minutes, stirring occasionally to prevent burning. Extinguish flame, add one teaspoon vanilla, and beat until the mixture is creamy. Pour into a buttered pan, cool, and mark in squares.

"Fudge" is an old English word but it came to denote a candy in America in Fannie Farmer's time. Processed chocolate like "Broma" was in great demand because candy-making was a popular pastime.

CHOCOLATE FUDGE

Makes 1½ lb/750 g fudge
2 oz/¼ cup/60 g butter
8 fl oz/1 cup/250 ml milk
1¼ lb/3 cups/600 g sugar
2½ oz/10 tbsp/75 g cocoa powder, or
  4 squares (4 oz/125 g) unsweetened
  chocolate, chopped
1 tsp vanilla extract/essence
8 inch/20 cm square cake pan/tin

1. Butter the pan/tin. Melt the butter in a large saucepan and add the milk and sugar. Cook over gentle heat, stirring, until the sugar dissolves. Add the cocoa powder or chopped chocolate and continue stirring over low heat until the cocoa dissolves or the chocolate melts. Bring to a boil and boil steadily until the mixture reaches the soft ball stage (240°F/115°C on a sugar thermometer).

2. Take from the heat and add the vanilla. Beat the fudge until the mixture loses its shine and stiffens slightly, 1-2 minutes. Do not overbeat or the fudge will harden. Pour at once into the prepared pan/tin and leave to cool slightly. Mark into squares with a knife.

ENTIRE WHEAT BREAD

Entire wheat flour, the equivalent of today's stone-ground whole wheat flour, was milled from the "entire" grain and so contained the protein-rich germ removed from all-purpose flour. As an invalid, Fannie had been more than casually interested in nutrition, and as a teacher she stressed the importance of protein "in the dietary," though she never mentioned vitamins, as they were not discovered until the twentieth century. *Gem pans are miniature loaf pans.*

**2 cups scalded milk.
¼ cup sugar or ⅓ cup molasses.
1 teaspoon salt.
¼ yeast cake dissolved in
¼ cup lukewarm water.
4⅓ cups entire wheat flour.**
Add sweetening and salt to milk, cool, and when lukewarm add dissolved yeast cake and flour; beat well, cover, and let rise to double its bulk. Again beat, and turn into greased bread pans, having pans one-half full; let rise, and bake. Entire Wheat Bread should not quite double its bulk during last rising. This mixture may be baked in gem pans.

A teacher training class at the Boston Cooking School lines up for the graduate photo, displaying the tools of their profession. Note the ingenious tabletop, which can be raised from a comfortable level for dining to worktop height.

WHOLE WHEAT BREAD

Makes 1 large loaf or 8 individual loaves
½ oz/15 g compressed yeast, or ¼ oz/7 g dry yeast
2 fl oz/¼ cup/60 ml lukewarm water
16 fl oz/2 cups/500 ml milk
1¾ oz/¼ cup/50 g sugar, or 2½ fl oz/ ⅓ cup/75 ml molasses
2 tsp salt
1½ lb/6 cups/750 g stone ground whole wheat flour, more if needed
1 egg beaten with ½ tsp salt (for glaze – optional)
9 × 5 × 4 inch/23 × 13 × 10 cm loaf pan/tin, or 8 individual loaf pans

1. Crumble or sprinkle the yeast over the warm water and let stand until dissolved, about 5 minutes. Scald the milk, let cool to tepid and stir in the sugar or molasses with the salt. Put the flour into a bowl, make a well in the center and add the yeast and milk mixtures. Stir with your hand and gradually draw in all the flour, adding more flour if necessary to make a soft, slightly sticky dough.
2. Sprinkle more flour on a board. Turn the dough on to the board and knead it, working in the flour, until smooth and elastic, about 5 minutes. Put the dough in a greased bowl, turn it so the top is greased also and cover with a damp cloth. Put the dough to rise in a warm place until doubled, 1-1½ hours.
3. Grease the loaf pans and heat the oven to No 6/400°F/200°C for small loaves or No 5/375°F/190°C for one large loaf. Knead the dough lightly to knock out the air, shape it into 1 large or 8 small loaves, and set in the pans – they should be filled half full. Cover and leave the dough to rise again almost to the top of the pans, 25-35 minutes. Brush the loaves with egg glaze. Bake in the heated oven until the bread sounds hollow when tapped on the bottom, allowing 30-35 minutes for small loaves or 55-60 minutes for one large loaf. Cool the loaves on a wire rack.

CREAM PIE

Cream pie is not a pie at all, but a cake baked in layer pans. Originally, it was probably baked in a pie pan. This recipe is typical of Fannie Farmer's many cake recipes; accurate though she was about spoon and cup measurements, it was not until later editions that she added details on the size of cake pans or baking temperatures.

⅓ cup butter.
1 cup sugar.
2 eggs.
½ cup milk.
1¾ cups flour.
2½ teaspoons baking powder.

Cream the butter, add sugar gradually, and eggs well beaten. Mix and sift flour and baking powder, add alternately with milk to first mixture. Bake in round layer cake pans. Put Cream Filling between layers and sprinkle top with powdered sugar.

BOSTON CREAM PIE

Makes one 9 inch/22 cm cake
2½ oz/⅓ cup/75 g butter
6½ oz/1 cup/200 g sugar
2 eggs, beaten to mix
7¼ oz/1¾ cups/225 g flour
2½ tsp baking powder
4 fl oz/½ cup/125 ml milk
French cream filling (see below)
confectioners'/icing sugar (for sprinkling)
Three 9 inch/22 cm cake pans/tins

1. Heat the oven to No 4/350°F/175°C. Butter and flour the cake pans/tins. Cream the butter, gradually beat in the sugar, and continue beating until the mixture is blended thoroughly. Gradually beat in the eggs, a little at a time, and beat until the mixture is smooth and light. Sift the flour with the baking powder. Stir the flour into the egg mixture in three batches, alternating with the milk.

2. Divide the mixture among the three prepared pans/tins and spread evenly over the bottom. Bake in the heated oven until the cake springs back when lightly pressed with a fingertip and draws away from the sides of the pan, 25-30 minutes. Turn the cakes out on to a rack to cool.
3. A short time before serving, sandwich the cake layers with the French cream filling. Sprinkle the top generously with confectioners'/icing sugar and set on a serving plate.

FRENCH CREAM FILLING

Fannie was not above endorsing selected products or equipment. The Dover egg beater mentioned in this recipe was one favored utensil.

¾ cup thick cream.
¼ cup milk.
¼ cup powdered sugar.

White one egg.
½ teaspoon vanilla.

Dilute cream with milk and beat until stiff, using Dover egg-beater. Add sugar, white of egg beaten until stiff, and vanilla.

FRENCH CREAM FILLING

Makes about 16 fl oz/2 cups/500 ml of filling
8 fl oz/1 cup/250 ml heavy/double cream
1 oz/¼ cup/30 g confectioners'/icing sugar
few drops/½ teaspoon vanilla extract/
*   essence*
1 egg white

Beat the cream until it holds a soft peak, add the sugar and vanilla extract/essence, and continue beating until stiff. Stiffly beat the egg white and fold into the cream. Use within 2 hours.

AUGUSTE ESCOFFIER

1846–1935

Escoffier has been hailed as the king of chefs and the chef of kings. He was the undisputed culinary leader in the thirty years before World War I, when crowned heads, led by the Prince of Wales, toured the fashionable resorts of Europe accompanied by the beauties of the day, and when the *Wagons-Lits* company ran a winter service from St Petersburg to Cannes. Escoffier was also the chef of chefs, redefining French cooking by reducing to essentials the elaborate structure of *haute cuisine* inherited from Carême.

London, Paris, Cannes, Monte Carlo, Nice, Lucerne – at one time or another between 1880 and the war, Escoffier headed the finest kitchens in them all. The situation was very different from the days of Carême – restaurants, from being a generally inferior alternative to dining at home, had taken the lead. No longer did the great chefs work in private houses for individual masters; instead the masters came to them in their restaurants and hotels. At the Café Anglais in Paris, headed by chef Dugléré of *sole Dugléré* fame, "one supped until midnight, the backcarat lasted until dawn and the Russian princes broke the house glasses with blows from the bottles of Champagne."

The achievements of Escoffier are hard to separate from those of César Ritz, the great hotelier whom Escoffier met in 1880 at a providential moment in his career.

OPPOSITE: This menu design by Alphonse Mucha (1860-1939) catches the spirit of the Belle Epoque – which was also Escoffier's heyday. Dishes such as Poulardes à l'Ivoire *and* Glace Coupe de Bohème *are typical of the time.*

Escoffier was thirty-four, with a thorough training behind him, but at the time of this meeting there seems to have been little hint of his special gifts. After a six-year apprenticeship at his uncle's restaurant in Nice (near Escoffier's home village of Villeneuve-Loubet), Escoffier had gone to Paris when he was nineteen, spending the next five years at the fashionable Le Petit Moulin. Later he admitted how hard he found the work; a sensitive man, the conditions of a busy kitchen with its incessant din and vulgar behavior were hard to bear. Worse still, being of small stature, Escoffier was forced to wear platform shoes to avoid suffocation by the burning heat of the stovetops. At the time of the siege of Paris in 1870 (famous for its culinary curiosities as the hungry population began to deplete the zoo), he was drafted as *chef de cuisine* at the headquarters of the Rhine army in Metz. Metz too was put under siege. "Horsemeat," Escoffier later remarked, "is delicious when you are in the condition to appreciate it . . . and as to rat meat, it approaches in delicacy the taste of roast pig."

Soon after this war ended Escoffier returned to Paris where he spent six years as head chef of Le Petit Moulin, followed by posts in several top restaurants. Then, at the height of the winter season at the Grand Hotel in Monte Carlo, César Ritz lost his chef Giroix to the rival Hotel de Paris. Escoffier

was called in, and so began the great partnership. In the next six years Escoffier divided his time between Monte Carlo and Ritz's Grand National Hotel in Lucerne, resorts frequented by such celebrities as the Emperor of Austria and the Prince of Wales, for whom Escoffier created his *poularde Derby*. Ritz was past master at attracting such a glittering clientele; his unerring chic was combined with a gift for making each guest personally welcome, to which Escoffier added the further seduction of his superb cuisine.

Escoffier cut down on the cumbersome garnishes that had survived from the eighteenth century, substituting instead a few simply-cooked vegetables and a sprinkling of parsley, insisting that all must be edible. He gave up the ornamental *hâtelets* (skewers) impaled with truffles, cockscombs, and crayfish, and the elaborate *socles* on which food had been mounted so as to be more impressively displayed. Food, he believed, should look like food. He had an equal abhorrence of a profusion of flavors and aimed instead to achieve the perfect balance of a few superb ingredients. Typical was his *sole Alice* (page 207), where sole, poached in wine, is heated in a chafing dish in a sauce flavored with shallots and thyme, to which oysters are added at the last moment. Escoffier quickly pointed out that his simplifications marked a development, not a decline, in the art of cooking: "What already existed in the time of Carême, which still exists in our time, and which will continue as long as cooking itself," he declared, "is the *fonds* [foundation] of that cooking. Because it is simplified on the surface, it does not lose its value. On the contrary, tastes are constantly being refined and cooking must be refined to satisfy them."

In 1889 the Ritz-Escoffier team took over the Savoy Hotel in London. By now their reputation was unrivaled, and they were followed at once by the Rothschilds, the Vanderbilts, the Morgans, the Crespis, and the rest of the *beau monde*. Escoffier was kept busy with his new dishes – *coupe Yvette*, *poularde Adelina Patti*, *consommé favori de Sarah Bernhardt*, and *salade Tosca* are just a few of the hundreds of creations of his fertile imagination.

Ritz, with his inimitable style, had persuaded ladies to dine in public for the first time; professional beauties like Lily Langtry were often to be seen at the Savoy, and Nellie Melba lived there whenever she was singing across the way at Covent Garden. It was after her performance in *Lohengrin* that Escoffier served the first version of *pêches Melba* (page 210) – poached peaches on a bed of vanilla ice cream set in a swan of ice, recalling the swan in the Wagnerian opera. (Not for several years did Escoffier add the crowning touch of fresh raspberry sauce.) When Ritz opened his hotel in the Place Vendôme in 1896, the story was the same, and all Paris flocked to sample Escoffier's cuisine.

In 1898 César Ritz opened the Carlton Hotel in London, where he was joined by Escoffier. Apparently moving from triumph to triumph, both of them had in fact been fired by the Savoy for theft and fraud involving back-handed dealings with suppliers and systematic re-sale of inventory. The Savoy company records note "the astounding disappearance of over £3,400 of wine and spirits in the first half of 1897". They also contain confessions, signed in January 1900 by Ritz, Escoffier and two other former employees, admitting to larceny.

The miscreants would have faced prison had the Savoy brought charges, but instead management chose to keep the affair quiet. One of Britain's leading food columnists, Paul Levy, who in 1985 discovered the secret archive at the Savoy, surmises that Ritz and Escoffier knew too much about other goings-on at the hotel – not least, the nocturnal escapades of the Prince of Wales, soon to be King Edward VII. The hotel bought their silence and, not surprisingly, they kept it.

The year 1902 is a landmark in culinary history because it marked the publication of Escoffier's first book, *Le Guide culinaire*. This is an astounding compendium of classic recipes and garnishes – over 5,000 in all. Starting with the *fonds* – the basic sauces, stocks, and pastries – Escoffier builds them like bricks into the great dishes for which he and the chefs before him were so famous. "A tool rather than a book" was his stated aim, and behind its somewhat forbidding façade of technicality lie forty years of practical experience in making almost every dish. What it is not, is a guide for the private kitchen. Even a layman who can follow the recipes would still be hard pressed to reproduce them at home. For example, the recipe for one of Escoffier's specialities, *tournedos Rossini*, in the space of five lines uses two technical terms (*sauter* and *déglacer*), two basic prepara-

tions (meat-glaze and demi-glace sauce) which take hours of advance cooking and which themselves demand other basic preparations, and an ingredient (fresh foie gras) which is a luxury even in Paris. To the professional chef, however, who knows cooking terms intimately and has all the basic sauces ready at hand, *Le Guide culinaire* is the perfect quick guide to thousands of classic recipes – it is indeed the "constant companion" that Escoffier hoped it would become.

Escoffier was not without his critics. "It would be difficult to serve these *suprêmes* in the way they were created," remarked a cookbook called *La grande cuisine illustrée*, referring to an Escoffier dish *suprêmes de volailles Otéro*. "Their only originality, hardly a recommendation, was to be placed on croûtons cut from truffles of which the smallest must have weighed a pound after peeling." The writers were two young chefs, Prosper Montagné and Prosper Salles, both trained under Giroix, Escoffier's rival in Monte Carlo. Their book shows even more clearly than *Le Guide culinaire* (which appeared two years later) how far cooking developed from the fulsome *pièces montées* of mid-century. However, theirs was a less comprehensive work than Escoffier's and never earned the same fame for its authors. It was more than thirty-five years before

With the help of César Ritz, Escoffier created a setting of unparalleled elegance at the Savoy Hotel. However, the two cannot have been pleased when a novice waiter tipped a dish of peas down a lady's dress. Stammering in broken English, the poor man tried to retrieve them one by one until he was knocked down by her outraged husband.

Prosper Montagné proved himself Escoffier's equal in influence and prestige as author of *Larousse gastronomique*, the outstanding encyclopedia of cookery to which Escoffier contributed a generous introduction just before his death.

Escoffier's greatest innovations were in menu-planning, which had already begun to change shortly after Carême's death in 1833. For hundreds of years, dinners had been served in the style called *à la française*, with a large number of different dishes set out on the table at once. The dishes might be changed twice or even three times to make three or four courses. The basic idea was to make an impressive show of luxury, with as great a variety of dishes as possible – a principle dating from medieval banquets.

Service à la russe, which gradually replaced *service à la française*, is the practice we know today of serving dishes consequently rather than simultaneously. It has two great advantages: food is served at once while at its best, and wastage is reduced because quantities can be estimated better. It is also more just, for each diner has a taste of every dish, rather than only sampling those nearest to him on the table. Carême had come across *service à la russe* during his time in Russia and it did not suit his love of show. "This manner of service is certainly

*Escoffier trained in bustling kitchens like these of Paris's Café Riche, shown in the 1860s. On the left, notice the **garde-manger**, set well away from the stove's heat, and the glass-enclosed office from which the head chef could command the kitchen.*

beneficial to good cooking," he admitted, "but our service in France is much more elegant and of a far grander and more sumptuous style."

For this reason *service à la russe* was slow to spread and it was not until 1856, when Urbain Dubois, who had cooked for twenty years in Russia, produced his massive *La Cuisine classique* with Emile Bernard (both "men of genius" in Escoffier's eyes) that the method caught on. By the 1870s, when Escoffier appeared on the scene, *service à la russe* was universal, enabling him to drastically reduce the number of dishes in his menus.

In *Le Livre des menus*, published in 1912, Escoffier outlines the principles that should underline a well-

planned meal: it should be appropriate to the occasion and to the guests; the season should always be borne in mind; if time is limited, the menu should be as well, and in any case a superfluity of courses should be avoided. A typical winter dinner served at the Carlton Hotel consisted of: blini and caviar; consommé; sole in white wine sauce; partridge and noodles with foie gras; lamb *noisettes* with artichoke hearts and peas; champagne sherbet (all such menus were broken up by a tart wine or fruit sherbet to refresh the palate); turkey with truffles; endive and asparagus salad; and various desserts. Even allowing for smaller helpings, such a repast is lavish by our standards, but nonetheless it called for but a fraction

of the dishes that Carême would have served for a comparable meal *à la française*.

Grey-haired and gentle of manner – according to Madame Ritz he "looked like a man of letters" – Escoffier would leave the kitchen rather than lose his temper with an erring subordinate. In this he was very different from the traditional loud-mouthed chef. At the beginning of his career, the profession had not been highly regarded, and with his own unhappy apprenticeship in mind, Escoffier was determined to improve it. He forbade the swearing and general brutality that had been the rule, insisting that a well-organised kitchen should at all times be calm. He himself never raised his voice and, symbolically, he changed the name of the *aboyeur* who barked out orders to *annonceur*. About the appalling heat he could do little, but he saw to it that a cauldron of barley water was always available for quenching thirst, thus cutting down on the consumption of beer and wine, the cook's habitual failing.

Even more important was Escoffier's revision of kitchen organization. Since medieval times, kitchen staff had been divided into sections, each of which was more or less independent. This meant that general preparations like sauces or pastry might be made several times by different sections – a wasteful duplication that also made quality hard to control. Escoffier reorganized his kitchens into five main areas, called *parties*, each dependent on the others. The *pâtissier* produced the pastry for every *partie*, the *garde-manger* supervised the cold dishes and supplies for the whole kitchen, while hot dishes came either from the *entremettier* (in charge of soups, vegetables, and desserts), or from the *rôtisseur*, responsible for roasts and broiled and fried dishes. Second in command under Escoffier, as befitted his importance, was the *saucier*. When a dish was ordered, not only could it be rapidly assembled by the appropriate *parties*, but Escoffier could more easily keep an eye on the finished result.

Though generally regarded as an exponent of the *grande cuisine* found in restaurants, Escoffier was able to translate his skills to a small domestic kitchen. Thanks to prompting from his publisher, Henri Flammarion, *Ma Cuisine* was published in 1934. It is an admirable survey of the *cuisine bourgeoise* that is still so popular today – the *soupe à l'oignon*, *brandade de morue*, and *blanquette de veau*

that are the backbone of French family cooking. The book is almost as comprehensive as *Le Guide culinaire* and much more usable. In Escoffier's own words, "It is not a simple aide-memoire, but truly a cookbook with recipes that are practical and as clear as possible." Nonetheless Escoffier takes for granted considerable cooking knowledge – he gives some quantities but not in a systematic manner. He makes no mention of oven heats, cooking times, or number of servings.

Escoffier remained at the Ritz Carlton until the end of World War I, retiring to Monte Carlo to join his wife when he was 73. He had spared little time for his family (he had three children) but he could look back on six decades of total commitment to cooking. In recent years, his style has been condemned as too elaborate, designed for a rich elite and requiring a prohibitive amount of labor. Nonetheless I believe Escoffier still ranks as the outstanding chef of the last hundred years. His *Guide culinaire* remains a primary reference book for the profession and none of the current generation of chef's cookbooks, charming and colorful though they may be, has succeeded in ousting it. In his day Escoffier was as revolutionary as the 1960s leaders of *nouvelle cuisine*. It is to him that we owe the familiar shape of modern menus, many of our favorite dishes. Above all, it is Escoffier who finally put an end to the medieval principle of luxuriant display. After 500 years, quantity had at last surrendered to quality, and gluttony to gourmandise.

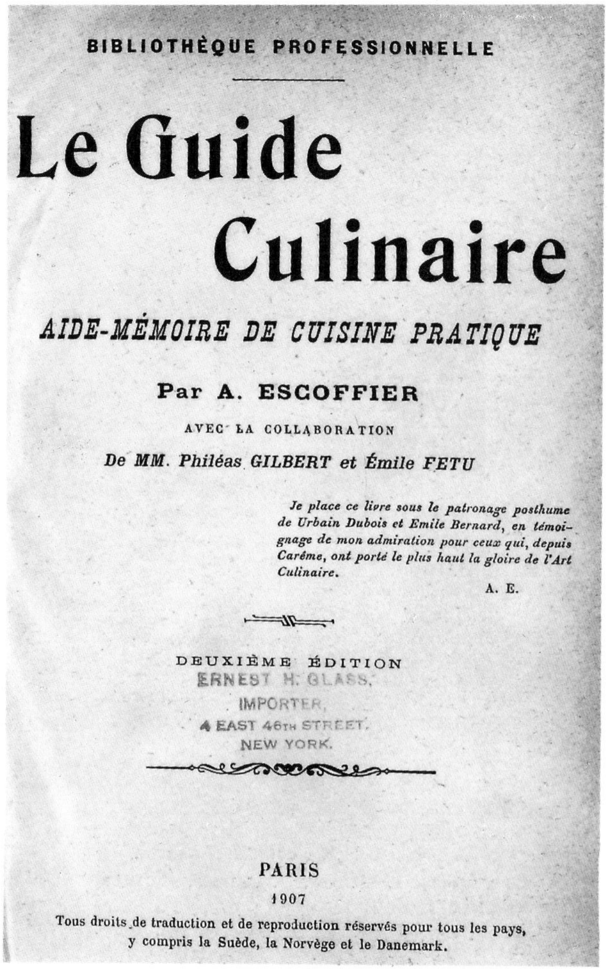

BIBLIOTHÈQUE PROFESSIONNELLE

Le Guide Culinaire

AIDE-MÉMOIRE DE CUISINE PRATIQUE

Par A. ESCOFFIER

AVEC LA COLLABORATION

De MM. Philéas GILBERT et Émile FETU

Je place ce livre sous le patronage posthume de Urbain Dubois et Emile Bernard, en témoignage de mon admiration pour ceux qui, depuis Carême, ont porté le plus haut la gloire de l'Art Culinaire.

A. E.

DEUXIÈME ÉDITION

ERNEST H. GLASS,
IMPORTER,
4 EAST 46TH STREET.
NEW YORK.

PARIS
1907

Tous droits de traduction et de reproduction réservés pour tous les pays, y compris la Suède, la Norvège et le Danemark.

OPPOSITE: *Sole Alice.*
ABOVE: *Escoffier's* Le Guide culinaire *is still today a standard work of reference in French professional kitchens. It not only includes recipes with the quantities standardized for restaurant use, but also keys them to literally thousands of variations.*

Escoffier's style of drafting recipes, with its complex series of cross-references, is hard to follow for anyone without considerable experience. *Le Guide culinaire* is intended as an aide memoire for professionals who know by heart the composition of such basics as meat glaze, sauce demi-glace and puff pastry. Most of the following recipes are adapted from his simpler, more personal book, *Ma Cuisine.*

PURÉE CRÉCY

This carrot soup illustrates how even the simplest ingredients are accorded meticulous attention by Escoffier. A *tamis* is a strainer of linen or wire mesh used to give a velvety consistency to soups and sauces.

Chop 5 or 6 carrots weighing 500 to 600 grams, put them in a pan in which 2 tablespoons of butter have been melted and add a chopped onion; season with a pinch of salt and a small pinch of sugar. Let stew a few minutes. Moisten with a liter of stock; add 125 grams of well-washed rice and cook gently. Strain through a fine *tamis*; thin the purée to just the right consistency with boiling stock and to finish, stir in 2 tablespoons butter.
Garnish: **little croûtons fried in butter.**
NOTA. – **to make the purée into *crème Crécy*, just before serving add 2 deciliters of boiling cream per liter of purée.**
The croûtons can be replaced, as you wish, with several spoons of rice or pearl tapioca cooked in consommé.

CREAM OF CARROT SOUP

Serves 6
2 tbsp butter
5-6 medium carrots (about 1 lb/500 g),
   chopped
1 medium onion, chopped
salt
small pinch of sugar
1⅔ pints/1 quart/1 liter beef or chicken
   stock, more if needed
3¼ oz/½ cup/100 g rice
FOR THE CROÛTONS:
3 slices bread, crusts discarded, diced
2 oz/¼ cup/60 g butter
2 fl oz/¼ cup/60 ml oil
TO FINISH:
6 fl oz/¾ cup/175 ml heavy/double cream
2 tbsp butter

1. In a heavy-based pan melt the 2 tablespoons butter and add the carrots, onion, salt, and sugar. Cover the pan and cook over low heat until the butter is absorbed and the vegetables are soft, 5-7 minutes. Add the stock and rice, bring to a boil, cover and simmer until the rice and carrots are very tender, 25-30 minutes.
2. For the croûtons: fry the bread in the butter and oil until golden brown, stirring so the bread browns evenly. Drain on paper towels and keep warm.

3. To finish: when the soup is cooked, purée it in a food processor or blender. Return it to the pan, bring just to a boil and add more stock if necessary to thin it to the consistency of thin cream. Add the cream, bring just back to a boil, and taste the soup for seasoning. Take from the heat, stir in the butter until melted and serve with the croûtons in a separate bowl.

SOLE ALICE

Sole Alice, one of the innumerable recipes Escoffier named for celebrities, honors Princess Alice of Athlone, a granddaughter of Queen Victoria. The cooking is completed in a chafing dish at the table.

Have ready an excellent fish stock, concentrated and very pale.– Trim the sole; place it in a special heatproof earthenware dish, with the base buttered, and poach it gently. At the right moment send it to the dining room with a plate on which are arranged separately: a little finely chopped onion, a little ground thyme, 3 finely ground rusks and 6 raw oysters.
At the table, the maître d'hôtel sets the dish on a burner, lifts out the sole, then detaches the fillets and puts them between two hot plates. To the cooking liquid from the sole he adds the onion and cooks it a few moments; then the thyme and enough breadcrumbs to bind the liquid; at the last moment, he adds the oysters and 30 grams of butter, in small pieces. As soon as the oysters are firm, he replaces the sole fillets in the dish, bastes them generously with the sauce and serves them at once, very hot.

SOLE ALICE

Serves 1
1 whole (about 12 oz/375 g) Dover or lemon sole, flounder or other flat white fish
2 tbsp finely chopped onion
½ tsp chopped thyme
1 oz/⅓ cup/ 30 g very fine browned breadcrumbs
6 shucked/shelled oysters, drained
2 tbsp butter, cut in small pieces
salt and pepper
FOR THE FISH STOCK:
8 oz/250 g fish heads and bones
12 fl oz/1½ cups/375 ml water
6 fl oz/¾ cup/175 ml dry white wine
1 slice onion
sprig of parsley
5-6 peppercorns

1. Heat the oven to No 4/350°F/175°C. For the fish stock: wash the fish heads and bones and put them in a pan with the water, wine, onion, parsley and peppercorns. Bring to a boil and simmer 20 minutes. Strain and boil until reduced to 6 fl oz/¾ cup/175 ml. Put the whole fish in a buttered baking dish, pour over the stock, cover with buttered paper, and bake in the heated oven until the fish is no longer transparent in the center, 15-20 minutes. Leave to cool, then drain most of the liquid.

2. To serve, take the fish on a plate to the table with the onion, thyme, breadcrumbs, oysters and butter. Heat the fish in the liquid over a table burner until hot; lift the fish out and bone it. Add the onion to the fish stock and simmer until soft, 1-2 minutes. Stir in the thyme and breadcrumbs – the sauce should be the consistency of thin cream. Add the oysters and butter and cook just until the edges of the oysters curl, shaking the pan so the butter melts into the sauce. Taste for seasoning; replace the fish fillets, baste them thoroughly with sauce, and serve as soon as the fish is very hot.

OEUFS À LA LORRAINE

By the time of Escoffier, the traditions begun by Carême of serving certain dishes only at certain meals had hardened into rules which are still followed in classic menus. An egg dish like this one, for instance, should only be served at lunch, as should hors d'oeuvres (of the antipasti type) and substantial cold dishes such as roast beef or lobster salad. At dinner at least one soup is mandatory, and in the old days a cream soup might be followed by a consommé. The garnish *à la lorraine* often refers to a combination of cheese and bacon, as in quiche lorraine. In his measurement of salt to the nearest centigram, Escoffier seems to be carrying precision a little too far!

General Principles: allow two eggs per person for this method of cooking. The normal amount of butter is 15 grams, of which half is spread in the dish and the rest melted and spooned over the egg yolks. The appropriate seasoning is 32 centigrams of salt for two eggs.
For eggs Lorraine: in the bottom of the dish place two slices of lean bacon, blanched and lightly broiled, with some thin slices of Gruyère cheese. Break the eggs on top; surround the yolks with a spoonful of cream and cook them as usual, with attention to the following points.
1. cook the white until it looks milky
2. the yolks should remain glistening
3. do not allow the eggs to catch on the bottom of the dish.

An advertisement for a kitchen supply house in England showing some of the typical hotel equipment of Escoffier's, and our own, time.

BAKED EGGS LORRAINE

Serves 4
8 slices (about 4 oz/125 g) bacon
2 oz/¼ cup/60 g butter
8 thin slices (about 4 oz/125 g) Gruyère cheese, halved
8 eggs
4 fl oz/½ cup/125 ml heavy/double cream
salt
4 shallow individual baking dishes, or 1 large shallow baking dish

Heat the oven to No 6/400°F/200°C. Broil/grill the bacon, keeping it as flat as possible. Spread half the butter in the baking dishes, set the bacon in the bottom and add the cheese, overlapping it so it does not spread up the sides of the dish. Carefully break in the eggs, spoon the cream around the edges of the yolks, and sprinkle with a little salt. Melt the remaining butter, sprinkle it on the yolks of the eggs, and bake them in the heated oven until the whites are milky, 12-15 minutes; the eggs will continue to cook in the heat of the dishes. Serve them at once.

POULET GRAND-MÈRE

This simple chicken dish from *Ma Cuisine* is bourgeois cooking at its best – an interesting contrast to the elegance of the more complex recipes. *Grand-mère* (grandmother-style) always means good home cooking.

Stuff the chicken with the following mixture:
Lightly brown in butter a spoonful of finely chopped onion, mix in 60 grams of minced sausage meat, the chopped liver of the chicken, a pinch of parsley and 2 spoonsful breadcrumbs, all moderately seasoned with salt and pepper. Truss the chicken and put it in an earthenware casserole with 50 grams of lean bacon cut in very small dice, a spoonful of butter and 10 baby onions. Cover the casserole, and set it over low heat. As soon as the chicken and the onions are golden brown, add 300 grams of potatoes, cut in small cubes; continue cooking over low heat.
Serve the chicken in the same casserole.

The market of Les Halles in Paris began to be disassembled in 1968 and had completely disappeared by 1972.

CHICKEN GRAND-MÈRE

Serves 2
3 lb/1.4 kg whole chicken, with the liver
3 tbsp butter
2 oz/½ cup/60 g diced lean bacon
10 baby onions, blanched and peeled
salt and pepper
2 medium potatoes, cubed
FOR THE STUFFING:
½ medium onion, finely chopped
1 tbsp butter
2 oz/¼ cup/60 g sausage meat
2 tsp chopped parsley
1 oz/⅓ cup/30 g fresh white breadcrumbs
salt and pepper
Trussing needle and string

1. For the stuffing: sauté the onion in the butter until lightly browned; add the sausage meat and stir to break it up. Chop the chicken liver, add it and cook 1 minute. Take the stuffing from the heat and stir in the parsley, bread-crumbs, and salt and pepper to taste. Let it cool, fill the chicken and truss it.

2. In a casserole melt the 3 tablespoons of butter, add the chicken, bacon and onions with salt and pepper to taste. Cover tightly and cook over very low heat for 20 minutes, stirring and turning the chicken from time to time; the chicken, bacon and onions should be lightly browned. Add the potatoes to the casserole. Cover and continue cooking, stirring occasionally, until the chicken is very tender and the potatoes are browned, 20-25 minutes. Remove the trussing strings from the chicken and serve it in the casserole.

PÊCHES MELBA

This most famous of all Escoffier's recipes is rarely made correctly; i.e., with fresh peaches, fresh raspberry purée, and homemade vanilla ice cream. A *timbale* is a high-sided metal dish, often made of silver plate; the name comes from the Arabic *at-thobal*, the drum.

Choose tender peaches with flesh that does not adhere to the pit; plunge them briefly in boiling water, lift them out quickly with a slotted spoon and put them in water with ice cubes; peel them, set them on a plate, sprinkle them with sugar and chill. Have ready a very creamy vanilla ice cream and a sweetened purée of the freshest possible raspberries.
Arrange the ice cream in a timbale or in a crystal bowl, set the peaches on the ice cream and coat with raspberry purée.
NOTA. – **During the season for fresh almonds, finely slivered almonds may be sprinkled on the peaches if you like; never use dried almonds.**

For centuries, capturing the essence of freshly-picked fruit has fascinated artists as well as chefs.

PEACH MELBA

Serves 6
6 ripe freestone peaches
1 lemon, halved
sugar (for sprinkling)
1¼ pints/3 cups/750 ml vanilla ice cream,
    preferably homemade
FOR THE PURÉE:
1 lb/500 g fresh raspberries, or 2 packages
    (1 lb/500 g) frozen raspberries
confectioners'/icing sugar
6 coupe or sherbet/sorbet glasses

1. Pour the boiling water over the peaches, let stand a few seconds, and transfer to a bowl of water containing ice cubes; if very ripe, the skin will peel easily after 10 seconds' soaking in boiling water, but longer may be necessary if they are less ripe. Rub the peeled peaches with the cut lemon and sprinkle at once with sugar to prevent browning. Set them on a plate, cover tightly with plastic wrap and chill. If this is done quickly, the peaches can be prepared 3-4 hours ahead and will not discolor.

2. For the purée: work the raspberries in a food processor or blender with sugar to taste – the purée should be fairly tart and if frozen raspberries are used, extra sugar may not be needed. Strain the purée to remove the seeds and chill it. Chill the coupe glasses.
3. Just before serving, spread vanilla ice cream in the base of the coupe glasses. Set a peach on top, spoon the raspberry purée over the peaches and serve at once.

SOUFFLÉ ROTHSCHILD

Soufflé Rothschild is enriched with candied fruits macerated in *Danziger goldwasser*, a liqueur appropriately flecked with gold leaf. The recipe is scattered over several pages of *Ma Cuisine*. Starting with the *soufflé Rothschild* ingredients, one must turn back to the mixture for *soufflé à la crème*, and back yet again to the method of cooking.

To the mixture for *soufflé à la crème*, add 80 grams of diced candied fruit macerated in a good Danziger goldwasser with plenty of gold flakes. Just before serving, surround the soufflé with a border of large fresh strawberries, or when they are out of season with preserved cherries.

Mixture for *soufflé à la crème* for four people: 1 deciliter milk; 35 grams sugar, a spoonful of flour; 10 grams of butter; 2 egg yolks; 3 egg whites, very stiffly beaten.
Bring the milk to a boil with the sugar, add the flour, mixed to a smooth paste with a little cold milk and cook the mixture for 2 minutes; take from the heat and finish it with the butter, egg yolks and egg whites. Presentation and cooking of soufflés: Soufflés are served in a timbale or in a special mold buttered and sprinkled with sugar. They should be cooked in a fairly moderate oven so that the heat slowly penetrates the mixture. Two minutes before taking the soufflé from the oven, sprinkle the top with sugar so it caramelizes and glazes the surface.
The decoration of soufflés is a matter of choice but should always be simple.

SOUFFLÉ ROTHSCHILD

Serves 4
2½ oz/¾ cup/75 g mixed candied fruit
2 fl oz/¼ cup/60 ml Danziger goldwasser or kirsch
confectioners'/icing sugar (for sprinkling)
8-10 large fresh strawberries, or 1 can (8 oz/250 g) cherries in light syrup, drained
FOR THE SOUFFLÉ MIXTURE:
5 fl oz/⅔ cup/150 ml milk
1¾ oz/¼ cup/50 g sugar
2 tbsp flour mixed to a paste with 3-4 tbsp milk
1 tbsp butter
4 egg yolks
6 egg whites
2⅓ pint/1½ quart/1.5 liter soufflé dish

1. Finely chop the candied fruit, add the liqueur, cover and leave to macerate at least 1 hour. Butter the soufflé dish.
2. For the soufflé mixture: heat the milk with the sugar until dissolved and stir in the flour paste. Bring to a boil, stirring constantly until the mixture thickens, and simmer it 2 minutes. Take from the heat, dot the top with the butter, and let cool until tepid. The butter will melt and prevent a skin from forming. This mixture can be prepared 2-3 hours ahead.

3. To finish the soufflé: heat the oven to No 5/375°F/190°C. Reheat the milk mixture to soften it. Beat in the egg yolks with the macerated fruit and liqueur, making sure the pieces of fruit do not stick together. Stiffly beat the egg whites and fold into the fruit mixture as lightly as possible. Spoon into the prepared soufflé dish and bake in the heated oven until the soufflé is puffed and brown, 15-18 minutes – it should still be soft in the center when served. Sprinkle the top of the soufflé with confectioners'/icing sugar and set it on a platter. Arrange the strawberries or cherries around the edge and serve at once.

AUGUSTE ESCOFFIER'S PÊCHES MELBA

SELECT BIBLIOGRAPHY

The following select bibliography does not list historical cookbooks except recent reprints which are of special significance because of an accompanying commentary. The best source of information about the many reprints/ fascimiles of old cookbooks, and about cookbook bibliographies which are now too numerous to list individually, is a specialized bookseller (see below). Works by most of the cooks cited in *Great Cooks* have been reprinted in the last 15 years, but few are available through regular trade channels. Unfortunately, many re-issues are expensive limited edition items.

American Heritage Magazine: *The American Heritage Cookbook and Illustrated History of American Eating and Drinking.* American Heritage Publishing Co., 1964.

Aresty, Esther B.: *The Delectable Past.* Simon and Schuster, 1964. Also *The Exquisite Table* (a history of French cuisine). Bobbs-Merrill, 1980.

Beck, Leonard N.: *Two 'Loaf-Givers'* (a tour through the gastronomic libraries of Katherine Golden Bitting and Elizabeth Robbins Pennell). Library of Congress, Washington, 1984. A knowledgeable survey with a long chapter on Platina.

Burnet, Regula: *Ann Cook and Friend.* Oxford University Press, 1936. This book recounts the bizarre tale of Ann Cook's attacks on Hannah Glasse.

Chiappini, Luciano: *La Corte Estense álla metà del Cinquecento* (notebooks of Cristofero di Messisbugo). Belriguardo, 1984.

Dodds, Madeleine Hope: "The Rival Cooks: Hannah Glasse and Ann Cook." *Archeologia Aeliana*, Society of Antiquaries, Newcastle upon Tyne, ser. 4, vol. 15, 1938. It was in this authoritative article that Hannah Glasse's origins were first unveiled. I am grateful to Mr L. G. Allgood, a direct descendant of Sir Lancelot Allgood (Hannah's half brother) for providing me with additional information about Hannah taken from family letters (now in the keeping of Newcastle Public Library) which Mr A.H.T. Robb-Smith summarized in some unpublished notes written in 1961.

Escoffier, Auguste: *Souvenirs Inédits, Editions Laffitte,* 1985. Interesting autobiographical notes and fragments edited for publication by Escoffier's grandson, Pierre.

Faccioli, Emilio, ed.: *Arte della cucina.* 2 vols. Edizione il Polifilo, 1966. Contains full text of Martino ms. and extracts from other classical Italian cookbooks.

Flandrin, J.-L. with Philip and Mary Hyman: *Le Cuisinier François.* Montalba, 1983. A reprint of both *Cuisinier* and *Pâtissier françois*, with a valuable commentary.

Freeman, Sarah: *Isabella and Sam* (the story of Mrs Beeton). Gollancz, 1977. Also *Mutton and Oysters* (the Victorians and their food). Gollancz, 1989.

Gottschalk, Alfred: *Histoire de l'alimentation et de la gastronomie.* 2 vols. Editions Hippocrate, 1948.

Guégan, Bertrand: *Le Cuisinier Français.* Emile Paul Frères, 1934. Reprinted by Belfond, Paris, 1980. The ninety-page introduction is one of the best historical surveys of French cooking.

Hartley, Dorothy: *Food in England.* Macdonald, 1954. A landmark in English culinary literature.

Herbert, A. Kenney: "The Literature of Cookery". *National Review*, 1895, pp. 676–684, 776–789.

Herbodeau, Eugene and Paul Thalamas: *Georges Auguste Escoffier.* Practical Press, 1955.

Hess, John L. and Karen: *The Taste of America,* Grossman, New York 1977. Includes a trenchant critique of Fannie Farmer.

Hieatt, Constance B. and Butler, Sharon (eds.): *Curye on Inglysh.* English culinary manuscripts of the fourteenth century, including the Forme of Cury. Early English Text Society, London, 1985. Constance Hieatt also edited *An Ordinance of Pottage* (Prospect Books, London, 1988) which features fifteenth-century culinary texts.

Layard, A.H.: "Renaissance Cookery". *Murray's Magazine*, March 1891.

Levy, Paul: *Out to Lunch.* Chatto and Windus, 1986. Contains account of Escoffier's dismissal from the Savoy Hotel.

Lotteringhi della Stufa, Maria Luisa: *Desinari e cene* and *Pranzi e conviti* (2 vols). Olimpia, 1965. Entertaining and well-documented histories of mainly Tuscan cooking through the centuries.

M.M.: "Gastronomy and Civilization". *Fraser's Magazine*, December 1851. (This article briefly quotes Voltaire's views on *nouvelle cuisine* – for full text, see his letter of September 6, 1765 to Comte d'Autrey.) M.M. is Mary Ellen Meredith, whose father (Thomas Love Peacock) and whose husband by a second marriage (George Meredith) were both novelists with a taste for the table. Her daughter by her first marriage, Edith Clarke, was also prominent in British cooking as head of the National Training School of Cookery in London.

Mallock, M.M.: "Old English Cookery". *Quarterly Review*, January 1894.

Manchester Collectanea: (proceedings of the Chetham Society, vol. 2, 1872): "Elizabeth Raffald" (a popular cookbook writer second only to Hannah Glasse in eighteenth-century England).

Mennell, Stephen: *All Manners of Food.* Basil Blackwell, 1985. (Penguin paperback, 1987.)

Moulin, Leo: *Les Liturgies de la Table.* Albin Michel, 1989. A good source for food and wine iconography.

Prospect Books: *Petits Propos Culinaires.* Essays and notes edited by Alan Davidson on food, cookery and cookery books. Available thrice yearly from 45 Lamont Road, London SW10. Prospect Books also publish facsimiles of old cookbooks and some important new English cookbook bibliographies.

Revel, Jean-François: *Un festin en paroles.* Pauvert, Paris, 1979.

Riley, Gillian (transl.): *The Fruit, Herbs and Vegetables of Italy* (Giacomo Castelvetro ms, 1614). Viking, 1989. A fascinating rediscovered account by an Italian exile in Jacobean England.

Scully, Terence (ed.): *The Viandier of Taillevent,* University of Ottawa Press, 1988. This scholarly edition compares all the different versions of the *Viandier*.

Tannahill, Reay: *Food in History.* Stein and Day, 1973. (Penguin paperback, 1988.)

Vehling, J.D.: "Martino and Platina, Exponents of Renaissance Cookery". *Hotel Bulletin and The Nation's Chefs,* vol. 49, no. 14, Chicago, 1932. Mr Vehling was the finder of the Martino ms. now in the Library of Congress. Since this ms. is identical not only to the recipe sections in Platina's *De honesta voluptate et valetudine* (1474) but also to the cookbook *Epulario* (1516), Vehling's assumption that the ms. dates from about 1450 – i.e., was extant before Platina wrote his work – is questionable. An article by Agostino Cavalcabo ("Platina, maestro dell'arte culinaria," in *Cremona,* no. 7, 1935) and Vehling's subsequent monograph (*Platina and the Rebirth of Man,* Chicago, 1941) throws no further light on dating.

Volant, F. and Warren, J.R.: *Memoirs of Alexis Soyer.* London, 1859. Reprinted by Cooks Books (see below). This book was the source for *Portrait of a Chef* by Helen Morris (Cambridge, 1938; Oxford University Press paperback, 1980).

Warner, Richard: *Antiquitates Culinariae.* London, 1791. Not a Latin work, but one of the earliest English histories of gastronomy; still makes racy reading. Reprinted by Prospect Books (q.v.).

Westbury, Lord: *Handlist of Italian Cookery Books.* Leo S. Olschki, Florence, 1963. The introductory essay in this bibliography stands on its own as the best overview of Italian culinary history available in English.

Wilson, C. Anne: *Food and Drink in Britain from the Stone Age to Recent Times.* Constable, 1973. An authoritative survey.

Wheaton, Barbara: *Savouring the Past.* University of Pennsylvania Press, 1983. One of the best recent histories of French cooking.

SPECIALIZED BOOKSELLERS

Booksellers who specialize in works about food and wine, and who take a particular interest in old cookbooks and in limited edition reprints/facsimiles, include the following:

United Kingdom	T. and M. McKirdy Cooks Books 34 Marine Drive Rottingdean, Sussex
	Catalogues include notes on culinary history *Jottings from the Dean.* The McKirdys assembled the evidence showing beyond reasonable doubt that Alexis Soyer was not the author of *The Pantropheon.*
	Books for Cooks 4 Blenheim Crescent London W11
	Janet Clarke 3 Woodside Cottages Freshford, Bath
United States	Nahum Waxman Kitchen Arts & Letters 1435 Lexington Avenue New York, NY 10128
	Jan Longone 1207 W. Madison St. Ann Arbor, MI 48103
France	Librarie Gourmande 4, rue Dante 75005 Paris
	La Verre et L'Assiette 1 rue du Val-de-Grâce 75005 Paris
Switzerland	H. Weiss Winzerstr. 5 8049 Zurich

PICTURE CREDITS

AGNESI: *p.27* Museo Storico degli Spaghetti – Collezione Agnesi, Pontedassio, Imperia, Italy; *p.114* Museo Storico degli Spaghetti – Collezione Agnesi, Pontedassio, Imperia, Italy; *p.126* Venditore di Maccheroni/Museo Storico degli Spaghetti – Collezione Agnesi, Pontedassio, Imperia, Italy

AMERICAN ANTIQUARIAN SOCIETY: *p.137*

ART INSTITUTE OF CHICAGO: *p.132* Picnic scene c.1853: Susan Merritt

AUTHOR'S ARCHIVES: *p.9*; *p.37*; *p.42* (left); *p.66*, Paris; *p.69* (top); *p.74*; *p.81*; *p.85*; *p.91*; *p.99*; *p.105*; *p.119*; *p.125*; *p.135*; *p.141*; *p.145*; *p.148*; *p.159* (bottom); *p.162*; *p.165*; *p.166*; *p.167*; *p.176*; *p.190*

BIBLIOTECA ESTENSE MODENA: *p.24* De Sphaera/transparency courtesy of Roncaglia, Modena; *p.34* Venditore de Cinnamamo/transparency courtesy of Roncaglia, Modena

BIBLIOTHEQUE NATIONALE: *p.15*; *p.53* (bottom): Larmessin; *p.59*: Larmessin; *p.61*; *p.156*

BOSTON ATHENAEUM: *p.187* Poster for C. Poole Jr. & Co, Boston; *p.188* Poster for New Household, White, Warner & Co; *p.195* Poster for W. Baker & Co. Chocolate; *p.196*

BRIDGEMAN ART LIBRARY: *p.11* Preparing Pheasant: Bibliothèque Nationale, Paris; *p.26* The Wedding Feast: Sandro Botticelli/Private Collection; *p.52* The Palace of Versailles in 1722: Pierre-Denis Martin/Château de Versailles, France; *p.56* The Fish Market: Frans Snyders/Louvre, Paris, Lauros-Giraudon; *p.71* An early London coffee house, 1688: signed A.S./British Museum; *p.78* Kitchen interior with still life, maid by the fire: Adriaen van Utrecht/Christie's, London; *p.84* Dinner at the temple of Prince of Conti: Michel Barthelemy Olivier/Château de Versailles, France; *p.86* La Chasse: Charles-Amedee-Philippe van Loo/Roy Miles Fine Paintings; *p.98* Covent Garden with St Paul's Church: Balthasar Nebot/Guildhall Art Gallery, London; *p.102* A Family at Tea: Richard Collins/Victoria & Albert Museum, London; *p.115* A meal at the St Benneto theatre: Gabrielle Bella/Galleria Querini-Stampalia, Venice; *p.120* The Grand Imperial Theatre, St Petersburg: Benjamin Patersson/British Library; *p.155* Banquet given by the Corporation to the Prince Regent with the Emperor of Russia and the King of Prussia, 1814: George Clint/Guildhall Art Gallery, London; *p.170* Leadenhall Market, 1865: Andreas Scheerboom/Guildhall

Art Gallery; *p.172* The Tea Table from Mrs. Beeton edition c.1907: Private Collection; *p.173* A picnic: Henry Nelson O'Neil/Christie's; *p.175* Billingsgate Fish Market: George Elgar Hicks/Fishmonger's Hall, London; *p.194* American forest scene – maple sugaring: Private Collection; *p.203* French Bakery: Joseph Bail/Gavin Graham Gallery, London

BRITISH LIBRARY: *p.17* Early painting of men chopping meat; *p.18* Early paintings of spit-roasting and of man cooking with large pot

COLONIAL WILLIAMSBURG FOUNDATION: *p.128* The Residence of David Twining (detail): Edward Hicks

EDIMEDIA: *p.19* Regnault de Montaubon: Bibliothèque Nationale, Paris; *p.41* Les Quatre Saisons – L'Automne: Arcimboldo/Bibliothèque Nationale, Paris; *p.62-3* Les Quatre Saisons – Le Printemps, l'Automne: 17th-century Flemish cabinet/© Roger Guillemot, Connaissance des Arts; *p.88* Cuisine provençale: Antoine Raspail; *p.103* The Milk Seller: Thomas Rowlandson/Victoria & Albert Museum; *p.121* Nature Morte: Luis Henendez/Musée de Piacio; *p.147* Marchande de Saucisse: Carle Vernet; *p.150* Les Halles en 1830: Canella/Musée Carnavelet, © Jacqueline Guillot, Connaissance des Arts; *p.152* Réunion Gastronomique ou les gourmands à table: Musée Carnavalet, Paris; *p.209* Le Carreau des Halles: Gilbert Victor Gabriel/Musée des Beaux Arts, Phototechnic, le Havre.

ELM TREE BOOKS ARCHIVES: *p.37* (bottom); *p.127*

E.T. ARCHIVE: *p.22* Marjoram (Origanum) from *Tacuinum Sanitatis*/Bibliothèque Nationale, Paris; *p.25* Pepper gathered in Kingdom of Quilon from *Livre des Merveilles*, 15th-century/Private Collection; *p.31* Aubergine (Meloneiana) from *Ortus Janitatis*; *p.32 Tractatis de Herbis*, Cesufa/Biblioteca Estense Modena; *p.49* Fruit seller: Vincenzo Campi/Brera, Milan; *p.93* La Cuisinière: M. Engelbrecht/Bibliothèque des Arts Decoratifs; *p.101* Rabbits, O'. – Street Crie: A. Courcell; *p.124* Tomatoes from Album Benary, Brussels/Kew Gardens Library; *p.130* Mode of drying fish, wild animals and other provisions: T. deBry/New York Public Library; *p.139* Indians carrying fruit in a dugout: T. deBry/New York Public Library; *p.158* London street scene with posters: John Orlando Parry/Alfred Dunhill Collection; *p.193* Le Cuisinier: 19th-century card

FINE ART PHOTOGRAPHIC LIBRARY LTD: *p.65* Still life of asparagus, cauliflower and strawberries: Adrienne Mols;

RECIPE INDEX

Original recipe titles are italicized.

INDEX

Original recipe titles are italicized.

ACKNOWLEDGEMENTS

I would like to thank the following people for their contributions to this book: Michael Boys and his assistant for the special photography, research associates Elizabeth Evans (for the three Italian chapters) and Margo Miller (for the American chapters), Emily Wright and Jenny Turtle for picture research, Sheryl Julian and Jenie Wright for recipe testing and development, La Varenne's *chef de cuisine* Claude Vauguet and pastry chef Laurent Terrasson for the dishes they prepared for photography at Château du Fey in Burgundy, editorial assistants Kate Krader and Cynthia Nims, Colin Webb, Gwen Edmonds and Gillian Young at Pavilion.

Special thanks to Michel A. Escoffier for kind permission to reproduce the Escoffier recipes. The recipes were taken variously from *Le guide culinaire* and *Ma cuisine* (Flammarion) by Auguste Escoffier. Escoffier's memory is preserved at the "Fondation Auguste Escoffier" and its Museum of Culinary Art at the small Provençal village of Villeneuve-Loubet, his birthplace near Nice.

And heartfelt thanks to my husband, Mark Cherniavsky, for contributing so much to the spirit and substance of this book.

A. W.